LIPPINCOTT'S
FAMILY LIFE SERIES

EDITED BY

BENJAMIN R. ANDREWS, Ph.D

TEACHERS COLLEGE, COLUMBIA UNIVERSITY

SOCIAL PROBLEMS
OF THE FAMILY

BY

ERNEST R. GROVES

LIPPINCOTT'S HOME MANUALS

Edited by BENJAMIN R. ANDREWS, PH.D.
Teachers College, Columbia University

CLOTHING FOR WOMEN

By LAURA I. BALDT, A.M., Teachers College, Columbia University.
454 Pages, 7 Colored Plates, 262 Illustrations in Text. Second Edition.

SUCCESSFUL CANNING AND PRESERVING

By OLA POWELL, Department of Agriculture, Washington, D. C.   425
Pages, 5 Colored Plates, 174 Illustrations in Text. Third Edition.

HOME AND COMMUNITY HYGIENE

By JEAN BROADHURST, Ph.D. 444 Pages, 1 Colored Plate, 118 Illustrations in Text. Third Edition, Revised and Enlarged.

THE BUSINESS OF THE HOUSEHOLD

By C. W. TABER, Author of *Taber's Dietetic Charts, Nurses' Medical Dic-
tionary*, etc. 438 Pages. Illustrated. Second Edition, Revised.

HOUSEWIFERY

By L. RAY BALDERSTON, A.M., Teachers College, Columbia University.
353 Pages. Colored Frontispiece, 175 Illustrations. Third Edition, Revised.

LAUNDERING

By LYDIA RAY BALDERSTON, A.M., Instructor in Housewifery and
Laundering, Teachers College, Columbia University. 389 Pages. 188 Illus.

HOUSE AND HOME

By GRETA GRAY, B.S., Director of Home Economics Department,
University of Wyoming. 356 Pages. 189 Illustrations.

LIPPINCOTT'S FAMILY LIFE SERIES

Edited by BENJAMIN R. ANDREWS, PH.D.
Teachers College, Columbia University

CLOTHING—CHOICE, CARE, COST

By MARY SCHENCK WOOLMAN, B.S. Illustrated. Second Edition.

SUCCESSFUL FAMILY LIFE ON THE MODERATE INCOME

By MARY HINMAN ABEL.   Second Edition

THE FAMILY AND ITS MEMBERS

By ANNA GARLIN SPENCER, Special Lecturer in Social Science, Teachers
College, Columbia University.

WOMAN'S SHARE IN SOCIAL CULTURE

By ANNA GARLIN SPENCER, Special Lecturer in Social Science, Teachers
College, Columbia University.

LIPPINCOTT'S FAMILY LIFE SERIES

EDITED BY BENJAMIN R. ANDREWS, PH.D., TEACHERS COLLEGE, COLUMBIA UNIVERSITY

SOCIAL PROBLEMS OF THE FAMILY

BY

ERNEST R. GROVES

PROFESSOR OF SOCIOLOGY AT BOSTON UNIVERSITY
AUTHOR OF "PERSONALITY AND SOCIAL ADJUSTMENT,"
"THE DRIFTING HOME," ETC.
CO-AUTHOR OF "WHOLESOME CHILDHOOD"

PHILADELPHIA, LONDON AND CHICAGO
J. B. LIPPINCOTT COMPANY

PRINTED BY J. B. LIPPINCOTT COMPANY
AT THE WASHINGTON SQUARE PRESS
PHILADELPHIA, U. S. A.

TO

CATHERINE, ERNESTINE, RUTH ELVA AND LOIS GROVES

COMRADES IN FAMILY FELLOWSHIP

AND

GLADYS HOAGLAND GROVES

THEIR UNDERSTANDING MOTHER

PREFACE

THIS book, written as a text for use in normal school and college classes, emphasizes, as its title suggests, the social function of the family. In spite of rapid and radical changes in its inner life, the family still remains the most significant of all our social institutions, for notwithstanding the ever-increasing competition from other social organizations, it continues to have the first and therefore the greatest opportunity to influence the character of children. It also provides for its adult members the most intimate form of association.

Sentiment naturally leads us to cling to conceptions of family life that are in harmony with the experiences of our own childhood, and in this way tempts us in thinking of the family to regard it as a static institution that exists by itself little influenced by the social conditions that are outside it. Actual facts show us, however, that the family is never sufficient unto itself, but rather at all times and in all places is in close contact with the general every-day life of people, influencing the motives and behavior of individuals and in like manner being itself influenced as an institution by the social experiences of its members.

A dynamic portrayal of family life which assumes that the family is always in process of adjustment in its attempt to minister to the needs of both the individual and the group in their practical life is the only treatment of the family that is in harmony with the thought of modern life. This book considers the family as a human relationship ever in such processes of adjustment, sensitive to the total social situation, and never a standardized and completed form of human activity. The faults and failures of the family therefore reveal the difficulties of an intimate group-life that cannot be more successful in its social activities than the individuals who comprise it. Thus the family and outside social conditions are in constant reciprocal relationship, and the two portions of social experience are so intertwined that neither can be understood by itself.

It is natural that tradition and prejudice should show themselves in discussions of family problems, since our personal attitudes toward the family are so tied up with our childhood experiences, our teaching and our affections. A scientific study of the family is not an ignoring of the values and ideals attached to the home, but an effort to put aside all subjective attitudes in order to understand the family as it actually is.

As the references and citations show, the literature on the family is extensive. There is, however, much less than one would wish that is scientific in attitude, and recent. The intimacies and reticence of family life create difficulty in its investigation and hamper scientific analysis. This explains in part why literature has attempted to interpret modern family life more often than has science.

I acknowledge my indebtedness to other students of marriage and family life, especially to those referred to in the text. I desire particularly to express my appreciation for the suggestions and stimulus given me in the writing of this book by Professor Benjamin R. Andrews of Teachers College, the editor of Lippincott's Family Life Series. Again I am indebted to my wife, Gladys Hoagland Groves, for her assistance in the preparation of my manuscript.

E. R. G.

January, 1927.

CONTENTS

SOCIAL PROBLEMS OF THE FAMILY

CHAPTER I

SOCIAL SIGNIFICANCE OF THE FAMILY

Social Importance of the Family.—The family had in its beginnings a biological purpose. It came into being to provide off-spring with the protection necessary for physical survival. As a biological institution the family may be found in simple form among the higher animals. For man, however, it has come to have a larger function. Not only has there been an enlargement of its original task; it also has developed a social purpose which has given it a complexity and significance characteristic of the human type of family life. It does more than minister to the physical needs of children; it serves society by its effect upon the various members of the family who live together within the home, and par-ticularly by its influence upon the personality of the growing child.

Thus the family has become of primary importance as an effec-tive socializing agency. It is chiefly through the family that culture is transmitted from generation to generation. Language is a good illustration of the influence of the family in the passing on of culture. From parent to child the fundamentals of culture, tradi-tions, mechanical processes, social habits descend, and in this man-ner the continuity of social life is assured.

The foundation of the family is sunk deeply in human nature. The family has developed to its present social significance because it provides satisfactions for the most compelling of human cravings. Sex, one of the most impetuous of the instincts, supports the ortho-dox family although, when unrestrained by modern social conven-tion, it also creates conditions hostile to the monogamous family. Parenthood, which in modern man and woman is usually a source of desires of supreme strength, conserves the family. Property-rights, law and order, the need of intimate comradeship, the wish for

1

the privacy and comforts of the home, and a host of lesser human wants add to the hold the family now has upon human nature.

Purpose of the Book.—This book treats the family as a social institution. It has for its purpose the description of the family in the United States, its outstanding problems and the suggestion of means for its improvement. There is naturally an immense amount of sentiment connected with the family. Because the home is so vivid a part of childhood and childhood so pleasant a portion of memory, it is easy for the emotions to color interpretations of the family. Problems of family life are favorite topics in the novel and the drama. Poetry portrays home experiences. In fiction and poetry the appeal to sentiment in the treatment of family topics is in harmony with the purpose of the author and is expected, even demanded, by the reader.

A scientific interpretation of the family requires, on the other hand, a purely objective attitude on the part of both author and reader. This does not mean that the human sympathies that relate to family experience are obstacles to the scientific understanding of the family. It is quite otherwise; but it is necessary that the emotional attitudes that would color the study of the family be held in check, for in no other social investigation is there such risk that personal experience or desire obstruct the effort to discover the facts. The chief value of a scientific study of the family as a social institution consists in the demand such an investigation makes that we consider the family with its problems apart from our own personal and emotional attitudes toward it. By disentangling our own experiences from the subject of our study, we gain a richer and more accurate understanding of the social significance of the family in modern life.

The Family and Human Nature.—Since the family has come into being as a means of satisfying human need and desire we find it revealing in clearest form the motives and mechanisms of human nature. It is easy to picture the family as something superimposed upon men and women to which they adapt themselves with effort as to something alien to their inborn dispositions, but this conception is contrary to the facts. Even when in individual cases we find the family unable to function in such a way as to satisfy the persons concerned, we discover that the family has added no outside foreign element to the situation, but has merely failed because as an institution it is helpless to do more than provide an opportunity for human nature to show itself freely and forcefully. The obstruction to the happiness of the home that fails lies in the clashing of the personalities of those who, in spite of contrary tendencies and lack of sympathy, are being tested by family contacts and intimacy. " You can know no one as he is unless you see him in his own home " is a true saying which brings out the value of the family as a revealer of the workings of human nature.

Intimacy of Family Life.—Family life, because of its intimacy and privacy, provides a unique opportunity for the free expression of personality. It is in this closeness of relationship that the family meets its severest strain. It is also in this very intimacy of home associations that we find the power of the family to influence character and satisfy human cravings. Thus the family permits in the largest possible manner " the intimate face to face associations and coöperation," which Cooley has told us are characteristic of the primary groups.[1]

With the closeness of contact of the members of the family, who in the privacy of their little group know each other as well as one person ever knows another and who deal with each other frankly in the everyday concerns of life, goes also in all normal homes the sympathy which makes possible that unity of interest characteristic of wholesome family life. History and literature are replete with illustrations of the social value of family intimacy. If, for example, Louis Pasteur " was the most perfect man who has ever entered the Kingdom of Science," [2] it is certain that his significance for society was as much the result of family ties as of inherited genius; for his youthful effort to please his parents was a great stimulus to him, his intense affection tended to turn his thought toward social welfare rather than personal ambition, and the death of his children attracted his attention to the prevention and cure of disease.

The family is the meeting place of adult and child. One, a social product already largely shaped, becomes the chief influence in fashioning the other and helping him to adapt himself to his social environment. The family is something more than the prototype

---

[1] Cooley, C. H., " Social Organization," Ch. III.
[2] Radot (Devonshire, tr.), " The Life of Pasteur," p. xvi.

of society; it is itself a society, the first into which we all enter, and the most powerful in changing raw human nature into a socialized personality.

The Family Socializes Human Nature.—Trustworthy experimental knowledge concerning heredity and environment is accumulating rapidly, especially in regard to plants and animals; but the relative importance of hereditary and environmental factors in the shaping of a human personality is, in spite of our ever-multiplying information, largely a matter of speculation. There is, indeed, an increasing agreement with reference to the immense part in the environmental influences that the happenings of the first six or seven years have in molding the development of an individual. No later social influences seem to get so deep down into human character as do those that come early to the child.

In the demonstration of this fact and the explanation of how it comes about, our psychology and sociology are making more clear and specific an idea which, built upon everyday observation, has been widely held by people of various times and places as a multitude of proverbs testify.

It is because of the significance of the child's first few years, physically, mentally and socially, that society is so largely a product of family conditions, for when the child leaves home to enter school he has already received a large part of the social influences coming out of his environment that determine character. It is this fact, coupled with the difficulty that many homes have in meeting the needs of the young child, that is bringing about the rapid growth of the nursery school for the pre-school child.

Home life, so far as the young child is concerned, is an introductory training station, and what the child gets, good or bad, profoundly affects his entire career. The home-child relationship is more complicated than appears on the surface. The child brings to his home life impulses clamoring for expression, and these are gradually formed into *conditioned reflexes* (associations dislodged from the original evoking stimulus and attached to some other stimulus), habit-trends, imitations, preferences and prejudices; because what the child presents is matched by what the other members of the family contribute, born also of impulses but more seasoned and conscious as a result of added years of experience.

The adults and older children stimulate, check, suppress and transform the attempts of the little child to obtain his satisfactions. Thus in the home there is a seething interplay of social influences to which the child is most open and sensitive, and against the force of which he has little power to protect himself. In this way the home circle becomes an arena of struggle, coöperation and adjustment, the young child being normally the one who must make the most radical efforts at adaptation to the social forces that play upon him.

Homes without children have much the same situation except for the fact that the interplay of personalities is all on the adult level, even though the emotions generated may be as undeveloped as children's, and compromise to a large extent takes the place of the conformity so commonly pressed upon the child. Even the family that is composed wholly of adults provides greater opportunity for the making and unmaking of character than do other human groupings. The home has no rival as the place to see human nature being formed.

There is, to be sure, a somewhat similar expression of human nature in the wider life outside the home, but without the frankness and intimacies of family contacts, and modified by the conventions and the various forms of superiority-inferiority relationships.

The Family and Social Change.—The family, although providing for its members a social microcosm, does not, of course, exist by itself uninfluenced by outside social conditions. Much of the family behavior is actually derivative, having its origin in the out-of-the-home experiences of the various members who compose it. In this way the family is kept in close contact with the social environment and is forced to adapt itself to the conditions of a group life larger than that of the home.

We are prone in thinking of the family to regard it as static, having reached by social evolution a final form which is fully adjusted to an unchanging situation. As we look backward we easily see the variations in family conditions and the necessity for them, but in our own time and place it is natural to feel that at last the family has arrived and must be protected against further change. It is our faulty human wish for permanence of conditions that have become comfortable by being made habitual that creates the idea of the family as an unalterable social institution.

Much of the pessimism regarding the family is born of the conviction, held with the tenacity characteristic of strong emotional bias, that any change in family life is an evil; or it comes from a failure to recognize that the family in its attempts at adaptation must suffer disturbances and losses. It is only by internal readjustments that the family in common with other institutions can adapt itself to human need and accomplish its social task.

The family must remain sensitive to the varying circumstances of group life; it cannot settle into a self-satisfied stiffness. Traditions passed from one generation to another within the family group frequently leave no place for family adaptability, but change takes place in spite of this, only with more emotional stress for the representatives of the two periods of time, who, with differing viewpoints, contend for power to shape the family.

Difficulty of Adaptability.—No social institution adjusts itself easily, for its organization always tends toward conservatism and the advocacy of letting things be as they have been. The family suffers especially in its attempts at social adaptation, for it has more of sentiment connected with it than have other institutions.

The meaning of individual family difficulties expressed in quarrels, separations and divorces is the failure of the persons concerned to adapt themselves to the needs of the family situation. Such failures bear testimony to the fact that for many people the shifting demands of business, morals and beliefs are more easily met than the demands of the home.

The difficulty is increased by the common notion that the family is a stable institution. Ideas of what constitutes a satisfactory family condition may clash, each individual assuming that the proper thing is what he or she has seen or personally experienced in other homes. Again, the conflict may result from an individual's attempting for selfish reasons to block changes that another member of the family believes imperative.

It would help not a little in solving the growing dissatisfaction with family life, evidenced by our increasing divorces, to exchange the conviction generally held that the family is our one unchanging human relationship for a clear recognition of the adaptation 'to actual conditions always required in the building up of a whole-some home.

Increasing Difficulty of Family Task.—The family in common with the other fundamental social institutions finds its task of adaptation becoming ever more difficult as a result of the growing complexity of civilization and the higher standards of living. In comparison with the family life of savages or even of people a half-century ago, the modern home has to make much more delicate adjustments or fail to bring to its members the satisfactions they want.

Social pressure in the form of fashion, conventional behavior, and such standards as are popularly regarded as ideals for home life, keeps the family ever in a process of attempting to do what is expected of it.

Of course it is true that this pressure is felt by the family members individually to a large degree rather than by the family as a whole, but the home group reacts to the situation as a result of the individuals' responses. If, for example, fashion demands of the marriageable daughter of the house, who contributes to the family income, the expenditure of a relatively larger part of her earnings that she may have the fur coat she needs to meet the matrimonial competition of her girl friends and rivals, then the family as a whole feels the drain made on her wages by a luxury she could not really afford.

The relationships of the various members of the family are more difficult to maintain satisfactorily to each person when there is an increase of leisure, with its heightening of desires and usually of sensitiveness, because there is time to develop the competitions that normally arise in the modern home. It often seems to children (and usually they are quite right about it) that what one of them has or does explains the necessity of the others' going without this or some other much-sought pleasure.

Then there are cross currents of social pressure. The mother may require the assistance of her adolescent daughter if her tea party is to be a success, while the assignment of work given by the high school may forbid the girl's helping at all. The child appeals to her mother as to what she had better do in her dilemma, and the mother finds herself from the family viewpoint interested in both of the child's duties, for the family will suffer a loss if either task is omitted.

It is also true that as the child comes more under the dominance of outside social organizations such as school and church—and such institutions are continually encroaching farther upon what was once entirely family territory—it is harder to adjust the various codes of conduct and the differing standards and purposes. The family has to assume the rôle of arbitrator; it must help the child adjust not only to the conflicting demands of outside institutions but also to the opposing interests expressed in the home program and that of other social organizations. The husband and wife in their response to out-of-the-home conditions have to meet difficulties similar to those encountered by the children. The family may have less function than in former times, but what it does becomes more complex and difficult.

Program for Reconstruction.—At a time when family defects and failures have become numerous and obvious there is need of a program which will tend to conserve family welfare. It is impossible to let the family meet its storm and stress with no effort to direct its course. Our other social institutions have the benefit of intelligent criticism, investigations and undertakings that attempt to strengthen them. At a time when people are so aware of their social needs, it is inevitable that movements and programs should originate that have for their purpose the betterment of family life.

Even the idea of giving specific training for parenthood and marriage is making headway. This is not entirely new, for in some form it is often present in savage society, but the present tendency is toward a kind of instruction that is different from that of the past.

There is common agreement that the ordinary home does not, indeed cannot, give such instruction satisfactorily although formerly under more simple conditions its failures were less costly. Specialization is required on the part of those who would teach the conditions of happy parenthood and marriage; the average parent and teacher realize that the information science has for them must be gathered by the expert and passed out in some popular form of instruction. Magazines have taken over a large part of such teaching and make increasing use of those specialists who can give in an entertaining and clear way what parents and other married people most need to know.

A great deal of this work has been done by the psychiatrist because his experience in dealing with personality problems has shown him the central significance of the family in maladjustment of an environmental nature, and also because patients have found him more helpful and understanding than others. It has also been an advantage to have help given by a specialist who is prepared to discover whether the social problem is only such or whether it is an expression of physical or mental disease.

The Study of the Family.—The student of the modern family meets all the difficulties that attend the study of any social institution and some that are peculiar to the family itself.

In no other experience is there so much of feeling and self-deception as is characteristic of family relationships. It is next to impossible for one to view without bias one's own home situation. The visitor in a brief period generally can see the significant conditions of a family in a clearer light than can the members themselves. Emotional attitudes are almost inevitable in the everyday contacts of a home. One's ideas of family matters are bound to be colored by feelings that forbid calm, objective judgments since everything which happens within the family is so likely to have a personal interest for each member.

Sentiment also hampers a just appraisal of any definite family. We look backward through the colored lights of emotion; our forward vision is distorted by our hopes, fears or wishes. The exact facts are hard to get. This does not mean necessarily that the interested person is trying to hide or change facts, but rather that our family relationships, past, present, and even future in so far as imagined, are too shot through with personal meaning to be treated with unprejudiced judgment.

The family also hides itself behind a privacy not shared by any other institution. If law regards a man's home as his castle, convention and tradition make the happenings of the home more private than the inner counsels of the most secret fraternal organizations. It is bad taste to talk without great care of one's own or even another's home conditions. Curiosity may wish to pry into the secrecy of family situations, but unless protected by the guise of serious purpose it is considered socially disreputable.

When we enter our homes we become by common consent socially isolated and our privacy is protected by a conventional code of conduct which the well-bred are expected to follow and which shuts in the family more effectively than high walls. Even those who turn to the court for legal separation or divorce are expected by public opinion to hide as far as possible the truth regarding their unhappiness. This regard for family privacy has become so ingrained in our social attitudes that we observe it without thought as a matter of course.

The idea of family rights is firmly fixed in law, and only an experienced social worker knows how heavy is the burden of proof assumed by one who asks of the court legal authority to interfere in a family situation which seems socially intolerable.

It is clear, therefore, that these emotional reactions, sentiments, and concealments hamper the scientist who attempts an objective study of the family. It is necessary to remember also that the word family is only a group term to generalize individual families and that we can have no satisfactory knowledge of family social life unless we can obtain trustworthy information of individual families.

Certain facts of great importance present no difficulty. We can, for example, tabulate the number of divorces, the marriage rate, the birth rate, and a quantity of valuable information. It is when we attempt the explanation of some of these facts in concrete human behavior that we find ourselves on uncertain ground. It is one thing to know that divorces are increasing; it is quite another to discover what motives are operating to produce this increase. We can easily discover the low birth rate record of college gradu-ates, both men and women, but it is not nearly so clear what social or psychic causes are at work to bring about this situation.

In spite of the perplexities in the way of a scientific interpreta-tion of family problems, the effort is bound to be made by students interested in the family, and not without result. We can at least bring together some suggestive material that will help those who must deal practically with family problems. All investigations of human behavior when they try to disclose psychic and social causes encounter baffling problems. Such studies are attempted, never-theless, and our fund of knowledge is slowly increased.

The family is essentially conduct. It is not an establishment as is the house, but a group of activities that have a core of common significance. It is not just people, but people who live together that make a home. The study of the social problems of the family is the investigation of human behavior in the relationships characteristic of family grouping. Family life is one type of social conduct, and everything we know about the behavior of men, women and children in their other relationships helps us to understand the problems of the family; every fact that we gather concerning family situations has a value in understanding human conduct in its wider aspects. The family is a social institution, but it is such because it is an organization which provides a peculiar opportunity for the interaction of individual human beings. It is essentially not a thing but life—life expressed at close quarters in ways characteristic of man.

CHAPTER II

THE PRIMITIVE FAMILY

The Evolution of the Family.—The student of the family naturally turns to the question: What has been its evolution? This is in part because it has become a habit to start every kind of study with the historic development of the subject of inquiry. To suppose that by studying the family life of the past one can get a great deal of help with reference to its present problems is a mistake. It is a fallacy to consider evolution as a continuous advancement. There is no such thing in social experience as consistent progress, and particularly is this true of the family.

The value of studying the primitive family is merely that one gains a background for appreciating its present-day characteristics. Nobody can safely go to the family of the past to get standards for the family of to-day. Much of the controversy of earlier students of savage society has been futile, for they have tried to determine by their investigations what is the normal home life for all time. Some writers have tried to show that our present conventional monogamy has always been the usual thing, fearing if they did not prove that, the family in its existing form would not be so secure. Others have tried to show that in the beginning mating was promiscuous, believing that would prove our present morals scientifically unsound. It matters little what the first form of marriage was, so far as the stability of married life today is concerned. We have no motive for reaching into the past and trying to force our findings into the preconceived form that seems to us necessary to establish the kind of family life we think good.

It is impossible to get at the very beginning of the family. Concerning the housing customs of primitive man we have a definite body of knowledge; we have discovered some of the caverns in which people lived a great many thousands of years ago, and we have seen a few of the utensils they used; we can tell something about their daily life from the pictures they left on the cavern walls. But in our attempt to ascertain the facts regarding their family life we cannot go beyond history because tradition does not help us. We therefore turn to the savages of to-day for our idea of what must have been true of primitive man; yet savages do not necessarily reproduce the life of earlier times, since they may be arrested or degenerate types or they may be more highly developed than prehistoric man.

We know very much more about animal than early human family life. Among the birds we find a high type of family life and among the apes, especially the gorillas, a very beautiful one. Concerning the gorillas we have only scanty information because it is almost impossible to come in contact with their family life, but the very few cases where definite knowledge has been obtained show it to be unusually stable and highly developed, with a sharp division of labor, the male protecting the wife and children who sleep in a tree. From what we know it seems probable that gorilla marriage is monogamous, one male to one female, rather than the mating of a number of males with a number of females, though it is claimed by some that there is evidence of this.

Generally speaking, savage life gives a definite background of simple family life, and that helps somewhat in understanding the modern family. The viewpoint we get from a study of savages that is most valuable in dealing with present-day situations is the conception that family life is constantly changing to adapt itself to its environment. Instead of continuing to suppose that one kind of family life is normal we are convinced that family life has to be adaptable, but we also learn that our form of family is the one that adapts itself most readily and persists because it is the most satisfactory type; though it is constantly varied by exceptions that are made in different places and times. For instance, until recently in modern European culture prostitution was an annex to the monogamous family life. The two went on together, whereas in the Mohammedan countries that had a polygamous family life there was no prostitution. Prostitution was an attempt to adapt monogamous family life to those not able to maintain it in its purity.

From the study of the savage family we get some clue to the tendencies of desires that express themselves in the home, so that we can be a little more sure of the kind of motives family life has to

satisfy. It helps us in investigating our present problems to realize
that the family must meet certain conditions in order to be stable.

The Family of the Savage.—The student of savage family life
is bewildered by the tremendous amount of variation in the customs
of the peoples he reads about, and most especially in their forms of
marriage. As he looks at the practices of individual tribes and
their changes in new circumstances, he finds much that is different
from modern life, but it seems as if there is nothing to make a
clear-cut picture, for there is no one definite form of savage family.
What the student does find is all sorts of family life, so that he must
generalize with a great deal of caution. The savage family varies
from place to place far more than the modern family as we know it,
though that differs from nation to nation.

Another thing that stands out clearly is the fact that there is
no progression from simple to complex family life so as to make
an increasing evolution. The typical characteristics of the family
at a certain level of experience differ from those at another level,
but it is impossible to say that one type is higher or lower; the
family life of a people is usually adapted to the life they have to
live, or at least to their ideas with reference to that life. Thus the
family has many different forms, each one fulfilling its function
fairly well.

Little is gained by merely recording what a certain savage
people believe concerning the status of women or the institution of
marriage, because that is largely theoretical. Only by following the
practices of the people throughout the whole of their social life can
the real characteristics of their family life be determined. For
instance, if it is the custom for the males to live by themselves, this
changes the entire complexion of the family. There can then be
only a limited family life with smaller function than where there
is no club life; and many of the functions that we think of
as peculiar to the family are carried on by the men in their club-
house, even the housekeeping duties of the women shrinking to a
very small place.

The difference between theory and practice in the savage home
is shown by the fact that the beliefs of a people may be such as to
make one infer that the woman is abused, while actually she may

receive fair treatment. Even though theoretically ill-used, she may be hedged about with protection.

A very marked economic division of labor is to be found in the family of the savage which throws light on the question whether the savage woman is exploited. When, for instance, the warrior coming home sees the camp fire and drops his game, which the wife goes out and gets, dragging it up to the fire and dressing it, because by custom no warrior brings home game when within sight of the camp fire, it sounds as if she were unfairly treated. Or if the wife and children may not eat until the men are satisfied, but must sit around on the hillside watching their menfolk feast and wondering if there will be anything but the scraps left for them, it seems to us like rank exploitation; but we do not take into account all the practical considerations. When there is not food enough for all, the men must be fed as well as may be, so they will be strong enough to go forth to seek more food for the group and able to repel the sudden attack of an enemy who have been waiting for a favorable time to make raids.

Both men and women often go hungry and overwork; neither of them is likely to be long-lived. The more we study the situation, the less sure we are that the woman is exploited compared with the man. Both are in hard circumstances and try to adjust themselves to the necessities of their existence. Some first hand investigators of savage life have concluded that the male does not live so long as the female, which makes us feel that he is more exploited by his environment, just as the modern male runs more hazard in his occupation than does the woman, a fact that has contributed to the greater death rate of man as compared with woman after the age of forty.

The strength of the primitive family is based on its economic rather than its social or moral value. This may be contrary to what we like to think but it is the fact. The family does, however, have social significance. The children are considered a wealth that belongs to the tribe, and a large part of the early history of the family revolves about the question: Who shall have control of the children? This is particularly true of the male children; it is often not true of the females because they are reckoned a less valuable tribal asset. They are worth enough when they are of an age that permits them to be sold or married, but the savage finds it hard to look forward to that time, and may put girl children to death when they are little, although the market price of brides is very high. When the girls are partially grown the tribe takes great interest in them because they do represent potential wealth and can be sold just as cattle are sold among peoples where such customs exist. Like other practices this differs from tribe to tribe.

Besides its significance as the producer of children, the savage family has another function that is socially valuable; it transmits culture just as the modern family does. The savage family transmits very satisfactorily and much more efficiently than our modern family because the culture to be handed on is so simple, with no perplexing problems or discords, whereas at the present time every family presents an enormous amount of discordant material to the child, who finds it impossible to reconcile the material he gets from parents, brothers and sisters, comrades, school, church and other sources. The savage child is taught just those things that seem important, consisting primarily of traditions, information leading to the skill which his way of living requires, and the ideas of magic and misinterpretation of causes which we label superstition and which occupy so large a place in savage culture.

The Happiness of the Savage Family.—Ordinarily the savage family is a happy family. This surprises those who cannot get away from the notion that the woman is exploited, but she seems to be at least as happy as the modern woman. She does not have the sensitiveness of the modern woman, but regards her life as the natural one and accepts it as it comes because she is accustomed to it; she does not complain because she has no motive for complaining.

Children are usually treated generously; indeed, they are sometimes indulged too much, contrary to our general thought; but as a rule they are so severely disciplined concerning the bigger things that they are very obedient, while in the smaller things they are allowed to do very much as they please and their life might seem enviable to the modern child whose life is so much regulated.

The elders are also treated very well, from a modern viewpoint too well, for they are often permitted to have too much power. One of the reasons why young boys and girls treat the elders so well is that among some tribes all the elders are relatives in the eyes of the child, there being in their thinking nothing like our idea of uncles and aunts but everybody being " related " if of the same clan. Even though the elders are sometimes put to death by their sons at the proper age for that proceeding, as has been true of the Eskimo, they are well treated up to that time.

The mother-in-law is controlled by very rigorous taboos, sometimes not being allowed even to speak to her son-in-law. Just why this should be is one of the puzzling questions. It is assuming a good deal to suppose that the savage plans this purposely to avoid trouble, for he is not so wise in other ways, but at any rate the taboo works out most advantageously. Freud thinks there is a feeling that the mother-in-law might be jealous of her daughter and have an affection for the son-in-law, but that seems absurd in view of other things we know about the savages. The two families often live together without any difficulty. Tozzer lived for a year beside a savage family, both houses having roofs but no walls to afford privacy, so that if there had been any quarrels he would have known it; the savage family consisted of a mother, three sons and three daughters-in-law, all living together with never a quarrel of any sort in all that time. This is a characteristic picture of savage family life. The fact that the modern family is more quarrelsome is an evidence of its progress, since the more complex and individualistic expression of personal desires means more collision, whereas a simpler and more thoroughly regulated life such as that of the savage is smoother. The very placid family life of the savage is not the kind we want or need in these days. It is generally true that any family to-day that has no conflicts is a bad family, for somebody is too much in control.

Position of Women.—The actual facts about the savage woman's life can only be estimated by looking at them in connection with the entire life of the people. When luxury begins to come so that the danger of starvation is a little further off, the woman gets a slight advantage as well as the man. It is only when both are near starvation that the woman has such a terribly hard time, and the man's life is then no easier than hers, though his hardships take a different form. Always, in savage as in modern life, woman's

2

real situation is governed more by custom than by law. In America to-day there is no legal discrimination against divorce in the rural sections. Legally there is no difference between getting a divorce in the country place and in the city, but custom enters at this point and makes it more disagreeable to get a divorce in the sparsely settled district than in the city. It is hard for a woman to go against public opinion in the country by getting a divorce, while in the city there is far less feeling about it. We read that a savage can divorce his wife by simply throwing a kitchen utensil after her as she goes out of the door. That sounds easy, but it does not often happen. The savage needs the help of his wife too much to think of sending her home on slight provocation. If he does not want her he prefers to exchange her for somebody else's wife. In theory savage divorce is easy, but in practice it is not common. With us the law is the same for a Catholic as for a Protestant, but religion enters and makes a difference. As regulations among savages operate on one side, public opinion is built up on the other side to prevent them from going too far.

Sex and Savage Family Life.—A superficial acquaintance with savage society leaves many people with the idea that sex control is a very modern thing and that savage people are lacking in sex discipline. There are so many variations from our way of living that it seems as if that must be the fact, and missionaries, travelers and traders, because they go so rapidly through the country or because they are so biased, often get this impression. But the theory that the evolution of man has been from a very loose to a very rigorous sex life is contrary to fact. What is true is that there are enormous differences among savages, some having a very pure sex life and others having considerable license, so that it is almost impossible to generalize. Often the facts have been misinterpreted by persons not scientific in their point of view, who do not linger long enough among a savage people to understand them. Sometimes the trouble has been an incorrect translation of words used by the savages. At other times the observers have not grasped the complexity of marriage relationships and have assumed that no standard marriage existed because they did not comprehend what it was.

Travelers get the notion that there is a communistic sex life among the savages they visit because there is an exchange of wives or because wives are offered to the travelers, not realizing that this may not often happen, and is no more standard than a house of prostitution in a modern city is a proof that most of the people in that city are not living a standard monogamous family life. Both the civilized and the savage situation only show that variations from the accepted standard exist.

The question of modesty also gives rise to misconceptions on the part of untrained observers. The savage is not immodest, but because his conventions are different from ours we are apt to think him so. He is usually much more modest than the modern European, according to the testimony of most anthropologists. It is true that the savage goes without clothes, or practically so; often it seems almost a death sentence to ask him to wear clothes, for experience shows that the rugged savage who suddenly begins to go about dressed like a European is very likely to lose his vitality and may sicken and die as a result of this drastic change in his habits. In going about unclad he is simply adapting himself to his climate. The death rate of the South Sea Islanders increased markedly among those who were induced to wear many clothes. Going naked is not an act of immodesty. The anthropologist says the wearing of clothes was the earliest immodest act; garments were first put on to attract attention, not for comfort.

The savage who comes in contact with the European thinks the European as immodest as the latter thinks him. What we think of when we say immodesty is a difference; that which is unlike the usual, accepted thing excites attention and is called immodest. In reality immodest dress is always relative, signifying the unusual, for the moment everybody adopts the new manner of dressing there is no longer any variation and therefore no immodesty.

It used to be claimed by some writers that in the beginning sex life was communistic. Soon after the evolutionary doctrine was pronounced, Lewis H. Morgan carried over this idea into a conjecture as to the development of family life; like a good Victorian he said the family life of his period was the pinnacle toward which the lower forms of family life had been tending from the beginning, which he assumed to have been promiscuity. Others took up this notion, which became a doctrine based purely on guesswork.

When the anthropologists began to study the question they could find no clear evidences of this promiscuous life, even among some of the higher animals. Birds are monogamous. Nowhere has promiscuity been found among savages. The theory has been largely abandoned now. One does find illustrations of something that seems to be a communistic sex life but rightly interpreted it is not that, rather it is a variation from a standard family life. As far as we can get evidence the first family life seems to have been very much like ours in that it was monogamous. Promiscuity may have occurred, but there is nothing to demonstrate its existence; its prevalence is a purely theoretical assumption. Morgan also said that among peoples with a rudimentary family life each generation married within itself promiscuously, so that all the younger men and women were mates, and the members of the elder generation, their parents; a child could not distinguish his own father and mother from the group of his potential fathers and mothers. This idea Morgan got from the fact that in the Hawaiian Islands, as elsewhere, the children call all the men father. The confusion apparently resulted from a misunderstanding of the meaning of the word, father; to Morgan the word meant what we mean by *father,* to the Hawaiians it meant men of the older generation. The savage was simply classifying the two generations. Likewise, when the young people used a certain term in speaking of each other it did not follow that they were mingling freely in their sex life, but that they were recognizing the fact that they belonged to the generation within which they would later marry.

Lowie's statement of the situation is representative of the modern viewpoint regarding the theory of promiscuity in human history:

Sexual communism as a condition taking the place of the individual family exists nowhere at the present time; and the arguments for its former existence must be rejected as unsatisfactory. This conclusion will find confirmation in the phenomena of primitive family life.[1]

Forms of Marriage.—Polygyny is one of the variations of marriage. We are apt to get the idea that it is common because it is permissible, but it cannot be common unless there are many more women than men. This does not often happen among savages. If one man has many wives, others will have none unless there is a

---

[1] "Primitive Society," p. 62.

great inequality of the sexes. Where permissible, it is often checked by the fact that it is too costly. On the other hand, it is sometimes not costly at all because the woman is an additional worker and it is an economic advantage to have more than one wife. Polygyny is frequently limited by the fact that the man has to live with his wife and she has to live with her kinspeople. Since she represents their property, the clan will not let her go outside their territory. A man who has several wives would have to live first with one, then with another, much as the Mormons used to do. This traveling household naturally restricted the polygynous type of family.

Polygyny is not necessarily unpopular with women. In the kind of life the savage lives, economic conditions may be so hard that the lone wife is overworked and urges her husband to take another wife so that she may have help with her household labors. As the first wife is the dominant one, every time the man adds another wife she gets an additional worker; while the new wives also benefit by the arrangement since the more women there are in the family, the lighter the duties of each and the more prosperous the group as a whole.

When polygyny thrives among people whose life is not so hard that many women are needed to do the work, it will usually be found to emphasize sex, as it has done in the very wealthy Turkish family of the past, where the women were little more than legalized sex companions of the man, keeping to their own part of the house, and sharing few interests or activities with the head of the house. This is the sort of polygynous family life we have in mind when we think of polygyny as degrading women and debasing the function of the home.

When the family lifts itself above the physical level to a possibility of comradeship and affection, the polygynous form of family life shows its handicap. Although Turkey has recently entirely done away with polygyny, making it a criminal offense for a man to have more than one wife, this is but the legal crystallization of a trend that was noticeable more than a decade ago. In 1914 Stanwood Cobb, a keen observer of Turkish life, wrote:

Polygamy is now a waning custom in Islam. The influence of European culture has been steadily creating a sentiment against it among progressives, and the Young Turk almost universally restricts himself to one wife.

It is only in the passing generation that the harem exists. The Young Turk aspires to the happiness of a real union—a home built up by the love and devotion of two people, one for the other—a partnership between man and wife. And he knows this is impossible if he has more than one wife. He also desires his wife to be educated, so that she can be his intellectual and spiritual companion.[2]

In America we have a peculiar sort of polygynous family life, in that ours is successive: a man does not have more than one wife at a time, but over a period of years he may have many wives because as soon as he tires of his wife or she of him they divorce and remarry, each of them perhaps repeating this experience with different marriage partners, so that alongside of this unavowed polygyny goes a corresponding polyandry. It seems evident that this fleeting family life is based too largely on sex; if it had a really affectionate basis there would not be the desire to exchange and get new mates for old.

Polyandry.—Polyandry is the opposite of polygyny, one woman having several husbands. It is very uncommon, only rarely being found among savages. When it does exist it may be due to an unusual disproportion between the sexes, caused perhaps by female infanticide or the carrying away of women by an alien tribe, or to such hard economic conditions that it takes the combined efforts of several men to support one family. Those who are familiar with the home life of immigrants in this country occasionally come across a polyandrous family, in which even as many as five or six men are supporting one wife between them; here it is obvious that the number of men migrating from a given locality far outnumbered the women, and also that the struggle to get ahead in the new land imposes on the workers virtually the same living conditions that would obtain if their economic situation were excessively harsh, since they must live very frugally in order to lay by the hoardings that are to furnish capital for advancement.

There are two kinds of polyandry, the fraternal and the non-fraternal. Fraternal polyandry is the marriage of brothers to one woman; non-fraternal polyandry is the marriage of several men not brothers to one woman. In the case of the brothers, the family usually lives in one place and the fatherhood of the children is likely to be decided by seniority, the first born being conceded to be the

[2] " The Real Turk," p. 74.

child of the eldest brother, the second child going to the second brother, and so on; though the fatherhood of the children may be decided in the fraternal as in the non-fraternal family by the performance of some such ceremony as the shooting of an arrow in a certain way. Each father has special control over his own child. The non-fraternal family is a migratory affair, the wife moving about and spending a few months with one husband after another, then coming back where she started.

Although polyandry is generally considered a result of oppressive poverty or an unnatural shortage of women, this is not always true. In Toda, a part of India, the people have been very poor and have maintained polyandry; when they became more prosperous, observers expected to see the polyandrous family disappear, but instead of that the Toda family became in many instances at the same time polyandrous and polygynous, the brothers continuing to live together but having several wives instead of one as in earlier times, so that the whole group was married, each woman having several husbands and each man several wives.

The Marriage Contract.—There has been much discussion about the history of the marriage contract. The old idea has been that most marriages at first were captures: the man went and got his wife by stealing or capturing her. Several ceremonies connected with savage weddings slightly hint at an earlier period of marriage by capture, and this is also suggested by some of our own marriage customs, but the present anthropological thought is that capture is a minor form of marriage contract which came about occasionally when men found it impossible to get enough wives and had to go out and steal them from some other tribe. If this had been common there would have been perpetual warfare among savages, and that was not true; besides, the weaker tribes would soon have lost all their women, which did not often happen. Moreover, a captured woman usually became not a wife but a concubine as in the Old Testament, the men seldom being allowed to marry the women they captured, though permitted to keep them as concubines. The anthropologists explain the suggestions of earlier marriage by capture which persist in savage and civilized wedding customs to-day by saying that those rites represent the male's desire to show his

strength and skill, or have perhaps been suggested by sporadic cases
of marriage by capture.

In the midst of the wedding feast the Bushman bridegroom suddenly snatches his bride away from her people, when he is immediately assailed by her relatives, who beat him unmercifully; if he
is able to endure this pommeling without letting go of his prize,
the young woman is declared his wife, but if his powers of endur-
ance fail and his bride eludes his grasp the whole performance must
be gone through successfully at a later date before the couple can
become man and wife.[3]

To argue that the carrying out of a mimic seizure of the bride
by forcible means in the face of the frenzied opposition of her kin
as part of a savage wedding ceremony is valid evidence of the
earlier prevalence of marriage by capture in that tribe is no more
sensible, says Westermarck, than to suppose that because some tribes
treat the bride and bridegroom as a king and queen is proof that
marriage used to be confined to royalty.[4]

Such modern customs as the wearing of the wedding-veil, the
honeymoon avoidance of friends and relatives, and the lifting of
the bride over the threshold when she first enters her new home
have been supposed by some writers to be relics of prehistoric marriage by capture. No such far-fetched explanation is needed, since
these conventions can be shown to have sprung directly from much
more simple and common impulses, such as "modesty." [5]

The most common marriage contracts were exchange and purchase. Exchange was the giving of one woman for another, one
family pledging its daughter to marry into another family, which
in turn promised a daughter to be given in marriage to a man in the
first family. Still oftener brides were bought from their parents
by the payment of animals or other goods. This enabled a wealthy
man to buy several wives if that were permitted in his tribe, while
a poor man might not be able to afford any.

The Old Testament story of Jacob working seven years for his
wife and then getting the wrong sister is an illustration of marriage by purchase. Marriage by purchase implies that the woman

[3] Westermarck, "History of Human Marriage," vol. ii, p. 255.
[4] *Ibid.*, p. 261.
[5] *Ibid.*, p. 277.

was considered property and was treated as such, but this does not necessarily follow; rather this type of marriage meant that a woman was recognized as having social value, and therefore was not carelessly allowed to drift about from one family attachment to another. In England in feudal times the lord of a manor demanded a considerable payment if the daughter of one of his villeins married a man living elsewhere, until finally it was seen that for every girl who married outside her home group a girl from another estate was brought in as bride to one of the tenants.

At times the gifts made to the relatives of a savage bride were replied to by presents from her kin to those of the bridegroom, much in the manner of our Christmas giving. This represented a ceremony, somewhat like our own giving of wedding presents, rather than actual marriage by purchase. Such an exchange of gifts takes place in the opera, " Madame Butterfly."

Not long ago a case of marriage by purchase in this country attracted wide attention. A gypsy sold his daughter to the man who wanted to marry her, and the characteristic gypsy wedding ceremony was enacted; but the girl soon afterward left her husband and ran away with the man of her choice, whereupon the man who had bought her as his bride wanted his money back from the father. In the ensuing publicity, it came out that the custom of buying their wives was widespread among the gypsies in America, but that the girls were growing less and less willing to abide by the conventions of their people, frequently running away from their allotted husbands, as this girl had done.

The Marriage Ceremony.—Marriage ceremonies are of all sorts. One of the commonest is simply to have the two people eat from the same dish. Eating has an enormous ceremonial significance to savage people, some refusing under any provocation to kill a person who has recently eaten with them. Underlying all the widely differing marriage ceremonies of savages two basic facts are obvious: one is that the bride and groom are doing something together that constitutes a legal contract, very much like the signing of a bond in these days; and the other is that since primitive man is very sure there is something bewitching in woman, which the South Pacific Islanders call *manu*, or magic, there being something about her that gives her power over spirits; and since she has more of this at some times than at others as her attraction waxes and wanes, the marriage rites often include a cleansing ceremony to take out of her this dangerous element of magic so that it will be safe for a man to marry her.[6] The idea that a woman is slightly dangerous appears in the Old Testament and is the basis of parts of the Israelitish code.

The Levirate.—A common practice in primitive life is the levirate, which provides that when a man dies his widow and children be taken over by his brother, no matter how many wives the brother has. That is because the family is responsible for the woman and when she loses her means of support she has to rely on the family that has entered into contract with her. This means that one of her brothers-in-law actually marries her. Such a case is provided for in the Old Testament when Onan is told he must take that attitude toward his brother's family.

Endogamy and Exogamy.—Endogamy and exogamy are very puzzling facts in savage society, and most difficult to explain. There is a strong taboo against what we call incest; one of the most forceful taboos of primitive life ordinarily prevents a man from marrying a near relative. Most savages have two kinds of regulations about marriage. One, called exogamy, is that a man must marry outside his own small family group, and usually that he must marry outside his clan, though he is almost always permitted to marry within his tribe. The other limitation, called endogamy, is that he must go into a certain definite clan for his wife; if he is a member of Clan A he can not take a wife from Clan A or from Clan B, but must go to Clan C for her. The two regulations, exogamy and endogamy, work together to prevent close inbreeding.

All sorts of explanations of endogamy and exogamy have been given. One, suggested by Freud, MacDougall and others, is that at first savages lived practically in herds of one male to many females, that one male not allowing any other males to stay in the herd after they reached maturity, just as the stallion described by Darwin maintained his position as head of the herd of horses by driving out the male colts as they grew up, perhaps trying to kill them, so that one strong male kept company with many females. If this

---

[6] Knight, Peters and Blanchard, "Taboo and Genetics," Part II.

was the early situation among humans it would account for the growing up of a deep-rooted custom of exogamy, since all save the dominant male in each group had for generations been forced to seek their mates outside their immediate circle; but we have no evidence that human beings ever lived in herds of many females to one male, nor does this happen among the apes.

Some say there is an instinct which makes it difficult for people closely related to mate. Westermarck emphasized this. But this does not necessarily operate, as shown by numerous cases of brothers and sisters, ignorant of their relationship, marrying or planning to marry, and at the last moment learning their true identity. It is true that constant familiar association from childhood tends to decrease sex attraction so that one naturally wants to marry someone he has not seen daily throughout his life. Moreover, the marriage of close cousins is widespread in savage life; all the young men and women in one family marry all those in another family, and the children resulting from these unions marry back and forth, although they are double cousins, the four parents of each member of the second generation coming directly from but two families, so that close inbreeding results.

Certain students of the problems of exogamy and endogamy hold that these practices represented a conscious attempt to prevent inbreeding. The trouble with this theory is that it is hard to see how the savage could find out that inbreeding was bad, if it was, for present-day biologists have no conclusive evidence that inbreeding of humans is necessarily harmful. Many biologists go so far as to maintain that the intermarriage of close relatives is dangerous only if the strain is markedly poor in important characteristics. On the other hand, the breeder of animals considers it important not to allow his stock to become inbred; if that happens he thinks he gets inferior results. Yet here again are conflicting stands; Darwin reported that the English race-horse was an example of as close inbreeding as one could hope to find. Some of the smaller animals, such as rats, which produce offspring at the age of three months, have been very closely inbred for many generations in laboratory experimentation without loss of vitality. Since it is so difficult to determine the status of human inbreeding to-day, one can scarcely imagine the savage holding such definite ideas on the subject as to impel him to set up the strong taboos of endogamy and exogamy.

Other theories as to the origin of these savage taboos vary widely. One is that savages wanted to bring the tribes into unity by scattering the marriages, much as the royal marriages of Europe are arranged with a view to bringing the nations into harmony. Another theory is that there is a feeling of mysticism involved: certain people must not marry because of a notion of fictitious kinship based on the idea of ancestral origin or similarity of clan name.[7]

Freud recently came out with the ingenious theory that the whole situation was due to the father complexes and mother complexes of the savages.

We end where we started. Nobody knows what is responsible for these taboos, which are two of the strongest in savage society. The puzzle is accentuated by this variation which rarely occurs: brothers and sisters who are physically related but magically unrelated, being members of different totems, are sometimes allowed to marry. Still more perplexing is the fact that throughout many of the peoples who subscribe to the principles of endogamy and exogamy it is marriage alone that is forbidden within the confines of one's own and certain outlying groups; sex relationships are quite another matter, entirely unaffected by the degree of relationship of the participants.

The Mother Right.—Bachofen's "Das Mutterrecht," published in 1861, influenced the writings of those advocating sex equality, asserting as it did that women were originally the dominant sex in early savage society, and in some way men stole their power and made them subordinate; this was based on the idea that the mother knew her child and the child followed her, while the father was not recognized as having any part in the child, so that the family consisted in the mother and child only. Lester Ward even said that woman was superior to man physically at that time, so that, politically and physically, sex made woman the centre of the group. Recent investigation demonstrates that these theories have no basis in fact.

---

[7] Tozzer, A. M., "Social Origins and Social Continuities," pp. 155–178. Read, C., "The Origin of Man," pp. 307–317.

We do find two ways of descent recognized by the savage, one through the mother and one through the father, though it is hard to say whether matrilineal or patrilineal descent occurs more commonly among the simpler savages, and therefore we have little basis for determining which came first in the evolution of society. The more important thing is not from whom descent may come, but who decides where the married couple live. If the family is matrilocal, it is not the woman but her father and brothers who are powerful; the husband loses his status but the wife does not gain it, it goes to the males of her family. When the family is patrilocal, the man becomes predominant. Once again it is not clear that the matrilocal family precedes the patrilocal, or *vice versa;* the two seem to come hit or miss.

One of the chief factors in savage life that tend to make the male prominent is the religious doctrines, for from the first the male has the advantage at this point since he gets control of the ceremonial part of life and often leaves out the woman, not permitting her to have any part in religion. As the family moves about, it is the male usually that has the larger opportunity because the moment the wife leaves her people she is at the mercy of her husband. Migratory life is, therefore, apt to emphasize the power of the husband.

Secret societies are often the key to the inequality of women. These societies are organized by men for men, against women. One that flourished among the natives of Africa had an occasional celebration, usually at night, when the members, wearing masks so they would not be known, would frighten the women and whip any who had been troublesome to men during the preceding season. This was a sort of taming society that kept women in their place.

CHAPTER III

HISTORY OF THE AMERICAN FAMILY

European Background.—With the settlement of America, European culture was introduced into a new environment. This culture of the Old World was no sooner injected into the new surroundings than it began to be changed by the effort of the colonists to adapt themselves better to their actual conditions of living. It was, of course, the European family that was transported to the western shores, particularly the traditional family of England. In the development of the thirteen colonies, in spite of a considerable proportion of non-English people in the population, made up of Dutch, Swedes and Germans, the culture of the Old World which influenced the inhabitants of the territory which was to become the United States was, in both its legal and social expressions, more and more predominantly English.[1]

The colonial family, therefore, attempted to set itself in the English form. The experiences of the Virginia plantation had early taught those interested in the settlement of the New World that the colonists could not become prosperous or stable unless some provision was made for the furnishing of wives to the single men who had migrated across the water. With the establishment of permanent homes, there began at once an evolution of American family life which disclosed the influences of the new physical, economic, religious and political conditions.

Home Life in the Colonial Period.—England in the seventeenth century was not without its class distinctions and religious parties. These differences were brought to the new continent by the original settlers and at once showed themselves in social customs and family life. The environmental differences of the thirteen colonies, especially as shown in their various kinds of economic activity, also made uniformity of family life from New Hampshire to Georgia impossible. In sketching the general characteristics of

---

[1] Harlow, "Growth of the United States," p. 70.

family life in the New World, one must not forget that the complete picture will contain religious, class and sectional variations.

The frontier character of the early settlements led, as one would suppose, to a closeness of family ties. The family of the pioneer had to be self-reliant, depending largely upon itself for existence. Food, clothing, education, religion, recreation and even medical care had to be provided by the family working as a unit, that its existence under hard circumstances might be maintained. The severity of life in the wilderness and scattered communities reinforced the natural sympathy of the family and encouraged its harmonious working. It is not surprising that under such circumstances family interests were intensified to such an extent as to produce the clannish spirit which still shows itself in rural New England, and the pride of family which became characteristic of Southern aristocracy.

There was hard work for all the members of the family, including the children old enough to contribute their labor, but the woman was given the heaviest load, since she had not only to be housewife but mother as well; even though she took her hard lot as a matter of course, she aged prematurely, just as does the woman of the pioneering family among the mountain whites of our own times.

The preponderance of men over women, usual in frontier life, undoubtedly acted as an advantage to the latter and mitigated to some extent the rigor of man's dominance. As each section developed into more thickly populated communities this disparity in the proportion of the sexes passed, but until recently the frontier persisted, ever moving westward, and with it went the tendency to grant women a nearer approach to equality of opportunity. Although this is by no means the only reason why woman suffrage came out of the West, it certainly played a part.

Colonial conditions led to early marriage. Of Connecticut youth, for example, it was said by one writing in 1704, " They generally marry very young, the males oftener, as I am told, under twenty years than above." The girls often married at sixteen or younger, and an unmarried woman at twenty-five entered the ranks of the old maids. Calhoun tells us that " New England family policy pressed as heavily upon the unattached man as on the isolated

woman. Bachelors were rare and were viewed with disapproval.
They were almost in the class of suspected criminals. . . . In
Hartford solitary men were taxed twenty shillings a week." [2]

After the Revolutionary War we find the same tendency toward
early marriage in the new frontier over the Alleghenies. In
Kentucky early marriages were common, men of eighteen or twenty
wedding girls of fourteen or sixteen.[3]

The social conditions that led to early marriage also encouraged
the re-marriage of widows and widowers and cut short their period
of formal mourning. Although the first marriage in Plymouth
Colony was an exceptional case, it was indicative of a situation that
demanded that family ties broken by death be replaced by others
as quickly as possible. In this marriage Edward Winslow, who had
been a widower only seven weeks, was married to Susannah White,
who had lost her husband twelve weeks earlier.[4]

It is stated that a governor of colonial New Hampshire married a lady whose previous husband had been dead just ten days.
It is possible, however, for us to exaggerate the influence of frontier
conditions in inducing early marriage and quick re-marriage. The
fact that we find these trends in the seventeenth century English
mores is evidence that we are not dealing here merely with the
difficulty of meeting pioneering conditions unmated. The
American frontier, nevertheless, favored the continuation of such
customs and also provided opportunity that made it easy for the
young people, accustomed to hard work, to leave the home of their
parents, knowing that courage and industry would soon enable
them to win from the unclaimed wilderness conditions as pleasant
as those they had left.

Early marriage and other social conditions stimulated the
American birth rate. As a consequence, the colonial fecundity
was one of the highest on record. Francis A. Walker, an authori-
tative American statistician, has said:

There is not the shadow of a statistical reason for attributing to the
native American population prior to the War of Secession a deficiency in
reproductive vigor compared with any people that ever lived.

---

[2] " Social History of the American Family," vol. i, pp. 67–68.
[3] Ibid., vol. ii, p. 14.
[4] Ibid., vol. i, p. 69.

Public opinion was favorable to the high birth rate. After the formation of the Union there was a national sentiment which encouraged large families. With the industrial development of the nation a rapid increase in population was also for the advantage of the large land-owner and of those engaged in trade and manufacturing. Along with the high birth rate went a correspondingly high death rate. In many a large family the majority of the children did not travel beyond childhood. Preventive medicine had not originated; even curative medicine could do little to curb most infectious diseases. An inscription on a Plymouth grave-stone is said to read, "Here lies ——— ——— with twenty small children." [5] Fortunately such a family history was not characteristic even of the colonial period. In spite of the high mortality of children, the excess of births over deaths was such as to send the population steadily upward.

Courtship was adjusted to the environmental conditions. It was, as one would expect, frank and generally brief. Although the conscientious parent kept a watchful eye upon his daughter, the frontier environment forbade seclusion. It was natural, also, in settlements made up of persons of kindred spirit, often largely relatives and friends, that the girl should be permitted greater freedom than would have been granted by the same parents on the other side. Courtship had to conform to the limited space of the houses, and until the singing school came in New England to help provide an opportunity for the youth to come together, much of the courting had to take place in the living-room, sometimes in the presence of their elders. Restricted quarters, without question, explain the revival of the old folkway, bundling, in colonial New England. Although from the beginning frowned upon by some, it was current from New York northward, but most common in Massachusetts and Connecticut. It is interesting to notice that it was attacked vigorously after the return of the colonial youth from the French and Indian wars, when their loose morals turned it to vice and it became a public scandal.[6]

The coarseness of manners in the colonies, both north and south, showed itself not only in courtship but in other elements of

---

[5] *Ibid.*, vol. i, p. 89.
[6] *Ibid.*, vol. i, p. 129.

3

family life. While this situation has been treated too lightly by those who have attempted to idealize history, it is only fair to remember that such conditions were characteristic of the period. Even the religious zeal and stern theology of the New Englanders could not protect them from the prevailing coarseness of the seventeenth and eighteenth centuries.

Status of the Colonial Wife.—The popular religion of the colonists, particularly in New England, though it can scarcely be said to be the product of the hard life of the frontier, was certainly in harmony with the setting in which the people found themselves. It was largely taken from the Old Testament and emphasized, so far as the family was concerned, the patriarchal character of the Jewish home. Family conditions were linked with the Scriptures until they appeared divinely sanctioned. The husband, of course, sat in the seat of power as the patriarch. It was the business of his spouse to demonstrate by obedience and subordination her piety and religious fervor.

In law woman's status was always that of inferiority. The colonists, whether Cavaliers or Puritans, had been trained among legal traditions that defined woman as legally inferior to man. The English law became our Common Law, and it placed woman in so great an economic dependence upon man that even the clothing and ornaments of a married woman were the property of the husband and could be disposed of by him according to his wish, while on the contrary his property was his absolute possession, to which she could lay no claim. The following excerpt taken from Blackstone's Commentaries, published in 1765, reveals the temper of the English law as it attempted to define the legal status of woman:

By marriage the husband and wife are one person in law: that is, the very being or legal existence of the woman is suspended during the marriage, or at least is incorporated and consolidated into that of the husband: under whose wing, protection, and *cover*, she performs everything; . . . Upon this principle, of an union of person in husband and wife, depend most of the legal rights, duties, and disabilities, that either of them acquire by the marriage. . . . For this reason a man cannot grant anything to his wife, or enter into covenant with her, for the grant would be to suppose her separate existence: and to covenant with her would be only to covenant with himself: and therefore it is also generally true that all compacts made between husband and wife, when single, are voided by the intermarriage. . . The husband also (by the old law) might give his wife moderate correction. For, as he is to answer for her behavior, the law thought it reasonable to intrust him with this power of restraining her, by domestic chastisement, in the same moderation that a man is allowed to correct his apprentices or children; for whom the master or parent is also liable in some cases to answer. But this power of correction was confined within reasonable bounds. . . . The civil law gave the husband the same, or a larger, authority over his wife: . . . But with us in the politer reign of Charles the Second, this power of coercion began to be doubted: and a wife may now have security of the peace against her husband; or, in return, a husband against his wife. Yet the lower rank of people, who were always fond of the old common law, still claim and exert their ancient privilege; and the courts of law still permit a husband to restrain a wife of her liberty, in case of any gross misbehavior.

These are the chief legal effects of marriage during the coverture; upon which we may observe, that even the disabilities which the wife lies under are for the most part intended for her protection and benefit. So great a favorite is the female sex of the laws of England.[7]

If the husband of the period was chiefly interested in defining his wife's subordination because of its significance for his control of the property of the family, his wife doubtless suffered most in her loss of legal rights from the greater power the husband had in the control of their children. How deeply this was embedded in the common law that colored American jurisprudence comes out when we learn of such facts as the following:

In 1911 there were, for instance, still seven states in which the father could by will prevent the mother from being the guardian of her own children after his death. There were twenty-four states in which the mother during the lifetime of the father had no legal right whatever in the control of the children, that is, states in which the father was the sole guardian.[8]

Harsh as was the definition of woman's status in the colonial period, it was nevertheless true that the husband was forced to accept some responsibilities in his marriage; he had to support her in the manner justified by his circumstances, and he was liable not only for the debts she contracted after marriage, but for those she had at the time of the ceremony. Colonial law also assured to the wife her dowry rights. In most of the colonies she was protected from the beating of the husband, although this was a right he had long enjoyed under English law.

Divorce in the Colonial Period.—The American colonies, as is the case at present in our states, differed greatly with respect to

---

[7] "Commentaries on the Laws of England," 15th edition, vol. i, pp. 441–445.

[8] Wolfe, "Readings in Social Problems," p. 447.

laws concerning divorce. In New England we find the idea of civil marriage in the place of an ecclesiastical marriage, and also divorce by the power of the colony. The Puritans were more influenced by what they considered the spirit of the New Testament than by the English law to which they had been accustomed. They practically did away with the canonical decree of separation "from bed and board" and replaced it with divorce, which was granted for various causes.

In Massachusetts after 1692, the control of matrimony and divorce was placed in the hands of the Governor and his Council. Governor Hutchinson, who for many years presided over the divorce court, states in his history of Massachusetts that what would have been considered a just cause for separation in a spiritual court was usually considered sufficient ground for an absolute divorce. Divorce was always granted automatically in the case of female adultery, and after considerable debate on the subject it was decided that in the case of male adultery divorce was not justified.

Connecticut was particularly liberal and modern in its attitude toward divorce; in 1670 this colony permitted remarriage to a woman who had not heard from her husband for eight years or more. Although the wives of New England received greater consideration than those of the other colonies, they were nevertheless discriminated against as compared with men. The trend in this section was to grant divorces most often on the grounds of cruelty, desertion and failure of the husband to support.

In the middle colonies we find a more conservative policy with reference to divorce. New Netherlands had granted few divorces for adultery or separation, but after the colony came under English rule it followed the English tradition, that placed the power to decree separation from bed and board in the ecclesiastical court, which, however, was denied the power of granting absolute divorce. As New York did not provide an ecclesiastical court for the trying of such cases, few separations were ever granted. The same situation existed in Pennsylvania, except that while New York had granted a few special separations by act of the Governor, who apparently acted without legal power, in the case of the neighboring colony the legislature acted in two cases to grant absolute divorce.

The southern colonies followed the teaching of the Church of England, but their failure to establish ecclesiastical courts to handle cases asking for separation resulted in there not being any power by which a legalized separation could be brought about. Separations, however, occurred and it was necessary for the courts to handle the question of maintenance. Record is made of such a case in Maryland; and in Virginia the county courts appear to have taken over the power of granting alimony, although they seem to have acted without statutory authority. It is interesting to notice that the English home government did not challenge the New England colonies in their policy of granting divorces, even though this was contrary to the English law.

Family Discipline.—The discipline of children was generally severe and the atmosphere of the home, at least in New England, repressive. Reverence for authority and respect for elders were taught children from their first years. There was great confidence in the value of the rod as a means of child-training. Fathers exercised their authority with the knowledge that the neighbor's eyes were on them and that any laxity would be frowned upon. The children were early introduced into the morbid teachings of New England theology, and all in all one gets the impression that to a child New England presented a sad and hard existence. It is possible, however, to exaggerate the burdens of the colonial child. There were undoubtedly parents who were sympathetic and affectionate, nor must it be forgotten that rigorous times tend to make stern parents.

The Family and the Western Frontier.—As the American population from the original settlements pressed over the Appalachian Mountains and scattered through the great stretches of wilderness, the frontier life of the early colonial period was continued, but with definite social modifications. Just as the English people who planted themselves along the Atlantic seaboard were gradually forced by their distance from the homeland and the changes in their environment to construct a new culture which, although English in its basic elements, was largely different, so also the American migrants from the South, New York and New England in like manner were led by the necessity of adapting themselves to new conditions into the building of a social life distinctly their own.[9]

The first settlers of the West were mostly from the South. Shortly an ever increasing number from New England, New York and the Middle States poured into the new territory. Later, an alien element from Europe, Germans, Irish and Scandinavians, appeared, and each of these groups of settlers added something to the social life of the towns and cities of the rapidly developing West. The family life that formed under these circumstances was of necessity a product of this mingling of people trained previously in such widely differing cultures, and of the influences that came out of the environment itself. While the New England habits and traditions largely prevailed, the family life was less stern, in part as a result of the contacts of Yankee parents with the more indulgent Southern and European fathers and mothers. The patriarchal home of the early New England theology was also out of season, for, with the passing of the years, this paternal authority had softened even in its place of origin in this country. The Western people, freer of ancient traditions and readier in adaptation, moved more rapidly toward a happier childhood and a greater equality of the sexes.

It was the more prolific families of the East that went into the frontier. The conditions of the West also encouraged parents in the having of children, for, as always when new and cheap lands are being brought under cultivation, a large family was an economic advantage.

Although manners were rough and conversation among the males often coarse, the prevailing domestic ethics were on a high level. Divorce was rare and vice uncommon. In the less settled parts everyone was well known to his neighbors and, as a consequence, there was a keen sense of the force of public opinion. Girls were given a large measure of social freedom in the belief, which was largely justified, that they were fully capable of taking care of themselves. The self-reliance of the modern American girl, which is everywhere recognized as a characteristic product of our culture, developed especially from the freedom of the girl on the western frontier.

---

[9] Turner, F. J., "The Frontier in American History," Ch. XIII.

It was to be expected that the coeducational college should start and thrive in the West. Its origin was not merely the economical desire to escape duplication of equipment. It was the natural issue of the free contacts of boys and girls from early childhood on through their schooling. When higher education was provided, it was the logical step and in accord with the attitude of public opinion that both men and women were given entrance into the new institutions, and thus continued their study in the advanced subjects in an association to which they had long been accustomed. Indiana, in its constitution of 1816, expressed the democratic trend of the West when it accepted as a matter of course the idea of equal educational opportunities for both sexes in its provision for a " general system of education ascending in regular gradations from township schools to a State University, wherein tuition shall be gratis and equally open to all." [10]

Slavery and Family Life.—In the colonial period we find slaves both North and South. The plantation system, and in particular the development of cotton growing as the major agricultural interest in the South, led to the prolongation and extension of the slave system of production in the section below the Mason and Dixon line. Once firmly established upon a slave basis, the Southern people found it difficult to discover the archaic and uneconomic character of slavery, especially after emotions were stirred by the bitter attacks of Northern reformers.

As slavery colored all the social life of the South, so it stamped its influence upon the family. The negroes on the whole had a meager and uncertain home life. Their domestic situation was largely dependent on the attitude of the owner. At best it was precarious; at its worst it reveals the most serious moral hazards of slavery.

White children on the plantations were not and could not be segregated from the negroes. Negro servants often cared for their master's children practically from birth. The black and white children came in contact constantly; not infrequently they played together. When cruelty was practised against the blacks, white children were coarsened and hurt. Because of their superstitious

---

[10] *Ibid.*, p. 282.

and vicious topics, negro conversations were not uncommonly harmful in the young life of listening children. Slavery of necessity perpetuated among the negroes the social standards of an illiterate and irresponsible people. White children could not be entirely protected from the influences of a social environment made up in part of elements contributed by the negro slaves.

Without exaggeration of the worst results of slavery as they appeared in miscegenation, and remembering the sympathy and affection which so often existed between the owner's family and the slaves, the strength of which was given vivid demonstration by the loyalty of slaves to their masters during the testing of the Civil War, it is nevertheless clear that slavery as a system struck at the roots of wholesome family life for the whites as well as the blacks. Family life tended to keep to a social level in accord with the attempt to continue a system which was becoming more and more an anachronism. The passing of slavery relieved the Southern family of burden in the same way that the wage system of industry has stimulated the prosperity of the Southern States.

It is a pity, however, that American statesmanship was unequal to the task of transmuting the slave system into that of free labor without the social costs of the Civil War. The war between the States struck the Southern home immediately a crushing blow, and the suffering that followed delayed the commercial and cultural contributions that the South is now giving in fuller measure to our national life.

The Civil War and Family Life.—The Civil War affected the Northern family also. The conflict was of course temporarily a great impetus to business, especially manufacturing. The number of producers being restricted, those who remained at home had plenty of employment and the mills multiplied, even though often working day and night. As men went out of industry women were drawn in. In the West, women, as in the recent World War, engaged in various forms of agriculture; in the East they were drained from rural sections into the towns and cities to carry on in mills work formerly given to men.

Many women had their horizons widened by the new occupations and opportunities that came to them through the war. Some acted as nurses and, through their service, exchanged their former environment for the more exciting contacts at Washington or some base hospital. Some entered government work as clerks at Washington. Others carried on activities that previously had been considered exclusively man's.

Women were taught by their humanitarian and patriotic enterprises to coöperate in various kinds of public activity. It was inevitable that these experiences should strengthen the demands of women for a greater share of self-expression and more social independence. Their growing sense of power was reflected in a less docile acceptance of the inferiority which men had come to consider one of the unchanging fundamentals of society. Agitation for social equality was stimulated.

The war with its great loss of life, North and South, accelerated the immigration of Europeans, who replaced the wastage of native stock and flooded industry with the cheap labor necessary for the rapid development of manufacturing. Cities became more magnetic and drew an ever increasing multitude from rural sections. Congestion of population arose in the Northern cities, creating slums as menacing to social welfare as those of the Old World.

The moral strain of the war showed itself in various experiences of corruption in the Government that were revealed in the years following the war.[11] The rapid growth of cities with the segregation of different nationalities in colonies that kept a considerable amount of their Old World customs made possible the political machine and boss and the low level of political life percolated back into the homes.

Many of the soldiers who had enlisted from rural communities when very young came into contact with vices of which they had previously known nothing. In the decades following the war commercial prostitution appeared in the cities in the proportions of a serious social evil, corrupting the police and becoming a most profitable source of graft. Although bound to grow with the rapid development of cities, particularly where immigration crowded into the Atlantic seaboard cities, prostitution without question got a firmer foothold because of the influence of war conditions.

Modern Industry and the American Family.—The industrial

[11] Harlow, "Growth of the United States," p. 556.

revolution, which changed manufacturing from a household factory system, developed more slowly in the United States than in England, in part because England attempted to keep secret its inventions and to prevent its machinery from being exported to the New World, and in part because the old country with its more thickly settled territory was riper for the change.

Factories did, however, develop in the Northern States, although delayed by English policy and by the rural character of the population. With the coming of the factories a new field of employment was offered women, since men continued in agriculture and trade, both of which seemed more profitable. The mills depended largely upon women from rural communities, and about 1830 we find the beginning of the movement of workers toward the mill towns.[12] These women who came to Lawrence, Lowell, New Bedford and other manufacturing places were mostly from the country; they entered the mills without loss of caste since mill-work at that time had the same dignity for women that farming had for their fathers and brothers. The situation changed later when the mills were filled with *foreigners* as a result of the influx of immigrants from Europe.

The women were young and were rarely married. Sometimes married women worked for a time to help their husbands pay for a home. Widows also found in the manufacturing towns opportunities to earn a living by keeping boarders. Dickens, a keen observer who visited Lowell, gives this testimony in his American Notes in 1842 regarding the condition of the young women workers:

These girls were all well dressed; and that phrase necessarily includes extreme cleanliness. They had serviceable bonnets, good warm cloaks and shawls; and were not above clogs and pattens. Moreover, there were places in the mill in which they could deposit these things without injury; and there were conveniences for washing. They were healthy in appearance, many of them remarkably so, and had the manners and deportment of young women: not of degraded brutes of burden. . .

The rooms in which they worked were as well ordered as themselves. In the windows of some, there were green plants, which were trained to shade the glass; in all there was as much fresh air, cleanliness, and comfort as the nature of the occupation would possibly admit of. . . . .

They reside in various boarding-houses near at hand. The owners of the

12 "Population Growth in Southern New England," *American Statistical Association Publications*, vol. xv, p. 813.

mills are particularly careful to allow no persons to enter upon the possession of these houses, whose characters have not undergone the most
searching and thorough inquiry. Any complaint that is made against
them, by the boarders, or by any one else, is fully investigated; and if good
ground of complaint be shown to exist against them, they are removed, and
their occupation is handed over to some more deserving person. . . . There
is a joint-stock piano in a great many of the boarding-houses. Nearly all
these young ladies subscribe to circulating libraries. They have got up
among themselves a periodical called *The Lowell Offering*, "A respository
of original articles, written exclusively by females actively employed in
the mills,"—which is duly printed, published, and sold; and whereof I
brought away from Lowell four hundred good solid pages, which I have
read from beginning to end. . . . Of the merits of *The Lowell Offering* as
a literary production, I will only observe, putting entirely out of sight
the fact of the articles having been written by these girls after the
arduous labours of the day, that it will compare advantageously with a
great many English Annuals.

Child Labor.—Children were also employed in the mills from
their first establishment. This was not strange, for child labor
was in accord with the Puritan's notion of childhood and his attitude toward play. The child was safe if at work. Idleness—
and play was not uncommonly interpreted as idleness—was the
Devil's opportunity.

It was of course nothing new for children to work. They had
long been accustomed to working with their parents either on the
farm or in the household industries. The factory merely provided
a different kind of work. There was no realization on the part of
many that machine industry necessarily meant overstrain for the
child and that an industry that was run for profits had no interest
in the child's welfare. Factory labor was nothing like the tasks of
the home as a training experience for life; the factory owner was,
even when humane in his purposes, unable to give his child workers
the safeguards furnished by parents of normal affection.

Samuel Slater, who started the first cotton mill in Rhode
Island, followed the English custom of employing entire families,
though it is stated that during 1790 and 1791 his operatives were
almost exclusively children of seven to twelve years of age.[13] The
Committee on Manufactures in 1816 estimated that there were
24,000 boys under seventeen and 66,000 women and girls in the
total number of 100,000 workers in cotton mills.

[13] Cheney, W. L., "Industry and Human Welfare," p. 51.

The first attack on child factory labor came from the governor of Rhode Island in 1818. Massachusetts in 1825 ordered an investigation of child labor in " incorporated manufacturing companies." It was stated after an investigation that the boys and girls in the mills worked twelve or thirteen hours a day. Beginning with Connecticut and Massachusetts in 1842, several states passed laws attempting to regulate the hours of child labor in the factories. None of these laws provided adequate means of enforcement and as a result they did little more than record a growing sentiment against the exploitation of child life by modern industry. Laws regarding school attendance were more effectual, and in this movement Massachusetts led with a law passed in 1836, which provided that children under fifteen years of age must attend school three months out of twelve. The report of the Massachusetts Labor Commission in 1866 proves that this law was not well enforced. From a Woonsocket manufacturer comes this statement regarding the working hours of children:

> From eight years old and upwards, they work full time—rise at four and a half A.M., having thirty minutes for breakfast, forty-five minutes for dinner, and leave work at seven P.M., fourteen and a half hours. . . . Manufacturers in Massachusetts and in Rhode Island pay little regard to the law respecting the employment of children.[14]

The following testimony was given by one who knew conditions in Fall River:

> Question.—Was there any one who ever tried to cause the children to be sent to school?
> Answer.—Not since old man Robeson died.
> Q.—Why do not the parents send them to school?
> A.—Small help is scarce; a great deal of the machinery has been stopped for want of small help, so the overseers have been going around to draw the small children from the schools into the mills; the same as a draft in the army.[15]

A laborer from the same city testified that children as young as seven were employed in the mills. He had his own children work because their earnings were necessary for the maintenance of the family. His attitude toward child labor was expressed with pathetic simplicity:

[14] *Ibid.*, p. 54.
[15] *Ibid.*, p. 55.

I don't know that I have any more to say, except that I have two little boys, one eleven and the other about eight and a half. I am no scholar myself because I have always been working in the mill, and I am sorry for it. I don't want my children to be brought up the same way. I wish to get them to work a little less hours so that I can send them to night school. I want, if it is possible, to get a law so that they can go to school and know how to read and write their own names.[16]

Child labor is by no means the dead issue many people think it. Its control by legislation is considered further in Chapter 15 on Conservation of the Family.

Unorthodox Family Life.—Of the various peculiar types of family life that developed in the United States, that of the Mormons is by far the most important. The doctrine of plural marriages based upon a literal imitation of Old Testament practices was not at first a part of the theology of the new church but appeared very early. It was without question due to their teaching of polygyny that the Mormons were treated with such hostility when as a rule all sorts of religious sects and doctrines were received with characteristic tolerance by the orthodox Americans. To the Mormons, in spite of early opposition on the part of some of the leaders, polygyny came to be the normal family form built upon a divine sanction. Marriage was for eternity, if accompanied by the ecclesiastical ceremony of " sealing," and was a necessary preparation for heavenly bliss. A man could be sealed to any number of women but a woman to only one man. Polygyny made possible the giving of earthly bodies to a multitude of spirits which had long waited opportunity for incarnation.

Eastern agitation against Mormon polygyny was carried on with a zeal only less than that which had marked the attack on southern slavery. The orthodox churches were determined to destroy the western monster that disgraced the land and when missionary enterprise proved futile they demanded laws forbidding polygyny. Laws were easy to pass in Washington but difficult to enforce in Utah. The eastern reformers forgot that the Mormon family life, although built upon a polygynous basis, had the same tenacious sentiments that always gather about the home and make regulations of the family difficult to legislate with success.

The student of the American family must, as Calhoun suggests,

---

[16] *Ibid.*

keep in mind that the Utah experiment was made possible by abnormal conditions that were certain to pass away. The country was a frontier, the people an alien minority who needed the strength of numbers for protection and prosperity. The surplus of unmarried women in the east, by providing a reservoir to be drawn from, alone made possible the plural marriages of Utah, for with the sexes in an approximate equality polygyny cannot exist.

The agitation against the plural marriage system came not from the women concerned but from eastern women. It is necessary to remember, however, that this may demonstrate the degree of the subordination of Mormon women rather than the success of their marriage form.

The Mormons gave up polygyny as a common practice as the price paid for admission into the Union as a State. Without question social conditions were already making ground against polygyny in a way law failed to do. Modern life with its economic competition and popularizing of high standards of life, coupled with the passing of cheap land, would in any case have put an end to Mormon polygyny except as the sporadic luxury of a few wealthy leaders. Already the existence of the early polygynous family has become to the younger Mormons of to-day a fact as much out of harmony with their personal preferences as it would be for any other group of American youth.[17]

Another interesting departure from the conventional form of marriage and family was developed by the Bible Communists or Oneida Community. The founder of this organization, as in the case of the Mormons, was a Vermonter who found it necessary to remove from local prejudices. Going from Putney, Vermont, the members of the new fellowship established themselves at Oneida, New York, where after a short period of hardship they began to prosper.

Their communism extended to the family and resulted in a definite kind of group marriage. In spite of their radical teaching and practices with reference to sex relations, the community was not disturbed; indeed as a result of their high business ethics the mem-

---

[17] Werner, M. R., "Brigham Young," p. 372.

bers enjoyed the respect and friendliness of those who came to know them locally.

The founder of this community, John H. Noyes, had from the first stated that social opposition might force them to abandon their peculiar family organization, and in 1879 as a result of agitation led by church organizations of central New York, they gave up their complex marriage and reorganized their business by incorporation as a stock company.

Noyes had no sympathy with what he termed free love; his statement is this:

> Our Communities are *families* as distinctly bounded and separated from promiscuous society as ordinary households. The tie that binds us together is as permanent and sacred, to say the least, as that of common marriage, for it is our religion. We receive no new members (except by deception and mistake) who do not give heart and hand to the family interest for life and for ever. Community of property extends just as far as freedom of love. Every man's care and every dollar of the common property are pledged for the maintenance and protection of the women and the education of the children of the Community.[18]

The Shaker experiment is interesting as an extraordinary basis for a religious organization but, built as it was on the idea of celibacy as one of the cardinal commands of the spiritual life, it could not have social significance. It has gradually dwindled and has now all but passed.

Robert Owen in his unsuccessful socialistic experiment at New Harmony, Indiana, appears not to have advocated the marriage ideas he expressed at a later time, but he did develop a dormitory care for the children as soon as they could leave their parents safely, and a nursery school. His enterprise has no greater interest for the student of the family than Brook Farm and the other communistic communities that during this period sprung up and died in various parts of the United States.

The Present American Family.—Since the Civil War the American family has been principally influenced by the following: the urban trend, the further development of capitalistic industry, the extension of public education, the social influences of immigration, and the greater equality of women. The home has responded to these conditions of modern life chiefly by the passing of the

---

[18] " Encyclopædia Britannica," 11th edition, vol. xx, p. 107.

patriarchal family, the decrease of the birth rate among the native stock, an increase in divorces, and the farming out to other institutions of many of the functions formerly carried on by the home. A description of the present family situation involves a discussion of the social problems of the modern home, a task that explains the purpose of this book.

The World War certainly influenced American family life, although we are still too near the event to detect all of its effects. It acted as did the Civil War as a means of opening up new opportunities to women, especially in industry, increased their experience in organizing public activities, gave them a larger social freedom, and to some extent stimulated among younger women more radical ideas regarding marriage. Women were quick to make use of the new advantages that war conditions provided for them, and as a consequence they are that much nearer equality with males.

The automobile is a new factor that has had and is still having a large influence upon the family. It affects the home in so many different ways that no consistent generalization can safely be made concerning it. As with all of man's inventions it increases social opportunity and at the same time makes possible evils that result from its misuse. On the one hand it has provided means for a multitude to live outside the crowded city in which they are employed, and has given all classes a fascinating recreation; on the other side we find it leading many to prefer luxury to home enjoyments, while for some it becomes an instrument for vice.

Causes of Agitation for Woman's Rights.—In the history of the American family the agitation for Woman's Rights holds a significant place. The leaders in the movement were anxious to gain more than suffrage for woman, but until this was finally granted they held to it as their immediate goal.

The demand for greater political and social opportunity for woman was an inevitable product of the evolution of modern civilization, but the trend away from female subordination was stimulated by the industrial revolution. Although this radical change in the form of production was attended with such suffering among the working classes that it appeared destructive of the old-time home life of these people, in the end it brought about conditions that made the denial of woman suffrage increasingly unjust. When the woman, whether married or single, went outside the home to take her place in the factory as a competitor with men for a daily wage, it became clear that she was handicapped by the fact that she had no vote.   This discrimination was plainly seen in England, once the male workers had been given the franchise.   In the American colonies women land-owners were theoretically entitled to the suffrage, but the legal and social status of a woman was too well established as inferior to that of man to permit woman suffrage to become a reality.   Even male suffrage was undemocratic, being governed by religious and property qualifications.

When the Constitution of the United States was adopted and the several States regulated the process of voting, the suffrage was definitely placed on a male basis.   Soon slight modifications occurred, as, for example, the permission granted widows in Kentucky to vote on educational matters.   As has been said, the frontier as it moved farther and farther westward developed a civilization freer from tradition and more open-minded with reference to the political rights of women.

Along with the industrial changes which had made woman a competitor of man's for the means of earning a livelihood, there went also a still greater tendency toward opening up to women political rights.   Gradually women obtained more and more opportunity to continue their education.   As they broke through tradition at this point and were admitted into high schools and finally into colleges and professional schools on equal terms with men, the political discrimination against women grew more and more indefensible.   It was the educated women who led in the fight, although it was obvious that the working women had more to gain by the privilege of registering their will through suffrage.

Slavery agitation early became allied with the Woman's Rights movement.   Women who took part in the attack upon slavery were also leaders in the drive for their own enfranchisement.   The experience that they obtained in organizing against slavery and to some extent speaking against it on the public platform gave them splendid preparation for work on the other reform of such significance to themselves.   On the whole, those interested in Woman's Rights joined heartily in efforts for social reform such as the abolition of the saloon and the doing away with slavery.   Many other

4

women actively fought those committed to woman suffrage, but the Anti-suffrage party was greatly handicapped because it seemed that by antagonizing the leaders engaged in the struggle for Woman's Rights they became the party defending the exploitations that the others were attacking. Thus they grew less and less influential as a result of their apparent conservatism and willingness to let social conditions remain as they were.

As the Mountain and Pacific States one by one granted suffrage to women for State elections, the political leverage exercised by the women engaged in agitation for a Federal woman suffrage law grew greater. Neither of the dominant political parties wanted to antagonize the women voters of the Western States. As the leaders of the two parties temporized with the growing agitation for complete suffrage for women, the industrial and educational and social influences that led toward women's full political rights gradually increased the number of thinking people who saw that eventually political rights could not be maintained on a sex basis.

Then came the war and, as in England, the part that women took in the ordeal gave them a reasonable ground for demanding what no longer could be denied without clear evidence of prejudice. The modern suffragists who adopted an aggressive program pushed to the utmost the opportunity the war brought them. Finally President Wilson reversed his former attitude that suffrage for women should come only through state legislation, and recommended a Federal law; the amendment which had twice passed the House of Representatives was voted June 4, 1919, by the Senate, and by the end of the year twenty-two States had ratified it. Thirty-six States were necessary, and the number was completed by Tennessee accepting the amendment in August, 1920. Wyoming had granted State suffrage in 1869, Colorado in 1893, Idaho and Utah in 1896, Washington in 1910, California in 1911, Arizona, Nevada, Kansas and Oregon in 1912, South Dakota in 1913, and Montana in 1914. It is clear that the Far West was most ready to act upon the logic of the changing social conditions of American women.

Advantages Expected from Suffrage.—The advocates of woman suffrage argued for the change because of its advantage both for women and for the State. It was claimed by many that woman's voting would be more rational than that of man because she entered the political arena free from the traditions that limited the insight of man. It was also urged that woman's practical interest in family matters, especially those having to do with children, would bring to the Government an element hitherto lacking because of its exclusively male character. Mothers could be depended upon to press forward the needs of children.

So far as women were concerned, they expected to help themselves by changing laws that discriminated against them, opening up greater educational opportunities and having means by which the Government could be made sensitive to the desires and needs of women, especially the working women.

Evils Prophesied from Woman Suffrage.—It is interesting and even rather startling to look back at the arguments advanced against suffrage. One of the favorite statements was that suffrage would ruin the home. Much was made of the possibility, which in the minds of the opponents of the suffrage seemed to be a certainty, that wives would have different political commitments from those of their husbands, thus leading to a division of the family. The increasing trend toward a democratic home was ignored by those who made this attack; they assumed that the family would be shattered unless it remained upon a foundation of man's dominance. It was also said that woman would be unsexed by her political activities; just what was meant by this was always difficult to determine. It was a sentimental attack upon the kind of woman that social conditions were inevitably producing; the protected and segregated woman was conceived of as normal. Any variation from this pattern was pronounced an unsexed specimen.

It was also claimed that politics would grow increasingly emotional and sentimental as a result of the appearance of women among the voters. This argument was based upon the common notion that women were more emotional and more given to sentiment than were men. It was prophesied by some that out of the voting of women would develop a sex antagonism between men and women. A Woman's Party would arise that would fight the interests and wishes of men. It is disconcerting to read from so careful an interpreter of history as Francis Parkman these dire predictions regarding the mischievous effects of woman suffrage:

Neither Congress, nor the States, nor the united voice of the whole people could permanently change the essential relations of the sexes. Universal female suffrage, even if decreed, would undo itself in time; but the attempt to establish it would work deplorable mischief. The question is whether the persistency of a few agitators shall plunge us blindfold into the most reckless of all experiments; whether we shall adopt this supreme device for developing the defects of women, and demolish their real power to build an ugly mockery instead. For the sake of womanhood, let us hope not. In spite of the effect on the popular mind of the incessant repetition of a few trite fallacies, and in spite of the squeamishness that prevents the vast majority averse to the movement from uttering a word against it, let us trust that the good sense of the American people will vindicate itself against this most unnatural and pestilent revolution. In the full and normal development of womanhood lie the best interests of the world. Let us labor earnestly for it; and, that we may not labor in vain, let us save women from the barren perturbations of American politics. Let us respect them; and, that we may do so, let us pray for deliverance from female suffrage.[19]

The Results of Woman Suffrage.—The most surprising thing about the voting of women has been the little difference that it has seemed to make in our political life. The disturbances prophesied failed to develop. At first it appeared merely that the number of voters had been greatly increased. As time passed, however, it became clear that woman had gained considerably in her progress toward social equality. The government did show a larger interest in matters that pertained to the home. The politician became more sensitive to woman's attitudes on social questions. Prohibition as a national policy is an illustration of the influence of women upon legislation, for women are much more committed to the prohibition policy than are men. They are also more solidly against commercialized prostitution. In such movements woman's power was felt before she had the vote, but her suffrage gives her greater opportunity to express her convictions in a way that carries political pressure.

Women are quite conscious that they have not yet obtained full social opportunity. Agitations for changes in the legal and economic status of women still continue. Attempts, for example, to make the salaries for men and women in corresponding positions in our public schools the same attest this effort on the part of women to reach full equality. Their attack upon the discrimination exercised by educational policy which discharges women who

_____
[19] Pamphlet issued some time between 1876 and 1880.

marry, while taking no notice at all of the marriage of males, is another testimony of the demand of women for complete equality.

Those who expected women to be little influenced by the existing political parties were disappointed, for if women came into politics free from former entanglements, they were easily brought into line and for the most part are at present allied to one of the dominant parties. It is not at all demonstrated yet, however, that eventually women may not bring into politics the pressure of a sex party which will transcend the less significant alignments of the old parties.

The most discouraging thing regarding the suffrage of women has been the considerable number of women who have not exercised their right of suffrage and who have had practically no interest in political matters. It must not be forgotten that many males take the same attitude. Indeed one of our recent Presidents did not care enough about practical politics to vote, so the records show, in the Presidential election previous to his own. Even if the suffrage is not exercised by women to the extent that was expected by those who led in the agitation for the franchise, the fact that they can vote if they will has no small political significance, which in the long run is bound to be for their advantage. It is not possible to trace clearly any effect on the home that has come out of suffrage, except that it has tended to strengthen the trend, inevitable in any case, toward a family firmly established on a democratic basis, with the inequalities of the paternal type of home life pushed aside.

Contemporary Movements.—What is known as the Woman's Movement did not come to an end with the granting of equal suffrage. There were and there still are various forms of discrimination in favor of men. With the coming of woman suffrage there were also new responsibilities for women. The Woman's Movement of today branches in two directions. On the one hand we find organized effort to induce women to meet their civic obligations and accept leadership in all kinds of educational and social undertakings. Working with this purpose are the National Federation and local organizations of women's clubs and the League of Women Voters. Although women, before they were given the vote, were performing a magnificent social service through their organizations, their attainment of suffrage increased their power and gave their efforts greater effectiveness.

Suffrage also stimulated agitation attacking the discrimination against women. The most radical attitude with reference to woman's social and political inferiority was taken by the National Woman's Party, which was formed in 1913 and is at present the organization which is most distinctively feministic. Some of the objectives of the present-day feministic movement are: the acceptance of the single standard for men and women, a clearer recognition of an absolute equality in marriage, the removal of all discrimination in education that limits women on account of their sex, a still greater financial independence for all women, the elimination in the education of the girl of the handicap imposed by traditions of physical and social inequality. Some of the more extreme feminists advocate doing away with the conventional marriage and the orthodox home, and urge the bringing up of children by the community.

Attacks are also made upon woman's legal and political handicaps that have been carried over from the home life of the past. Some of the legal reforms women are demanding are: the guardianship control of children by mothers without discrimination in favor of fathers, the abolition of the idea of the husband as the legal head of the household, a legal residence apart from the husband when the woman finds this separation necessary or desirable, increased legal freedom for wives in business transactions, the removal of all legal discriminations against women in matters that have to do with sex, modification of the Citizenship Law of 1922 so as to give women an absolute political equality with men. In short, women persist in their agitation for a nearer approach to an equality with men. With reference to goal and methods there are differences of opinion among leaders in the contemporary Woman's Movement. All recognize the necessity of educating public opinion, but the National Woman's Party stresses the need of an amendment to the Constitution giving women more substantial equality, while the League of Women Voters directs its effort to the winning of civic reforms by the improvement of the legislation of the individual States.

CHAPTER IV

HUMAN NEED OF THE FAMILY

Advantage of Marriage.—Some think the human need of the family is so strong and so self-evident that it needs no argument: others that nothing can prove its value. The other day a woman who had been studying family life said, " Now frankly, what does a man get out of marriage? " Several years ago a very thoughtful man who was just about to marry asked me, " Why does a woman want to marry? I can see why a man wants to, but what does a woman get out of it? "

Economic Advantage of Marriage.—The first test one would naturally make of marriage in these days would be to determine whether it is an economic advantage. In the country it is, as it always has been. An unmarried man finds it almost impossible to carry on a farm. In the frontier period of America when most people were farmers it was almost unheard of for anyone to remain unmarried. A man who lost his wife remarried very soon, perhaps in a few days, and the woman who lost her husband did the same. Seldom did anyone wait a year before remarrying. Calhoun shows us that the conventional thing was an immediate remarriage; it was so difficult for the widow or widower with a farm and children to go on unmarried that convention adapted itself to that condition. Our attitude toward remarriage was not present.

Almost everywhere in the world where farming is carried on it is still true that people need to be married. Some farmers have housekeepers, but that often represents common law marriage which is more or less taken for granted by rural people because of the economic difficulties of the unmarried man.

The financial advantage of marriage in the city is hard to demonstrate. On the surface marriage is a decided disadvantage for city people. One would hesitate to advise young couples in the city to marry for purely economic reasons. A man is often obliged to support a family on just what he previously had for himself alone. When children come the wife usually has to give up her work. In many cases the wife clings to her work and the family has no children; the family life is then a sort of compromise, with little housekeeping, scanty home life and a preponderance of business interests. There is a tendency in some of our cities for a temporary, common consent, unlawful family life to occur as a result of this economic condition. A paper delivered at a recent scientific meeting in Chicago reported on an investigation of ninety blocks in the rooming area of that city; although 38 per cent. of the renters of these furnished rooms were living together as " married," it was determined that 60 per cent. of the couples were actually unmarried.[1] This extraordinary situation suggests that the companionate without a legal basis is more prominent in some of our cities than we think.

In certain professions marriage is an economic advantage. The doctor finds it so, the school administrator who is married has an advantage over his unmarried competitor in getting and holding a position, and the minister receives from marriage a protection from social troubles. These individual cases demonstrate that, at least for some, marriage is an economic advantage.

It may be fair to say that if we dig under the surface we will see that most persons in the city find an economic advantage in marriage. Marriage is a very stimulating experience. Many a man who is not very energetic before marriage becomes so as a result of his entrance upon family life. A man who has children is likely to become eager to do the best he can for his wife and children. For a number of years, unless he gets discouraged, he is very ambitious. It is a great thing to be pushed forward in this way to do one's utmost; even though there are no immediate economic returns, perhaps at first only added expenses incident to study or other preparation for greater responsibilities, active ambition is an asset.

By the steadying effect it has on many men marriage helps their economic situation. Before marriage the man is often restless and adventurous; when married and unable to move about freely, following his emotions, he learns self-control and stays permanently in one place, so that he becomes more prosperous and successful. The employer generally feels that he is getting a steadier type of worker when he hires a married man, though the statistical evi-

[1] See p. 145.

dence is not so conclusive on this point as one would expect. In a report on the chauffeurs of the Checker Taxi Company of New York it was found, to the surprise of the officials of the company, that the unmarried men had a better record for dependability than the married men. The company had been employing largely married men because they wanted a dependable type, but they discovered that the facts were quite the other way. If this report was accurate,[2] there are several possible explanations for the conditions it revealed; doubtless many of these unmarried chauffeurs are actually maintaining families, supporting their mothers or bringing up younger brothers and sisters, which makes them as steady as if they were married; some are looking forward to marriage and are therefore more reliable than they would otherwise be; a part of the unreliability of the married group can be charged up to unsatisfactory marriages, for a man who has married unhappily is often less steady than when he was expecting to be happily married.

An economic advantage which is not always present in married life, but has value when it does occur, is due to the fact that most persons prosper more when they have opportunity for consultation because "two heads are better than one." A man often wonders what to do when he meets a puzzling problem. He goes home and talks it over with his wife. Because he waits and thinks it over and looks at the question a little differently with the addition of his wife's point of view he makes a wiser decision than if he had acted on a snap judgment. The economic advantage of consultation is seldom to be found outside marriage, for nobody but a wife or husband can ordinarily be trusted to give a perfectly frank answer to a concrete question of policy.

Economic advantage depends not only on the amount of money earned, but on the amount spent. The significance of the wife's housekeeping contribution must not be forgotten, for she takes the raw materials purchased by the man's money income and turns them into finished goods and services which give the family a better living than is represented in terms of its bank account.[3] Some men never save until they add another factor to their economic situation by marrying a woman who makes them save. Other men

[2] Taken from a newspaper report unconfirmed by the company.
[3] See Andrews, B. R., "Economics of the Household," Ch. III.

marry women who are extravagant and make it impossible for anything to be saved. In thinking of the economic ins and outs of
marriage, these two conditions must be balanced. It is probably
true that in the majority of cases, over a period of years, marriage
will be found an economic advantage, though in some cases, and
perhaps in many others for a short time, it will not be.

Suppose we consider not the question whether the married or
unmarried have the greater amount of income to spend for personal pleasures but which are the more likely to get the greater satisfaction from their expenditure. In such a comparison, of course,
much depends upon the individual and the passing of a group
judgment is difficult. We find many expressions and slogans that
suggest the superior comforts enjoyed by the married home-makers,
such as the common advertising argument " as good as in your own
home." " Home cooking " is the slogan of the commercial baker;
hotels have " all the comforts of home " ; the church has " home
atmosphere." What is it that makes the traveler exclaim when he
returns to his family, even though he has been having the luxuries
of the well-appointed hotel, "there is no place like home" ? It may
be easy to prove that the unmarried have the greater opportunity
for spending for personal enjoyment, but it does not follow that
they all obtain by their expenditure more pleasures and
greater comfort.

Marriage and Sex.—There is another argument for marriage
that has great force and social significance. Marriage has for one
of its most important functions the regulation and legalizing of
sex relationship. Sex has a profound interest for human nature,
and marriage offers for most men and women the only satisfactory
expression of this vehement impulse. It is true that sex experience is not confined to the family, but there is a vital difference
between sex that is kept apart from affection and that which has
been incorporated into love. Marriage is the normal result of the
second and superior type of sex relationship. Marriage con-
solidates sex and makes it a constituent of affection. Certainly as
a rule the unmarried cannot think of an illicit sex experience as
do the married of their socially recognized relationship, for in the
case of the latter sex is not an isolated act but a natural expression
of intense affection, whereas the man or woman who is getting the

sex experience without the family connection is forcing the physical element to be detached, magnified and made a thing by itself so that, as a rule, it is a purely physical experience.

The question at issue is: Does the normal man or woman find sex by itself apart from affection a more satisfying human experience than when it is incorporated in affection? It can be easily demonstrated that those men who have detached their sex life are sooner or later dissatisfied with it and are the ones most anxious somehow to build up a normal family life. Leaving out all question of exploitation and morals and taking the matter of sex on a mere basis of satisfaction, human experience seems to testify that the detached sex life brings a greater amount of dissatisfaction and makes the man or woman who has had it crave the family sex experience even though this is increasingly hard to obtain. Moreover, the detached experience brings all sorts of worries: for the woman, the danger of pregnancy; for the man, the thought of exploiting another human being, with the possibility of all sorts of complications; for both, the risk of venereal disease and social stigma.

The more satisfying and prudent as well as the more human sex experience is that incorporated in family life. In other forms of sex life, after the sex craving is satisfied there is still a void because the human element is lacking. In view of this situation there need not be worry about the future of the family, since even though morals might permit unorthodox relationships it would still be true that the majority of human beings would crave a well-regulated, firmly established family life as the most satisfying experience.

Comradeship.—Another asset to be credited to the family is comradeship. Man and woman both crave comradeship, and this they can get in various ways, from parents, brothers, sisters, neighbors, fellow-workers; but of all the possible friendly relationships none has quite the flavor of that of husband and wife. As an association of pure comradeship marriage represents something that is highly desired by most people.

Several qualities of marriage fellowship make it stand out as different from other relationships. In the first place, it is more likely than any other to be an absolutely sincere and frank comradeship. When a friend asks for counsel, one advises him but one does not always give him perfectly frank counsel, because he might resent it. One has to be delicate, suggest and hint rather than say straight out just what one thinks If one were to give one's friend a full and free statement that he does not expect or want he might end the fellowship, but his wife can speak more frankly, and if she has the wit she will.

Seldom can one get a perfectly frank statement from teacher, neighbor, minister or parent. The parent is a little more likely to be frank than the others, but even here prejudice or dread of openness is almost bound to enter. Nobody can dare be so frank as a wife in talking with her husband or a husband in talking with his wife, and that makes their comradeship a peculiar thing, precious because of its possibility of sincerity. Of course, that is not true in every marriage, but this relationship offers an opportunity for frankness beyond anything else because husband and wife are both in so intimate an association that it is for the interest of each to be frank with the other, since the welfare of one means the welfare of the other. If they are clear-headed they will be likely to see that.

It is very difficult in talking with other people to know whether they are altogether friendly. One's friend is often one's rival to a certain extent, especially when there is vivid sense of competition; if he gives one adverse criticism one sometimes feels that this is only an attempt to advance his own self-regard, while his favorable criticism occasionally appears to be an unconscious attempt to trick one into going ahead and making a mistake that will be for his advantage or at least will give him an opportunity for indulging in feelings of superiority. In the home deceit leads in the long run to trouble for both. The wife is, therefore, likely to be as trustworthy as she can be in talking with her husband, and the same is true of him in counseling with her.

It is amazing how easily friends can forget former friends in trouble, how busy people are when demands are made on their time by friends. For most people friendship is a bright-season experience, it does not go through bad weather; but the marriage ceremony as generally spoken brings out plainly that the essence of marriage is a security against possible trials and difficulties. We do not believe the wife should leave the husband because he gets cancer or that when the man becomes blind his wife has any right to divorce him for that. If the woman develops tuberculosis we condemn the man who runs from her and leaves her to the pity of strangers. We assume that marriage means standing by one another in hardship. No other comradeship carries with it such an obligation, backed up by social convention, to protect people in their period of weakness. Not everybody passes this test, but we can say without hesitation that more people pass it in the fellowship of marriage than in any other voluntarily assumed relationship. Many a man who would not live with a woman on the mere basis of passion does stay with her through trial when married.

Married couples profit from the fact that the consolidation of the two lives, persistently maintained, gives a supplementary experience which everybody craves but finds it hard to get. Some people feel this need more than others; it is more or less an individual reaction with which age has something to do, the older person being more likely to feel it. Plato once said the man and woman were two parts of one whole that had been severed and each hunted to find the other half that they might have a complete life. Normally we like to supplement our life; we want the advantage of seeing life from the point of view of somebody else. We get this a little from our friends, but it is transitory and intermittent, made up mostly of quick interpretations; only in the fellowship of marriage do we get the organized point of view of another person steadily presented day after day.

Moreover, man and woman, perhaps because of their social training, see life somewhat differently, not that one is right as compared with the other who is wrong, but the two are unlike and both viewpoints seem necessary to give a clear outlook. Ordinarily no man can hope to get a woman's point of view unless she is his wife because there cannot be the necessary steady fellowship, conventionally, without marriage; he needs to get this from a wife that is with him and contributes to him day by day. It is not different in the case of the woman. When marriage fails to yield this supplementary experience to one of its members he or she is likely to be so dissatisfied as to go seeking it elsewhere, with the result that the married life of the couple courts disaster.

The Coming of Children.—The economic advantage of marriage is a lesser matter than its opportunity for wholesome sex life, and that is far less than its fellowship; the most significant asset of married life is the coming of children. The normal human being who is aware of his needs will find that nothing in his life is so deep as his desire for children. To suppose that this is true only of women is to go counter to the facts. To say that the craving for children is not intense is to overlook the fact that even among animals offspring take precedence over everything else during the period of helplessness of the young and that as we go higher in life the imagination is able to forecast the intense emotions of parenthood before they are awakened by the arrival of children so that human beings do not merely respond to the needs of existent offspring, but consciously desire to produce their young.

Some there are who tell us that we can have children without being married; but there are grave complications that make this a disadvantage. One can have an illegitimate child, but the child is very unfortunate, being hurt at the start by not having a normal beginning in life. It is remarkable how few illegitimate children have become distinguished persons. When very young the illegitimate child encounters difficulties of adjustment that may seriously affect his whole life. In view of the hardships involved for the child, nobody would lightly decide to substitute illegitimate offspring for lawful children.

It is true that one can adopt a child, but even when this is done in the most normal way, by husband and wife, there is always some doubt as to the heredity of the child; just how important this is no scientist can now say but none says it has no importance. Often the foster-parents do not know both father and mother of the child they are adopting. There is still a lack in the life of the husband and wife, for they will miss the joy of tracing resemblances to themselves and the pride of creation they would have if the child were their own offspring. Adopting a child is a way of making the best of hard circumstances and accepting the nearest substitute that can be found for the normal experience of producing children.

Another kind of adoption is that where the unmarried person adopts a child. Of late there has been a slight tendency among middle-aged single women to adopt very young children, two or three women sometimes living together to form a home circle in which the child is brought up. This is often an advantage to the child compared with what his life otherwise would be, but his environment is very one-sided; he not only has no foster-father, but when several women join forces to bring him up he has an over-supply of the mother-element in his life. Nobody would choose to have children in this way unless the more normal family circle was out of the question.

One of the advantages of having one's own home is the fact that nothing matures responsibility like becoming a parent. Untrustworthy, reckless young people are often tamed by the coming of their first child. There is a proverb in many languages, " Nothing holds a man under control like having a child." Since his presence develops the character of his parents and makes them grow up, the child is an asset in the home.

The care of a child also acts as a socializing process. We have all known people who were completely shut up within themselves, caring for nothing outside their own little circle, until their child came when they were forced to be concerned with the doings of others. Up to that time they had paid no attention to the health work of their community; hospitals, the Red Cross, movements for securing pure, clean milk meant nothing to them, but when their child came and had to drink the milk, be in places where possible contagion lurked, immediately they began to take an interest in sanitary conditions according to their thoughtfulness and real affection for their child. The same thing happens in the case of recreation. The husband and wife have said, " Let the dance halls be as they are; if people want vicious conditions, what do we care? " But when their child became older, the parents were alert to these dangers also. (Nothing socializes adults so much as children. Every kind of moral virtue is fundamentally based on the extension of the family attitude from one's immediate family circle to the larger social group. Parenthood is especially important because of its socializing function.)

More than anything else parenthood provides the renewal of life, though many parents never fully realize their power to go back by means of their children and taste again some of the joys of their earlier experience. The more a parent has been dulled by his adult life, the harder it is for him to benefit in this way from the presence of his children, yet here lies one of the possible resources of all parents. The old idea of immortality, which is almost the only one to be found in the Old Testament until we come to the Prophets, is the idea of racial immortality through children. While living a mature life the parent also lives the life of the child because he loves the child and through his offspring perpetuates himself.

Children furnish satisfaction for the parents' craving for intimate response; however much husband and wife may fulfill each other's needs in this respect, the interaction between parent and child is qualitatively so different that it can never be duplicated. There is hardly anybody that is not touched by the affection of a child. We have countless illustrations of that in the theatre and the novel. The effect of being with a child and being loved by a child gives us something we get nowhere else because on one side are helplessness and trust and on the other ability and the consciousness of power. It is an enormous price to pay for any other satisfaction to go through life without knowing the satisfaction of intimate response between parent and child.

Children as Security.—It may seem like anticlimax to suggest that children are a protection for the future. This is a smaller thing than some of the other advantages of having children but it is worthy of consideration. While not an absolute security, children are better than an annuity or a savings bank account because a living person who cares for one is more likely to give one the help needed in sickness or old age than any impersonal organization. Children have always been thought of as a surety, not only against dire want, but against loneliness and discomfort. The insurance of comfort, security and companionship represented by children is of course open to the hazards of life because the child does not always live, or if he does he may be sickly, incapable of supporting anyone, or neglectful of his parents.

When there are no children at all the husband and wife are occasionally thrown together by the void they face. Though they suffer a loss they also draw together because of the depth of emotional stress they share. It is especially the death of a child, rather than the inability of the couple to have children, that draws husband and wife together in this way, intensifying their affection for each other. In such cases there is a very deep bedrock foundation for the fellowship of the man and woman because they have suffered together and each understands how the other feels. Even a childless marriage gives a greater degree of satisfaction than the unmarried state since it provides enduring comradeship which mitigates the increasing loneliness of advancing age.

[In spite of the mistakes and failures of married people and the restlessness of the unhappily married, the institution of marriage will endure because it is built, not on convenience or coercion, but on human craving; behind it are centuries of human experience that demonstrate that the home has come to meet the greatest human need, the desire for intimate response based on an affection that is trustworthy.]

CHAPTER V

ECONOMIC CONDITIONS AFFECTING FAMILY LIFE

The Family and Economic Conditions.—The history of the family reveals the large place that economic influences have had in shaping family life. In savage society we find the form of marriage determined in large degree by the economic life of the tribe or, in cases where varying forms of marriage exist contemporaneously, by the economic status of individuals. Even though in primitive life economic conditions do not by themselves explain the prevalence of polygyny, polyandry or monogamy, it is clear that the economic is one of the major factors.

In its attempt to perform a biological and social function the family was necessarily forced to assume economic responsibilities and as a result became an economic unit. In the agricultural stage particularly we see family life constructing itself under the influence of its economic activities. Until invention, by making possible machine processes, created factory production the family was an industrial as well as an economic unit. By making the different members of the family conscious of their common interests the economic struggle contributed to a well-knit home life.

With the advent of the Industrial Revolution the family rapidly lost its industrial function and instead of forming a producing unit the members of the working-class homes who were old enough to work were drawn into mills and factories and so scattered about that they no longer labored in association. Nothing has happened to the modern family of greater consequence than this transference of production from the family to capitalistic organizations. At once the economic pressure that formerly had consolidated family unity began to weaken family ties by the disintegration of common interests.

Although it is true that the changes in the processes of manufacturing and commercial organization which we are wont to describe as the Industrial Revolution forced upon the family a rapid transition and to a large extent, outside of agriculture, destroyed the former function of the family as a producing institution, it is easy to exaggerate the change and also to over-paint the losses of the family, while forgetting that the family through its members shared in the advantages that came eventually to all classes from the evolution of modern industry.[1]

When the husband, wife and children in what we are accustomed to call the working classes went their several ways outside the family enclosure to enter the mill as help, although they still continued to have common interests as wage-getters they ceased to be fellow-workers in a family environment, and the consuming activities of the family replaced its former producing functions as the centre of interest. Thus a family sense of common enterprise was lost and the essential economic task of the family became the problem of distributing an income, usually inadequate, so as to meet the needs and if possible satisfy the desires of its different members.

As a result of this subtle transformation the new family found itself dealing less with activities that stressed unity and more with those that tended to emphasize the clashing of individual desires. We get a glimpse of the significance of this transference of function by observing the forces that tend toward unity in a rural family and contrasting this with the urban family, which is confined largely, so far as economic activity is concerned, to the problem of justly dealing out an income earned by the members of the family who work outside.

Economic Independence of Woman.—Woman's economic contribution is by no means recent. As far back as we can go in tracing social experience we find woman carrying her share of the economic burden. She was, as the anthropologists have so clearly shown, a pioneer not only in household arts but also in large measure in the beginnings of industrial activity.[2] It was woman who took over the rude cultivation of plants and fruits. Thus we are indebted to her for the origin of the means of food production. At the lowest levels of savage culture we find the men chiefly engaged in hunting and fishing, and although these occupations

---

[1] Stone, G. E., " The History of Labor," p. 197.
[2] Mason, O. T., " Woman's Share in Primitive Culture."

may have had a greater emotional appeal social progress depended upon the development of the crude toil carried on by the women, who cooked what the hunters brought, made garments from the skins of animals or from barks or grasses, invented the manufacture of domestic utensils and the tools that they used in the rough form of gardening which they evolved as a secondary source of food material.[3]

The new and perplexing problems that we now associate with woman's modern economic condition originate, not because for the first time she is making a substantial industrial contribution, but rather because since the Industrial Revolution she has gradually been obtaining economic independence. This does not mean, of course, that she has grown free from the dominance of the industrial system into which she entered as a worker, but that within the system itself she is more and more gaining the same status as man. Specialization, organization and the increasing complexity of modern industry have made both man and woman unable to maintain individual self-support, since the comforts, even the necessities, of life depend upon myriad forms of interrelations.

The great economic happening in the modern world, as far as the woman is concerned, is the fact that she has emerged from her family background and become an economic individual. She is, indeed, dependent upon the system that prevails, and by which the industrial world is maintained; but she is not, as for centuries she has been, forced to rely upon a male for her support and opportunities for social experience. When the Industrial Revolution changed the form of the family as an economic unit a multitude of women found themselves driven from household occupations in the very same way that men were expelled from household industry. For a time, as was natural, woman remained a dependent member of the family although she, like her husband or brother, earned her living outside the family domain in the sharp competition of modern industry.

Obviously such a situation was too illogical to continue long. Woman could not be at the same time man's competitor and his dependent. The industrial revolution actually affected her more

[3] Groves, " Rural Mind and Social Welfare," p. 17.

profoundly than man; for him the experience was like a volcanic eruption which destroyed former habits of livelihood and forced new adjustments necessarily painful to acquire, while for woman the new industrial situation forced a division in her life that made satisfactory adjustment for most concerned impossible.

Motherhood laid upon woman a burden the father did not share. The birth and care of children linked her to the home and hampered her industrial career. The married working woman therefore found her industrial experiences spasmodic. She worked when she could and returned to the domestic occupation if children and housekeeping made this imperative. Thus, though she counted greatly as a mass in the industrial world outside the home, individually she was largely a bird of passage or even worse, one who had to divide her attention between work that brought her family an income supplementary to the inadequate wage of her husband and the labor which it was necessary for her still to continue within the house itself in order that a semblance of home life might be maintained.

Difficult as the industrial situation was for man, it required of him merely readjustment to the new type of vocational experience, while woman was forced to re-adapt herself to two different and frequently antagonistic centres of interest, with the inevitable consequence that as soon as she entered the mill as a worker her domestic duties began to be sacrificed.[4] We can only sense the disastrous effect of these conditions upon family life by recalling the length of the working day at the time of the industrial revolution and the irksome discipline imposed by mill-owners. The woman introduced into the factory from the freer and less systematic routine of household work found that the monotony, restrictions, and rigid schedule which she encountered in her new type of labor sucked out her vitality and left her too exhausted and disheartened to bring to such home life as she still had the normal attitudes of affection.

It is, of course, to England that we must turn to see the full force of this undermining of home life. At the advent of the new industrial system the United States was too rural to receive such

---

[4] Hammond and Hammond, " The Town Laborer," p. 23.

a staggering blow as was inflicted upon the working classes of England. Nevertheless, the United States did not entirely escape these first social fruits of the modernizing of industry; and at a later stage, when fortunately the evils of factory labor as they affected family life were somewhat mitigated, conditions detrimental to family life, due to the employment of women and children, became serious enough to attract the attention of all students of social welfare.

Employment and the Fertility of Women.—We have evidence that the conflict between woman as wage-earner and woman as home-maker still persists. A very careful English report on the fertility of marriage shows us that the employment of women, as a rule, lowers the birth rate and that there is a higher death rate among the children of those women working outside the home than among the children of those who keep house. We do not have at present a similar study of conditions in this country, but such material as we have leads toward the same conclusion. According to the United States Census Report for 1888 there were 2, 500,-000 women occupied in industry, while in 1920 the number had increased to 8,500,000, of whom nearly 2,000,000 were married. In 1920, 9 per cent. of all married women fifteen years of age and over were gainfully employed, while in 1890 the percentage was only 4.6. This rapid growth in the industrial employment of women means increasing trouble for the modern family unless society can find ways by which the home may be protected from the baneful influences that have in the past been associated with the employment of mothers and wives in industry.

According to the British report regarding the fertility of women in industry the characteristic birth rate of married women less than forty-five years of age who work outside the home is low.[5] Actresses, for example, as might be expected from the migratory character of their occupation, have the extremely low rate of 43 per cent. of the average for the whole population, of similar marital duration; teachers, 52 per cent.; musicians, 54 per cent.; clerks, 55 per cent.; bar maids, 63 per cent.; while the important textile indus-

[5] Report on the Fertility of Marriage, vol. xiii of the 1911 Census of England and Wales, published by His Majesty's Stationery Office, London, 1923.

tries employing large numbers of women run from 59 to 75 per cent., with the exception of silk, lace and canvas manufacturers and cotton spinners, where the percentage was 77, 98, 96 and 82, respectively.[6]

In this country there has been a rapid increase in the number of women employed in clerical and professional work. The English investigation shows a low birth rate for these classes, women clerks having, as stated above, a birth rate of 55 per cent. of the average, while married professional workers stand near the bottom of the list. A study of the family status of bread-winning women in Passaic, New Jersey, conducted by the Women's Bureau, revealed some interesting facts with reference to the size of families. This is summarized in the following table with a comment regarding it published in the report.

TABLE I.

Number of children of breadwinning mothers, by marital status of mother

Marital status	Total women having children	Women having specified number of children										Average number of children per mother
		One	Two	Three	Four	Five	Six	Seven	Eight	Nine	Ten	
Total: Number..	3,271	1,073	926	590	370	176	82	34	12	6	2	2.4
Per cent..	100.0	32.8	28.3	18.0	11.3	5.4	2.5	1.0	0.4	0.2	0.1	....
Married, husband breadwinner: Number.......	2,608	787	755	489	306	157	68	31	9	4	2	2.5
Per cent.......	100.0	30.2	28.9	18.8	11.7	6.0	2.6	1.2	0.3	0.2	0.1	....
Married, husband not a breadwinner Number.......	35	13	7	7	4	1	2	...	...	1	...	2.6
Per cent.......	100.0	37.1	20.0	20.0	11.4	2.9	5.7	...	...	2.9	...	....
Married, husband not living with family: Number.......	151	84	41	16	6	1	1	1	1	...	...	1.7
Per cent.......	100.0	55.6	27.2	10.6	4.0	.7	.7	.7	.7	...	...	....
Widowed: Number.......	456	178	117	76	52	17	11	2	2	1	...	2.3
Per cent.......	100.0	39.0	25.7	16.7	11.4	3.7	2.4	.4	.4	.2	...	....
Divorced: Number.......	21	11	6	2	2	...	...	...	...	...	...	1.8
Per cent.......	100.0	(a)	(a)	(a)	(a)	...	...	...	...	...	...	....

a Not computed, owing to small number involved.

Though the families of working mothers were not large, the children were young. Approximately 60 per cent. of the employed mothers had

[6] Metropolitan Life Insurance Bulletin, May, 1926, pp. 2–3.

children under five years of age, 20 per cent. had children of five to seven years of age who had not yet entered school, although the New Jersey school regulations permit children to go to school at the age of five years. These percentages are not mutually exclusive, as mothers with children under five years may also have had children between five and seven years.[7]

The attempt to measure the effect of the married woman's working outside the home upon the death rate of children is hopelessly complicated by the fact that it is impossible to separate the effect of the mother's absence from home from the poverty, lack of sanitation, poor nutrition, and ignorance of child-care that are so likely to be found in households where the mother goes out to work. A study made in Scotland of over five thousand records of working mothers, married less than fifteen years, compared with the same number of mothers who did not go out to work revealed an excess mortality of about 62 per cent. for the children of the mothers who worked out.[8]   An excess in the mortality of infants whose mothers were gainfully employed in the year preceding the child's birth was found in every city but one investigated by the Children's Bureau in their series of studies made in different parts of the United States to determine the influence of economic conditions on the death rate of children.

The following statement and table[9] appear in Number II of the "Infant Mortality" series published by the Children's Bureau, consisting of the study made of conditions in Akron, Ohio.

In this table are shown rates of infant mortality according to whether or not the mother was gainfully employed during the year before the infant's birth. The mortality among infants whose mothers were gainfully employed was 107.4 as contrasted with only 77.2 where the mothers were not employed. The mortality among infants whose mothers were gainfully employed at home appears higher than that for infants whose mothers were employed away from home, the rates being 114.5 and 88.2, respectively.

None of the thirty-seven infants whose mothers resumed work away from home during the lifetime of their infants died in the first year of life.

It is clear from the findings of the English study already mentioned that the death rate of these children is high not merely because the mothers work, but, as one would naturally suppose, because the children are neglected as a consequence of the mothers'

[7] Women's Bureau U. S. Dept. of Labor, *Bulletin No. 23*, p. 36.
[8] Dunlop, J. C., "The Fertility of Marriage in Scotland: A Census Study," *Journal of the Royal Statistical Society*, February, 1914, p. 282.
[9] *Bureau Publication No. 72*, p. 43.

inefficient homekeeping and low standards. In the industrial classes where the mothers are most likely to obtain an adequate substitute for their services, as it is true generally of post-office officials, teachers, actresses, clerks and shop-keepers, the mortality rate shows that the children suffer little; on the other hand, in the

TABLE II.

Total births during selected year, live births, infant deaths, infant mortality rate, and per cent. of stillbirths, according to gainful employment of mother at home and away from home during year before infant's birth, and nativity of mother.

Employment of mother during year before infant's birth, and nativity of mother	Total births	Live Births	Infant deaths	Infant mortality rate a	Stillbirths	
					Number	Per cent. of total births a
All mothers............	2,322	2,253	193	85.7	69	3.0
Not gainfully employed....	1,666	1,620	125	77.2	46	2.8
Gainfully employed........	656	633	68	107.4	23	3.5
At home................	481	463	53	114.5	18	3.7
Away from home........	175	170	15	88.2	5	2.9
Native mothers.......	1,402	1,356	95	70.1	46	3.3
Not gainfully employed....	1,125	1,090	69	63.3	35	3.1
Gainfully employed........	277	266	26	97.7	11	4.0
At home................	216	207	18	87.0	9	4.2
Away from home........	61	59	8	......	2	......
Foreign-born mothers..	920	897	98	109.3	23	2.5
Not gainfully employed....	541	530	56	105.7	11	2.0
Gainfully employed........	379	367	42	114.4	12	3.2
At home................	265	256	35	136.7	9	3.4
Away from home.......	114	111	7	63.1	3	2.6

a Not shown where base is less than 100.

homes where the mothers work in the textile industries, in the printing, earthenware and leather goods trades, the employment of the mother is frequently a contributing influence to the death of the child.

The Social Consequences of Woman's Economic Independence.—Eventually, when the evolution of the family has progressed further than at present, it will be clear to students of

social institutions that no more radical change in the entire history
of the human family has ever happened than that through which
we are now passing, based fundamentally upon woman's economic
independence. The family in all its aspects, and other social institutions in so far as they came in contact with the family, had
become firmly adjusted to woman as a dependent of man. Costly as
was the Industrial Revolution in the hardship it imposed upon
woman, the price paid was not too great for her emergence
into independence.

It would be historically unfair to describe woman's social and
political inferiority as a product of man's deliberate attempt to
exploit her; the dependent relationship of woman was in the past
as much taken for granted as in our day is that of the child: law
defined it, religion explained and defended it, social traditions
solidified it and educational partiality perpetuated it. Woman was
man's helpmate and her subserviency to male dominance was for
all women a conventional theory and for the majority an actual
fact which in countless ways hampered them and made impossible
the free and full expression of their real desires.

Although the most influential factor in bringing about the new
status of women has been her increasing economic opportunities,
this force has not acted separately. Her progress has been cumulative. Greater economic opportunity, increased educational facilities, larger political freedom and other advantages have all
contributed to her advance. Her gain at any one point has made
it possible for her to move forward along some other line. Had
she not obtained increasing educational opportunities for her
development, her entrance into industry would have sunk her
deeper into social and economic inferiority. Her education doubtless would have been limited to a small minority born to wealth or
brought up in the atmosphere of the professional classes, and chiefly
confined to the accomplishments that marked the graduate of the
one-time boarding school, satisfied with covering its pupils with a
cultural veneer which in social circles was a desirable substitute for
intellectual development.

As woman made progress in economic independence she was
able to demand more political rights; as she decreased her political
inequality she improved her economic status. As the different

changes in woman's social situation occurred, society in its various aspects was forced to make new adjustments in harmony with her progress. Upon woman, herself, fell the greater burden of reconstruction, but the task was not exclusively hers. The new conditions that followed woman's advance toward social opportunity and equality demanded new habits and attitudes from men.

Adaptation to the new order of things could not be an abstract or generalized process, but in actual experience was expressed in countless problems that arose in individual households and in the relationships of individual men and women. The perplexities, disappointments and contentions involved have been best portrayed in the more serious literature of the period. We turn to the novel for a picture of the fascinating struggle for conduct in harmony with the new order of things because only in fiction is it possible to present the atmosphere of this great social transformation. With the advent of the psychological novel and its more subtle interpretation of human motives and desires, literature threw in bold relief the new life of women which was clashing with the old life of men. The writing of novels gave women a medium of expression which they could use in practical equality with men.

The increasing economic independence of women and their approach to social equality has created other problems than those of personal adjustment. The entire social environment of men and women has been and still is being modified. We can easily detect the new influences operating upon the mores and upon the social institutions. For example, the legal status of woman has been of necessity redefined; her state of legal dependence, expressed so clearly by Blackstone, sounds ridiculous when in actual fact woman has arrived at such a degree of economic independence that legal decisions have increasingly moved away from the earlier positions of the English Common Law as a result of new legislation because the court has been forced to recognize the logic of actual facts. In the United States all of the several States have not kept abreast of this movement, and as a consequence woman's rights differ in the various States. Everywhere, however, changes are occurring.

The legal adjustment is complicated by the presence of laws and decisions that originated in the effort to protect women because of their former position of inferiority or on account of the prevailing belief that they were physically weaker than men or handicapped by their character as potential mothers. Naturally we find among the women themselves those who desire to press forward to an absolute equality with men as soon as this just rôle can be attained, while others are fearful that women who need help most will suffer first if the legal safeguards that have been built up for their protection be pushed aside in an unstrategic effort to obtain the deceptive prize of fictitious equality.

Education is another aspect of American society that has felt the impress of woman's new status. It is remarkable that women have come to such a degree of educational equality in view of the short period of time they have been permitted substantial educational opportunities. There are still social prejudices that hamper women in getting or using their education, though some of these are melting slowly. For example, recently the president of a woman's college, of course a man, who has had men and women on his staff, stated in a letter that henceforth as vacancies occurred in his teaching positions he would appoint only male instructors. Anyone familiar with the advantages men have in obtaining posts as teachers in the higher institutions of learning will look with some misgivings upon the long line of women graduate students who come forward for their diplomas at the Commencement exercises of our large universities. They can indeed go into high school teaching, but many of them must carry into their work the conviction that were it not for their sex they would be permitted to do the kind of teaching that is their preference and for which they have trained themselves.

The woman student who senses the significance of her educational experiences realizes as she presses forward into advanced study that she suffers handicap resting on a sex rather than a personal basis long before she graduates and goes out to practice her profession. Just a few years ago a thoroughly competent student, studying for her doctorate in a division of social science at one of our oldest universities where it has long been the practice to give women opportunity for graduate study, was not permitted to enter a course within her chosen field of study because it had long been the tradition of the department concerned that only male students could elect the courses offered. No doubt was expressed regarding the young woman's ability to do the work, nor was it charged that her presence would create difficult problems of class instruction; it was merely a matter of well-entrenched prejudice, permitted to issue in a bias of discrimination that would have seemed intolerable had it not been for the fact that in the institution woman's educational inequality in one form or another had long been taken as a matter of course. There was an element of humor in this particular instance, for it so happened that the wife of one of the colleagues of the instructor who thought women students unfitted for his particular subject had already obtained a well-established reputation as a scholar in that very branch of social science.

A study of the salaries paid public school teachers reveals how extensive is the discrimination against women. Although this disparity in salaries is not entirely a matter of prejudice, since there are other factors involved, one cannot investigate any school system where this policy of discrimination exists without quickly discovering in concrete cases that it is based essentially on sex. The procedure is defended by arguments that suggest rationalization, but actually it is largely traditional, expressing in dollars and cents a former belief still widely held, that a man in competition with a woman in the same line of work is more efficient and deserves a larger wage, a position that the neutrally-minded person will find it difficult to defend when applied to a comparison of individual men and women in the teaching profession.

As more women become economically independent and women as a class push forward to a larger measure of social equality, the present prejudice favoring men who compete with women in the same line and under the same conditions of work will be less and less maintained; and as social opinion changes, driven to a new attitude by the logic of existing facts, man as a competing individual will be forced to surrender the advantages he now obtains from being a member of the group of males.

More than any other expression of social experience public opinion discloses increasingly the influence of woman's attainment of economic independence. No force in the past has done more to compel her to accept conventional limitations and to hamper her development than the necessity of conforming to the accepted fact.

Woman in the modern era has won by heroic struggle, little by little, the opportunity of sharing the process of making public opinion.

So much coercion of woman's self-expression has issued forth from conventional public opinion that it is still impossible to distinguish in feminine behavior that which originates as a characteristic product of biological sex from that which is constructed by the pressure of social environment. Even yet, almost from early infancy hampering forces begin to operate upon the girl, consciously and unconsciously administered by those who care for the child, and interfere with her growth in a way that would not happen were she a male. Public opinion, including the mores, constructed in harmony with the ideals of male dominance, touches so constantly in the sensitive years of childhood the developing personality of the female child that no woman escapes its modifying influence. As a consequence the personality of the developing girl is so largely a product of the conditioning of her reflexes in harmony with the prevailing ideas of the disparity between the sexes that the real nature of woman cannot emerge.

No small amount of the difficulty that American parents are now having in dealing with adolescents is due to the fact that this generation of youth, particularly the girls, as a result of present ways of living have opportunity to escape from many of the coercing influences that in the past have operated to stamp the character of the growing child with the prejudices of adults. The change is more significant for the girl than for the boy; indeed, much of the change in the boy's behavior is an attempt on his part to adapt himself to the difference in attitude of the modernized girl.

It is in the realm of public opinion that we must expect to find serious social disturbances as women climb closer to social equality by advancing their economic status. One of the centres of conflict between the ideals of the old and the new order where a new social judgment must be established is the changing of the double standard of sex morality, built in the atmosphere of male dominance, to a code that demands the same standard of both male and female. In the confusion of making so radical a transformation in social ideas many minor trends are to be expected, but the main current shows itself unmistakably as a sweeping aside of the former code that exacted little of men in their self-control and much of women.

In the political world changes regarding woman's status have taken place so recently and with such rapidity that we are not yet in a position to recognize the social consequences of women's having nearly attained full political equality. Since practical politics and political institutions go on, superficially considered, in much the same way as has been the habit of the past, the tendency is to discount the significance of woman suffrage and the increase in women holding public office by appointment or by election. Under the surface there are trends in government that disclose already the contribution of political influence that women are beginning to make. Although we do not see the startling results in public life that were formerly prophesied by woman suffrage advocates or feared by its opponents, the government shows itself susceptible to the influence of women voters. Already the game of politics has become more difficult to play, and the strategy of its management more complicated.

Modern statesmanship, carried on under the social conditions of male dominance, came to its end with the World War. Henceforth government must adjust itself more and more in progressive countries to the impulses of both men and women, and at present these differ though we do not know whether the variation is a consequence of sex inheritance or social pressure or both. Even though a multitude of women take no interest in politics and do not so much as vote, as potential voters their influence reaches the government and shows itself in political policy. The professional politician would without doubt prefer a male constituency, but he must forget his choice and take heed of the feelings of women as well as men.

Woman suffrage is significant socially, not because women can claim a superior virtue, but because the forces that operate on government must now come from two centres of influence rather than one and the program of government can neither be maintained in accord with man's impulses nor constructed to echo woman's but must become more characteristically human in its expression in that, like the home, it represents the interplay of man's nature and woman's nature as at present they are constituted.

Women are finding suffrage a distinct advantage in their effort to establish more firmly their economic independence: their right of voting permits them to safeguard their economic progress; it also affords them a weapon which they can constantly use in attacking their social inequality in many of its expressions. It is evident that they have not yet learned how to make the fullest use of their new opportunity, but in this respect they do not at all differ from the men who in the past have won increased political rights as democracy has gone forward. As woman makes headway in her economic condition she will learn from experience the value of suffrage in her life.

In recent years the American woman has not only deepened her economic status; she also has widened it by entering all sorts of vocations. This tendency to increase the number of occupations by means of which women can earn their livelihood was greatly stimulated by the World War. If that cataclysm was a test of modern man's courage, it was equally a test of the efficiency of the modern woman. Wherever there was a scarcity of male workers, there women entered, and they generally demonstrated that they could perform successfully work from which before the war they had been excluded. As was to be expected, they were unable to hold permanently all the economic territory that they occupied during the war, but the experience uncovered the check that social convention had been putting upon the vocational activities of women. It was evident that women were not unfitted to enter trades and businesses from which they had been long excluded. At the end of the war it was interesting to notice how often the returned soldier laid claim to his old job with the argument, not of his superior efficiency, but that it was unfair to deprive him of his means of livelihood in return for his service overseas.

In many cases employers were glad to turn back to men, not because their women workers were unsatisfactory, but because they could not be depended upon as can men. The single woman was likely to leave her industrial position just as soon as she was able to accomplish the marriage which was her real goal, whereas the single man who married was likely to continue in the same line of employment. In other words, woman's industrial handicap proved to be not so much inferior physical strength or mental ability as her double function of home-maker and worker. As at the beginning of the industrial revolution, the vexing problem of woman's labor showed itself again to be her two centres of interest, home-making and wage-earning.

The Home and Woman's Economic Independence.—If the results of woman's entrance into industry are showing in every kind of social experience, it is in the home primarily that the profoundest problems are created by the new situation. Nowhere else was the idea of man's dominance so firmly established or with such practical consequences. The authority of the male as the head of the house was in accord with woman's actual dependence. Social tradition transmitted this concept of family relationship, religion sanctioned it, and law attempted to define it.

Family life, moreover, had become accustomed to the division of labor which sent the husband out of the home to earn the family income while the wife took over the responsibilities of housekeeping. In spite of the fact that with the advent of the industrial revolution numbers of women, both single and married, became wage-earners, social convention persisted in thinking of the husband as a worker and the wife as a housekeeper. It was not until the middle class woman entered employment and in many instances refused to leave her business or profession even after she married that it became apparent that the traditional type of home was by no means standard. Just as soon as social pressure was a bit loosened it became clear that there were women who refused to choose between marriage and industrial experience, but who were determined to try to satisfy both their domestic and their vocational impulses.

It was chiefly in the city that this ambitious program could be undertaken with any possibility of success. Urban life, that was squeezing out of the old-fashioned home the undertakings of the homestead family, gave the modern woman who wanted marriage without sacrificing her industrial or professional career the opportunity she desired. The small flat with its conveniences for light housekeeping furnished the resources for the new experiment.

In cases not a few, as is well known by all social workers, the woman married and left her occupation, expecting like her mother to devote her time to housekeeping. The small flat, however—all that could be afforded—led quickly to the discovery that there was so little work to do that the woman had to choose between once again going into industry, becoming a parasitic wife, or assuming

6

motherhood, which involved economic risk that the slender income of the husband could not justify. Many such women eventually have gone back to their former work, often with the expectation of later undertaking housekeeping on a larger scale.

Woman's Employment and Marriage Selection.—Without doubt the entrance of women into modern industry has some selective influence upon marriage. This influence operates not upon the birds of passage who enter employment temporarily with the idea of leaving their work as soon as they find their mate, but upon those who commit themselves to a life vocation after having obtained the needed training. Women who take their work so seriously necessarily develop an attitude of independence and self-reliance which hampers their winning the affection of the average man. Men have long looked upon themselves as protectors of women and children, and the majority of them intuitively shun the kind of woman who not only can take care of herself but even finds intolerable the masculine attitude of social guardianship.

In spite of this preference on the part of men for what we have been wont to call the old-fashioned woman, the mating that occurs on the higher level of absolute equality of relationship constitutes the marriage that is representative of the modern trend. Men who are reluctant to accept the implications that issue from woman's economic independence must pay the penalty by seeking their mates among the less progressive and efficient young women. If men's selection of the less advanced women operates at present to influence marriage choices, it is nevertheless a decreasing fact, for there is no masculine instinct which forces men to assume the protective attitude; rather it is a product in accord with the conditions that have prevailed in the social life of the immediate past.

The freer contact of the present-day adolescents, which accustoms boys and girls to normal comradeship, is bound to show itself in the recognition by a great number of men of the advantage of a feminine character in harmony with the modern self-expression of woman. In other words, the new type will increasingly make the stronger emotional appeal as men through association become more familiar with the typical character-reactions of the girl who has developed in the social atmosphere that now prevails in this country.

It must be remembered that we have no evidence that the more independent type of woman is lacking in sex energy, reproductive capacity or love of home as compared with her sister of opposite disposition. The domestic traits of the clinging type, when subjected to analysis, are revealed as purely negative; the home shelters her lack of maturity or deficient aggressiveness more than it provides for her a means of conscious commitment to the kind of experiences that she has learned to value most. To be sure she is more likely to marry, to have more children if married, and to become more easily buried in household routine than the woman who has achieved economic independence and demands a mate that appreciates the values of a co-partnership, but these facts do not signify that the clinging type of woman has more sex or more motherhood possibilities, but rather that her social retardation permits her to tolerate the easier home life characteristic of the time when women were subservient to men.

Problems of Woman's Employment.—It is evident that the new order puts a double burden on woman. This appears even in the educational preparation for life. If the young woman is to look forward to life employment with the same seriousness as the young man she must attempt an equally long and exacting preparation. At once she runs risk not only of not getting adequate training for marriage and motherhood, but her effort to get ready for her chosen vocation is likely to lessen her contacts with men and decrease her opportunities for successful mating. If she regards the successful pursuit of her ambitions as incompatible with marriage, she steels herself against possible temptation that would lead her to turn aside from the path she has chosen to become a wife and mother. It is a commonplace observation that the man in obtaining his preparation faces no such dilemma as does the woman who seems to reach the fork of the road where serious training for a livelihood diverges from the attainment of a complete home life.

It is at this point of strain that the economic independence of

woman is bound to force social changes that will either protect her
from the necessity of making so hard a choice or will permit her
to compromise, in a way that is now difficult, her two interests.
The student of modern family life in our cities is aware that
experimentation at this point is already taking place. Some women,
at least, are finding that they can marry and have home life and
continue their business or profession exactly as does the man,
provided they accept a different sort of home life from that of their
parents. Even motherhood, although a much more difficult problem to surmount, is for some merely a temporary interruption of
their outside work. The nursery school prophesies the way of relief
for those women who insist upon both motherhood and a permanent
industrial or professional career.

The Rural Home.—The country woman does not have the
facilities that would permit her to reduce her family responsibilities
in the way the city wife can. However in the rural districts the
married woman is rarely the type to lessen her home duties in
order to carry on employment away from the house. The farming
industry still offers a large measure of family coöperation and the
wife of the farmer seldom feels the antagonistic forces tugging
toward and away from the home. Many of the young women who
shy away from the concentration on home duties that the farmer's
wife usually takes as a matter of course go cityward and if they
marry it is with the expectation of assuming less exacting home
responsibilities than the country environment requires.

The urban trend toward a smaller house and the lessening
of the burden of housekeeping reacts to some extent upon the
country. The country wife becomes acquainted with the inventions
and architectural improvements that make housekeeping easier
and simpler and, stimulated by the difficulty of getting household
help, she also decreases considerably the drudgery of housekeeping
as compared with the practices of her mother. The popularity
of the automobile has encouraged this departure from the former
program of the rural home, since the household tasks must be
minimized or the housewife will have little opportunity to share
in the recreation provided by the family car. Although the rural
family is not in the throes of such disturbances as city life has

created, it is gradually changing toward a simpler and less independent home life.[10]

The Gregarious Effects of Woman's Employment.—The
love of being with people is obviously not a masculine trait; it is
a normal human impulse, shared alike by men, women and children.
The wife of the past, during the régime of the homestead type of
family, was much alone as she worked, for even when fortunate she
rarely had more than one servant or, part of the time, her older children as associates while she toiled. She seldom appreciated the extent
of her deprivation even when she suffered from chronic depression,
because she had never been accustomed to anything else. Employment, however, which brings women into group contact, even the
monotonous labor of the factory, provides the thrills and satisfactions of gregarious experience.

Once the woman has learned the pleasure of working in company
with others, keeping house in isolation becomes irksome. A social
worker connected with a large department store, who is familiar
with the home life of the sales girls who marry and leave the store
to begin housekeeping, testifies that in a very little while—often
a few months—a great proportion of these young women return to
the store, stating that they want their old job back, not because
they are unhappy in their marriage or contemplate leaving their
husbands, but because they find working alone in the house so
dull that they are driven to tears. Their indictment of housekeeping is that it is a lonesome occupation; they want to be back
where they can enjoy human contacts, and are willing to move into
smaller quarters and farm out a greater quantity of their home
activities in order to obtain relief.

A recent writer gives a vivid illustration of the depth of craving
women workers experience for group contacts. Visiting a sick
widow who had been supporting her small children by working in
a factory, the caller was surprised to find that the chief regret of
the sick woman was not her suffering or illness but the fact that
she was prevented by her condition from sharing the sociability of
her former place of occupation.

Woman's economic experience has profoundly influenced her by
awakening her desire for gregarious satisfaction. It is not economic

[10] Groves, "Rural Problems of To-day," pp. 23–25.

motive alone—in some cases it is not at all the desire for gain—that makes so many married women who have worked in industry before they started housekeeping crave intensely a return to employment outside of the house. Without question the restlessness of a considerable number of so-called "nervous housewives " is actually rooted in unsatisfied gregarious hankerings, even though the source of the difficulty is kept out of consciousness because it would seem treason against affection to admit that the home does not fully satisfy them.

There are, of course, women who for one reason or another are glad to flee from the strain of irritation they have received in industry. To them marriage is a happy relief, but this reaction certainly is not characteristic of the modern young woman who enters industry.

The women of our times are less likely to smother or conceal from themselves their genuine desires than has been the habit of women in the past. It is to be expected, therefore, that modern woman will not only, through her industrial experience, decide that like man she desires to be with others as she works; but she will frankly face this and recognize that a marriage that denies her a reasonable quantity of associations is a hardship that risks happiness.

In judging women's contribution along lines that bring distinction, critics fail to take into account the unstimulating character of housekeeping. Work that lacks the zest of personal contact and rivalry and that holds an individual in isolation lowers mental vitality and discourages the development of talent. It is not necessary to assume that men tend to inherit greater intellectual capacity to explain the lesser attainment of distinction of women, since not only have men had more opportunity, but also the majority of men as compared with the majority of women have enjoyed a more stimulating environment. The economic independence of woman is bound to open the way for a greater number of ambitious and gifted women to achieve social recognition.

The Wage-earning Woman.—Woman's industrial experience acts at times as a cause of friction between husband and wife. One of the well-established prerogatives enjoyed by man in the not-distant past has been the command of the family purse. This was natural, even inevitable, during the régime of male dominance.

This financial program still persists, without question, in the majority of American homes at the present time but it frequently produces friction in the home where the woman previously has had a large measure of economic experience and financial independence. The woman who has worked for wages before marriage is irritated by the necessity of asking her husband for money and being forced, perhaps, to account for every penny spent. Sometimes the wife eventually seeks divorce through a loss of affection that was started by quarrels over money matters; other women gradually adjust themselves to a condition which has given them many unhappy thoughts, the only flaw, it may be, in an otherwise successful marriage. Still others attempt to seek what they consider their rights by subterfuge and deceit.

A rational preparation of men for marriage in these days includes a clear understanding that what the husband earns out in industry while his wife keeps house must be regarded as a family income, and not conceived of as something to which he has prior rights. Some women return to a wage-paying occupation after their marriage in order to escape bickering over expenditures; they have been accustomed to having money of their own and spending it in their own way and they find the husband's archaic attitude toward family finances intolerable.

The Family Budget.—There is only one right and intelligent way to deal with the family income, and that is to establish some kind of budget, well adapted to the circumstances and needs of the particular family. Income, from whatever source, then becomes a family and not an individual possession, and is spent in accordance with a program that recognizes the equal rights of husband and wife. The budget does more than provide an equitable distribution of the family funds; it educates all the members of the home in the spending of the money and leads the family to protect itself against future needs by reasonable savings.

A budget program cannot remain static and provide for the needs of a family constantly changing. One who has intimate knowledge of family life occasionally learns of a woman who has overworked and over-worried in the effort to keep within the allowance apportioned for household expenses, in spite of the fact that the husband's income has considerably increased beyond what it was when the budget arrangement was first made.

Employment and Woman's Standards of Living.—One of the unfortunate facts connected with woman's employment is her temptation to dress beyond her means. In her competition with other women for a mate she sees the value of attractive clothes. In counseling with the middle-class working-girl who, in the middle twenties, has come to realize frankly her need of marriage and who wishes to know how she can legitimately obtain a chance to win a home of her own, I have learned what a problem she has in deciding how much to spend on clothes. The girl who dresses beyond her means does indeed attract the attention of men, but she also often frightens her serious admirers, upon whom she must depend for her offer of matrimony. Hardly able to support themselves, and unwilling to jeopardize their future career by assuming through marriage too great an economic hazard, the more thoughtful young men postpone marriage. Thus the extravagant working-girl by her policy tends to delay the consummation of courtship in marriage which she is seeking.

The girl accustomed to standards of living that she has been able to maintain by spending on herself all her earnings while living with her parents finds it difficult to start marriage on the level necessitated by the earnings of her young husband. Inexperienced in the management of a home, she tends to spend beyond what can be afforded and soon financial worries begin to devour the peace and sympathy of the couple.

Sometimes the man is the more at fault, for he also during his single career may become captive to luxuries that he cannot wisely continue after marriage. Preparation for marriage, now so desperately needed by young people as a consequence of the prevailing conditions of social life, should include among other things instruction and if possible experience in family expenditures. Love is too valuable a family wealth to be lost through inexperienced buying or selfish gratification of cravings for superficial comforts.

CHAPTER VI

THE ARRESTED FAMILY

The Companionate.—The term *companionate* first appeared in an article written by Dr. M. M. Knight of Barnard College, published in the *Journal of Social Hygiene,* May, 1924. The expression was at once incorporated into the technical vocabulary used by scientists in the discussion of family problems. Doctor Knight has hit upon a happy word to describe a modern variation from the historic type of family. It was recognized by all students of the family of today that many married couples were attempting a relationship consciously based upon a program of pleasure and mutual advantage which deliberately sought to sidestep all possible social responsibilities, particularly those connected with the having and rearing of children. Marriages of this sort were clearly in contrast with the orthodox family, and for clarity of discussion a distinguishing term for the modern variant from the family was needed.

With the introduction of the term it became apparent that even the companionate could be broken up into different types. According to Doctor Knight's statement, "we may call the state of lawful wedlock, entered into solely for companionship, and not contributing children to society, the 'companionate,' using the term 'family' in its true historical sense, as the institution for regulating reproduction, early education, property inheritance, and some other things."[1]

A later conception of the companionate added the idea that the union was of temporary character, and that those who entered upon it should be allowed to choose for themselves divorce and remarriage, but only after some delay and conformably to regulations.[2]

In the discussions that followed the introduction of the term companionate, it became evident that some of the advocates of the new relationship stressed as its distinguishing mark the fact that

---

[1] *Loc. cit.,* p. 258.
[2] Kirkpatrick, *Journal of Social Hygiene,* Nov., 1924, vol. x, p. 473.

it rested on a contract between the two persons concerned, which, even if its registration was required by the state, did not entail the assumption of permanency or the social responsibilities belonging to legalized marriage.

It is evident that the common characteristic of these different ideas of the meanings of the companionate is the deliberate intent of those entering upon it to escape children and all possible social responsibilities. It is with this meaning that the word companionate is used in this text.

The Social Significance of the Companionate.—The companionate is an attempt at an arrested type of family life. There have always been married couples who have had no children; in the past this has been thought of as a defective family life. Because of physiological conditions such as the sterility of one or both members of the marriage partnership due perhaps to venereal disease, children were not born, a situation which, from the point of view of the orthodox family, has been looked upon as a misfortune. In the program of the companionate a similar situation, differently produced, becomes desirable for the success of the relationship.

An understanding of the motives that lead to the establishment of the companionate requires an analysis of the social conditions influencing family life. These conditions are discussed elsewhere in this text, especially in Chapter V. The companionate is a social product and can be interpreted satisfactorily only if it is looked upon from the point of view of the general social situation and the conditions that are operating upon men and women in these days.

It is clear that economic motives play a large part in the factors that encourage the establishment of the companionate. It is equally apparent that the companionate as a conscious program rests upon the widespread confidence that science has at last obtained control of the birth processes so that those who desire can enter marriage with the certainty that children will not be born. In spite of the growing confidence in the efficacy of contraceptive methods of birth control it is the conservative statement of scientific authority that there is not yet any satisfactory or dependable method of birth control. Therefore the companionate as a determined effort to protect the marriage from children rests upon a precarious foundation, and in cases not a few the contemplated companionate passes, by the accidental coming of children, into the orthodox family; so that the companionate occasionally represents a conscious desire rather than a successful policy.

The fact that some who attempt the companionate are frustrated because of their inability to carry out their program does not in the slightest degree lessen the social significance of the companionate as a marriage objective. It is the desire to escape children and social responsibility that has the greater meaning, and not the failure of those who because of faulty methods of working out their desires are driven into the orthodox family responsibilities. So far as prevailing social conditions hamper the growth of normal family life and restrain individuals from accepting the biological function of the family, a social situation exists which will necessarily popularize the idea of the companionate.

Moreover, there can be no doubt that science is making progress in its attempt to gain greater control of the birth process, and no one can guarantee that science will never discover harmless and satisfactory methods of birth control. Indeed, the premature confidence of some may merely be a prophecy of what is soon to be with us, and if science accomplishes this in the near future neither legislative prohibition nor religious hostility is likely to prevent the rapid dissemination of the new knowledge among all classes throughout the civilized world.

Motives for the Companionate.—Although the companionate is an expression of certain trends in modern social life, there are personal motives of various sorts that influence individuals who enter the new type of relationship. Sometimes the husband or wife is fearful of the physical dangers of childbirth; occasionally one comes in contact with a situation that is literally a fear complex, often started in early childhood. Familiarity with a case where the mother has died in giving birth to a child, or the undue stressing of the dangers of maternity by the mother, may arouse in a child a fear tendency which increases with advancing years until the individual in maturity regards pregnancy with literal terror. It may be either the husband or the wife that suffers from the fear complex; rarely, both of them feel the same dread. At other times husband or wife fears having children because of an actual or imagined hereditary trait; of course not all such cases are genuine, for rationalization takes place here frequently and a reluctance to accept the birth of children is justified by concentrating upon some ancestral defect so as to protect the individual from self-criticism. There are, however, conscientious persons who establish companionates because they feel that their family history does not justify their bringing children into the world.

Chronic illness on the part of the man or woman explains some cases of companionate. A, for example, married a young woman whom he knew to be in the advanced stages of consumption; the disease had appeared during their courtship and the circumstances were such that there seemed no way to give the woman the rest she needed unless her lover married her. Both of them understood that death was not likely to permit their relationship to continue long. The man entered upon the marriage in the belief that he was doing the only just thing, but it was also clear that for this marriage to issue in the bringing of a child into the world would be a wrong against both mother and child.

Another motive that leads many to attempt the companionate is professional interest. Newly married couples entering missionary service in a trying climate may be given medical advice not to have children, at least for several years. Even though the postponement of children is planned for, rather than a permanent companionate, the result may be childlessness. A typical case is that of Mr. and Mrs. X, an ambitious young couple who married while they were both working their way through college; the husband continued his professional training for several years, while the wife worked as a stenographer to eke out the money he was able to earn during vacations. Children were out of the question during these years of self-denial, but the moment Mr. X finished his training and accepted his first position the happy couple planned to start raising a family. To their dismay no children came to round out their family circle, and for ten years they deeply regretted the course they had pursued in the beginning of their married life; then one child was born to them, and with that abnormally small family they had to be content.

The Marriage Program of the Past.—It is of course wrong

to suppose that the condition of childlessness is an entirely new experience in married life. Ordinarily men and women have not married in order to propagate children, they have merely followed personal impulses and have been led by the natural coming of the child into the more complete and mature form of family life. There have always been marriages consciously planned for the having of children, but such marriages have been rare and certainly not characteristic. The young man and woman in the fervor of courtship have wished each other; and the possible coming of a child, although it may have been in the background of their thoughts, has not received attention; it has been a remote contingency, a distant fruition but not one that was consciously sought. The difference now is that nature can often be thwarted in her attempt to lead marriage to its full development. Those who successfully maintain a companionate are limiting their marriage career so as to protect themselves from the responsibilities that in the past were accepted as a necessary complication of marriage even when they were undesired.

Abortion.—There can be no doubt that in the past, and even in savage life, a determined effort has been made by some to keep marriage on a companionate level. The desire to control birth is by no means a new thing in the history of mankind: it is the increasing ability to do this by scientific methods that is new, so that the desire to escape children is more often satisfied than formerly. It must not be forgotten, however, that in the distant past abortion has often been used either to prevent the coming of any children or to limit the size of the family. Savage life discloses that the use of abortion for such purposes has had a real social significance.

Nomadic tribes, those living chiefly on meat or fish, and all that do not have a constant supply of soft food such as milk or grains that furnish pap for the feeding of young children must allow an interval of several years between the rearing of the several offspring of each woman, since the child is dependent on the mother's milk for from two to six years, according to the living conditions of the people. Infanticide is a common means of thus spacing the children to be brought up; continence, enforced by taboo and aided in some cases by polygyny, is the rule among many peoples; and abortion or mutilation resulting in sterility is practiced in some tribes.[3]

Although these methods of influencing the size of the family were primarily efforts to keep the population from becoming too great for the safety of the group, there is no reason to suppose that individual and family motives played no part. Indeed we are specifically told by one anthropologist that the women of a certain tribe employed abortion to spare themselves the labor of rearing many children.[4]

In the recent past abortion has been more extensively practiced than common thought supposes. The wife of a struggling New England farmer reports that she was violently berated by her mother-in-law whenever the approaching advent of another child became obvious, the older woman doing her best to get the young mother to make use of the crude methods of abortion which had limited her own offspring to two children. " How can you expect your husband to get on, with so many mouths to feed? He can't never get nowhere with you having another baby every year or two. Where's your pride? Do like I did and *be* somebody." This was the burden of the less scathing of her remarks.

Reliable statistics are naturally impossible to obtain, for not only has abortion been illegal, but also it has been socially reprehensible so that individuals who have resorted to it have endeavored by concealment both to satisfy their personal desire to escape the burden of children and to hold the respect of neighbors and friends. Such information as we have, chiefly based on the estimates of doctors, makes it clear that abortion has had a larger place in modern life than the moralist likes to admit. The abortion rate has been estimated at from two millions to a half million annually in the United States. East considers the latter figure nearer the right guess, which he would place somewhat lower than this. He says: " Whatever the rate in any country it is too high. Leaving moral considerations aside, the physical consequences of

[3] Descamps, " Comment les Conditions de Vie des Sauvages Influencent leur Natalité." *Revue de l'Institut de Sociologie, Tome I. No. 2.* Septembre, 1922, pp. 175, 183.

See also Westermarck, *op. cit.*, vol. iii, pp. 68, 79.

[4] Skeat and Blagden, " Savage Races of the Malay Peninsula," vol. ii, p. 23.

induced abortion are so distressing as to make it an economic crime." [5]

The Problem of Sterility.—It would be a great mistake to suppose all childless families are the result of the deliberate choice of husband and wife. It is estimated that at least 10 per cent. of our population are infertile. Many of those who assume they are protecting themselves from parenthood are actually sterile, and if they made no effort at all to avoid children they would still remain barren.

The question of marriage infertility is a complicated biological problem about which we know much less than we wish. Of course the infertility may be the result of the sterility of either the man or the woman. Gonorrhœa is held responsible for a considerable share of these cases of sterility, but no one supposes this to be the only cause. We have every reason to believe that there are many factors that increase or destroy fertility. In cases not a few couples who are infertile when together can yet have children when they separate and contract second marriages. Experiments with the breeding of animals and medical research are adding knowledge that reveals how complicated the problem of sterility is. For example even the endocrines, concerning which all our knowledge is so recent, according to some authorities influence fertility as well as general health and emotional behavior, and it is claimed that curable cases of sterility are successfully treated by endocrine therapy.[6]

Pleasure Basis of Companionate.—The companionate, in so far as it represents a determined policy to prevent marriage from developing into the orthodox family, is in the majority of cases a program that expresses a craving for personal advantage or the seeking of pleasure. Ambition, professional or social, tempts some to establish a companionate rather than risk success by assuming the liability of children; but for the most part the companionate issues from the desire to have the pleasures of comradeship and sex without undertaking the social task nature in the past so often thrust upon even those unwilling to have children, as a consequence of their entering the intimate relationship

[5] "Mankind at the Crossroads," p. 263.
[6] Bandler, S. W., "The Endocrines," Ch. IX.

of marriage. Sex obviously impels toward marriage, but the family is something more than the legalizing of sex attraction. In some of the higher animals and in most human beings sex as an experience naturally passes into parental affection; it is the companionate's blocking of this development that makes it an arrested type of family life.

The companionate has to support itself by one or more of the following motives: the professional or economic advantage of a marriage partnership, the craving for intimate response, or sex pleasure. It is sex, however, that looms large in the companionate. Although sex is well fitted to drive toward marriage, it is not so satisfactory a basis for perpetuating the marriage status. In the past the decrease of sex attraction has been accomplished by the development of parental interest in the child, who has drawn forth a new element of common sympathy. Sex thus became incorporated in a larger whole and the orthodox family profited from the combination of interests that held the husband and wife together. The companionate has a smaller province and in so far as it is predominantly sexual in character it is more likely to dwindle with time than to increase. This explains the influence of children in preventing divorce. In short, the companionate is a wilful attempt to keep marriage on the level of pleasure and expediency by cutting off its normal passage into parenthood.

Education and the Companionate.—The popularizing of education and its lengthening, especially for the woman, necessarily favor the establishment of a companionate. The ambitious woman who wishes to get as complete an educational preparation for life as possible tends not only to delay marriage, but when married is more tempted than was her untrained ancestor to continue her mental growth by protecting herself from the obligations of motherhood. The young woman who has been looking forward for several years to a life of professional activity does not easily reconcile herself to being cut off from these interests and confined to the domain of her mother. She is skeptical about the possibility of swinging the double responsibility of a profession and an old-time home, when she sees how hard it is for an unattached woman to forge ahead in her chosen line because of the prejudices of those in power.

Even by maintaining a companionate the professional woman handicaps herself, for she is tied to the locality where her husband's interests are best served, and this often means that she can not make a move that would be beneficial to her or that she must give up a good opening to try her fortunes elsewhere in order that her husband may advance in his career; a salary raise may be denied her for the simple reason that it is assumed that she is not free to move to another place and is therefore at the mercy of the institution employing her. So strong is the feeling that a married woman can not do justice to her work on account of her attention being divided between work and home that she is quite likely to be engaged at a lower salary than would be offered to an unmarried woman of inferior ability. When a man and woman who are employed in the same institution marry, it occasionally happens that the management no longer wish the services of the woman because they have a notion that the man will show favoritism to his wife if his position gives him any opportunity, or that the couple will side together on questions of policy so that the man's opinions will carry more weight than those of another individual.

Not only is the trained woman tempted to set up a companionate rather than a more usual type of married life, but the man who has been educated for a profession finds himself confronted with serious reasons for delay in the coming of children. As a consequence, what may have been planned as a temporary childlessness sometimes becomes a permanent companionate either because of ensuing sterility or because the couple never reach the point of being ready to assume the parental task until surprised by the fact that for them children have become impossible.

The keen competition which faces the professional person at the beginning of his career makes one who is financially insecure hesitate to undertake the rearing of a family. Thus, though education usually fits the man and woman more adequately for parenthood, at the same time it multiplies the motives that lead to the companionate and encourages a program of postponement or repudiation of the historic family responsibilities. It is not merely that education, by taking over an increasing amount of time, delays marriage and creates standards that hamper the

7

development of the marriage into its complete form, but also that the attitudes and interests of the young couple are turned away from parenthood and concentrated upon intellectual experience or social opportunity.

Recognizing the Companionate.—According to Havelock Ellis, America is a pioneer in frankly recognizing the presence of a new type of marriage, called the companionate. He states that it is a matter of common knowledge that unions for sexual and social comradeship, with no thought of the procreation of children, are with us and to ignore the fact of their presence is neither wise nor courageous. It is his opinion that the decrease of prostitution and the growing need of control and deliberation regarding the bringing of children into the world necessarily produces this trend toward a new type of sexual union. He would relieve those forming a companionate from the necessity of receiving the instruction for parenthood which those establishing the orthodox family need to be given. He also suggests that the companionate marriage might well be formed and ended with less formality and regulation than is necessary for the historic family. Ellis considers the recognition of the companionate and a sincere effort to deal with it on a different basis from ordinary marriage a first step in wholesome social reform.[7]

The Companionate an Arrested Family.—As Havelock Ellis suggests in his statement concerning the companionate, the new form of marriage puts much stress upon sex. This, of course, does not mean that the sex impulse is ever absent from the motives that lead men and women into normal marriage, but the companionate is a deliberate attempt to hold the marriage on the plane of experience which hitherto has been characteristic of the early period of the historic home. In the past the sex impulse has, by the natural progress of events, led the couple into the higher level of parenthood experience. It is this change, which used to be taken as a matter of course, that those establishing a companionate desire to avoid. As a consequence their union must derive its stability from sex satisfactions and social advantages. Such a marriage loses the cohesion that comes from the growth of parental interest and this loss forbids the full development of their rela-

[7] "Life *Versus* Lives," *Forum*, December, 1925.

tionship. Even though the individuals concerned have never been awakened to any sense of loss, their union represents an effort to block the characteristic unfolding of their powers, and, however satisfying to those involved, it represents not only to the state but also from the point of view of the personality-growth of husband and wife a social arrest. In so far as sex is the predominating motive of union the risk of transitoriness is increased, for where sex attraction is reënforced by the addition of attributes brought out by parental sympathy the home has a deeper and more enduring foundation.

Children a Liability.—The appearance of the companionate in our modern life is evidence that children are becoming more and more a liability, particularly to parents of the middle class. If marriage no longer seems an advantage in one's economic career, as has been pointed out in Chapter IV, the same situation arises even more clearly with reference to the coming of children. The worker who looks to his child for economic assistance finds that child labor laws and the constantly advancing requirements of educational preparation are taking away from him the asset he once had in children. Social conditions have become such that for many homes the child is distinctly not a material help in the economic struggle and it is not strange that the family should react sensitively to this situation and adapt itself by the forming of the companionate.

It is in the city especially that the child is liable to be an economic burden as well as a social problem. The parent is handicapped even in the renting of a house as compared with his married friend who has remained childless. The parent's ease of mobility is also decreased so that he does not have equal opportunity in quickly changing employment and place of residence in order to raise his income and advance to higher and more desirable business openings. It is obvious to the onlooker that the conscientious parent who is forced to bring up his child in the city has much to worry about, and there are those who avoid a responsibility which seems to them too serious to be undertaken.

Public Opinion and the Companionate.—The companionate could not occupy its present place of importance in our society were it not for recent changes in public opinion. No satisfactory means can be discovered for the measurement of the pressure of public opinion as exercised in the past in keeping the family in its orthodox form. It is clear that both husband and wife when their union has remained barren have felt that they were somewhat frowned upon by neighbors and friends who were doing the expected thing. The legal stress put upon barrenness is a striking illustration of the way public opinion has regarded parenthood. How far this attitude of public thought has pressed individuals into parenthood undesired we have no way of knowing, but there can be no doubt that it is these changes in public opinion that are giving the companionate its opportunity. Indeed, in the case of many the movement of thought has completely reversed, and the coming of the child is regarded as a real misfortune by others who have successfully avoided parenthood.

The new social attitude reveals the temper of modern life as it operates upon the family. As the companionate program becomes increasingly secure by advances in the technique of birth control it will be apparent that married couples cannot be scolded, tricked or bribed into parenthood. Society itself must develop conditions that favor the home or a growing proportion of persons will choose the easier and safer and freer companionate, preferring to keep their union on the sex and comradeship level rather than undertake the burdens that befall parents.

Mothers by Coercion.—The task of the mother, as Professor Leta S. Hollingworth shows, is similar to that of the soldier as a contributor to the state. This writer's indictment of social leadership for using the processes of control to induce women to bear children and confine themselves to home duties is justified by the facts. The desire for population has expressed itself in social attitudes that in the past have made the childless woman at least uncomfortable. Professor Hollingworth points out that not only have the costs and dangers of childbirth been minimized, but also that the average woman has been led, through the construction of her ideals as well as by art, education, public opinion, belief and the law, to look upon childbirth as her inevitable destiny without reference to her own personal wishes.

It is not too much to say that in the past there has been a conspiracy against childlessness, which has been built not upon the desire for good homes but rather upon exploitation, mass dominance and national confidence in the security of a multiplying population. It is no longer possible to manipulate social control to such an extent for the stimulating of births by means of pressure upon women. In the better homes children are not likely to come unwanted. Their appearance must more and more depend upon the sincere wish of both husband and wife for children and a willingness to assume the kind of handicaps that children bring.

The family can compete with the companionate only by providing for many people a more desirable type of experience. The companionate will not be lessened by attack. The more complete form of married life can be encouraged by creating social situations that permit it to furnish more adequate satisfaction for most married men and women. Certainly the companionate is to be a persistent rival of the orthodox family and the family must maintain itself by social superiority. How many unwilling mothers we have had under the former régime can never be known, but it is most fortunate that society has at last progressed to the point where the home with children in it will be for most of those who establish it a definite choice. If in the past individuals have been pushed from the level of impulse to the more complete experience of parenthood, in our time they who go beyond the reaches of the companionate will more often proceed by conscious and deliberate volition.

The Social Value of the Companionate.—It is well that modern youth are not made to choose between living a single life and parenthood. The possibility of the companionate experience offers a compromise of decided social value. No one who recognizes the motives that influence people to postpone and refuse marriage will question the utility of the companionate. This new type of marriage relation will induce some to marry who, faced with the probability of becoming parents, would hesitate to enter matrimony. As the social currents are now moving, the reasons that make men and women delay or reject marriage will grow more compelling.

The companionate is not without its responsibilities. It asks more of human nature than does single life; it contributes to the maturing of personality and the stabilizing of the emotions as well as to a larger sense of public obligations and even to more exacting morals. It is well to remember also in a discussion of the companionate that those who form it do not always remain steadfast in their program. The experience itself tends toward greater maturity and a finer sense of values and often those who would not have married without confidence that they could maintain the companionate voluntarily go beyond this into the more difficult and more satisfying experiences of parenthood.

It is especially likely to be true of the woman that not until she has enjoyed several years of the comradeship of married life does she realize the strength of her own longing for children; then, finding that the companionship of her husband is not enough to feed her craving for intimate response, she determines to have children. This maturing of the maternal instinct is hastened by the pleasure the woman gets from her companionate opportunity of mothering her husband. There will always be some for whom the companionate will act as a prelude to the more complete type of family life. If the companionate is an arrested human relationship, single life for the biologically mature is even more an obstruction of human development. Here again social pressure will be found unavailing except as society brings about conditions that make marriage more desirable and the single life less satisfying.

Legislation.—Legislation can of course affect the growth of the companionate. Legislation that adds to the handicap of parents will automatically act as an encouragement of the easier type of marriage relationship. The influence of legislation upon home life is often practically forgotten by those who pass laws with attention upon certain objectives, which, although desirable in themselves, are obtained by regulations that hamper the having and rearing children. Our income tax laws have been written with much more thought of the possibility of easily bringing in the necessary funds with the least disturbance of business than of their effect upon child birth. Lawmakers will become more conscious of the need of keeping the interests of the home ever in mind in passing legislation that influences family life as the trend toward the companionate grows more apparent. In the effort more nearly to equalize the social burdens of the orthodox family and the companionate, legislators must beware of fixing upon the companionate too great handicaps by the passing of taxation regulations, for it will be easy to induce a more ominous trend toward single life and the avoidance of all marriage by over-penalizing the companionate.

A Positive Program.—The companionate must be treated as a serious change in family relationships. For many it is to be the desirable, even the conscientious type of family. The prosperity of the more mature form of family life demands a positive program. It is only by building up the most favorable conditions for wholesome and successful parenthood that society can meet the problem thrust upon it by the coming of the companionate.

Education, that does so little specifically to foster family life, must assume a new task with zeal and with skill. Our more thoughtful youth are most emphatic in their demand that they be given instruction that will help them to enter marriage well prepared. Likewise from young mothers of intelligence is coming a request, which has become irresistible, for concrete assistance in dealing wisely with their children. The friends of the family must look to education rather than to legislation or social pressure for the means by which the orthodox family may win its fair share of adherents. The companionate is itself in no small measure evidence of an inadequate and uninterpretive education which distorts the values of life. If the companionate reduces the number of families with children, it will at the same time tend to elevate the general level of family life.

The companionate is not born of new motives in human experience. It would have come in the past if it had been possible and if social conditions had stimulated its development as modern life has done. The right sort of educational preparation for marriage and home life will give the great majority of youth the courage to undertake the full task of home-keeping. It will be seen that the more complete form of relationship calls forth moral qualities that more than compensate for the limitations placed upon the parents by their obligations. It is only in the superficial sense that there is real conflict between parent and child. When Sumner said: " The interests of parents and children are antagonistic; the fact that there are or may be compensations does not affect the primary relation between the two," [8] he was oblivious to

[8] " Folkways," p. 310.

the deeper and more significant moral advantages that the child brings the parent.

The Problem of Population.—It is necessary in considering the social significance of the companionate to consider its relation with what is known as the problem of population. The relation between the number of people that must be fed and the food available for their support is a matter of the largest concern to society and one that since the publication of Malthus' famous "Essay on Population" has been much discussed. The great growth in the world's population during the nineteenth century, an increase of approximately one hundred per cent, naturally brought forth the question how long the people of the earth could continue to multiply at such a rate without a necessary decline in the standards of living. In the years before the Civil War the population of the United States increased over one-third of its total population each decade. With this increase of numbers there occurred a noticeable advance in the general standards of living.

During the latter half of the nineteenth century we have in most European countries and in the United States a decline in the birth-rate. In this country immigration has had an important influence upon the increase of population and upon the birth-rate of the native stock. Partly because of economic competition between the natives and the new settlers and in part as a result of other social and economic conditions which would have operated had there been no immigration, the size of the families of native American stock has constantly decreased and this gradual displacement of the original stock by the later arrivals and their offspring is popularly known as our problem of race suicide.

It is clear that the influences which have tended to decrease births in this country have also encouraged the companionate. From this viewpoint the companionate may be regarded as one of the preventive checks that work against a too great birth-rate. Even if desirable from this larger social outlook the companionate may nevertheless constitute, when considered in its domestic aspects, a serious social problem for the home. The fact that it is a means of giving social relief from excessive births does not change its influence upon those who maintain it. It may be both an advantage from the standpoint of population and also an obstacle that prevents many from receiving the full satisfactions of marriage.

The problem of population, however, is not merely one of quantity. The question of the quality of a people is also included and it is in this fact that the social risk of the popularity of the companionate is revealed. Many of those who choose to marry and go through life childless are just the people who by inheritance and favorable environment are well fitted to have children and give them a good preparation for life.

The companionate cannot be treated merely as an effective means of decreasing births; it also is a relationship that influences the distribution of population. It leads a large proportion of those who are gifted and fortunate in material resources to deny themselves children and leaves to those less favored the opportunity to supply in excessive measure the population of the nation.

CHAPTER VII

COURTSHIP

History of Courtship.—Courtship has existed longer than man himself. We find it among the animals, particularly the birds, where it appears in a highly developed form. Anyone familiar with bird-life has seen in the pairing season the male wooing the female in a way suggestive of modern human courtship. The male tries to attract the attention of the female by strutting, display of feathers, flying about and uttering cries; the female assumes a more passive rôle, but when he shows discouragement she at once changes her disposition and incites him to new interest. This play element in animal courtship is said to have an important biological function, since it acts as a stimulus for the male and the female and prepares them the better for the act of reproduction. The same element of play appears in modern courtship, where it has chiefly a social function.

There is also a combative element in animal courtship, especially among the higher animals, where two males fiercely contend for the possession of the female, not uncommonly in her presence. The struggle acts as a selective process, for in most cases the more vital animal becomes victor and transmits his qualities to the next generation. It apparently also acts as a sex stimulus, at least for the female. In modern human courtship this element of combativeness also appears, but like the play element its function is primarily social.

It is not possible to make a satisfactory general description of courtship among savage people because of the diverse customs and differing interpretations made of them by European students. The problem of adequately picturing courtship among savage peoples is bound up with the more comprehensive task of directly estimating the position of woman. Speculations of half a century ago regarding the position of the savage woman, built upon the idea of the matriarchate and given extreme expression in the gynæcocentric theory, have been discarded by common consent among the anthropologists, in view of the information which we now have, showing explicitly that the older positions are untenable. Perhaps, however, of late there has been a tendency for the anthropologists to go too far in their statements of woman's inferior social status. Not only is the problem baffling on account of the difference between the social theory and actual practice among primitive people, but particularly because of the temptation of the European to contrast savage situations with those familiar to him in his own society.

It is clear from the immense amount of concrete data that has been gathered regarding the courtship habits of savage peoples that often the woman, as in modern life, has a real choice of mates and has to be won by her suitor by practices not essentially different from what we have in our own courtship. A savage Besisi in Kuala Langat on the Malay Peninsula, when asked how a man would speak to a woman he wanted to marry, and who was willing to accept him, replied by giving the following dialogue:

"*Man.*—Are you willing to take me, say?

"*Woman.*—What mean you? I merely follow you. How can I refuse?

"*Man.*—I wish that too.

"*Woman.*—How can I refuse? It is the man with whom it rests. I merely follow you, since I am but a woman. As I am a woman, I merely follow you.

"*Man.*—If that is truth, so be it. I will be father and mother to you, rest assured.

"*Woman.*—What mean you? I follow you for a single day, but not for long.

"*Man.*—That is also my desire.

"*Woman.*—If you are savage, overbearing, harsh-spoken, if you are like that, if you are like a hornet, I shall be unable to endure it beyond tomorrow." [1]

There have been great changes in the form of courtship during the historic era and at the present time the variations between nations and even sections of the same nation are considerable. In our own country the history of courtship shows marked changes and the evolution is still going on. Just now the tendency is unmistak-

[1] Skeat and Bladgen, "Pagan Races of the Malay Peninsula," vol. ii, p. 69.

ably toward permitting the woman to have a more open part in the courtship without meeting social disapproval. She has always had a larger place than appears on the surface, but she is now more free to exercise openly and frankly prerogatives that in the past were supposed to be primarily man's and which formerly she assumed with safety only when she was skillful in concealing her leading part.

In this discussion it will be necessary to confine ourselves to modern American courtship. Among us today courtship may be said to have three purposes: first, it provides opportunity for the getting acquainted of the two persons; second, it permits their testing; and finally it allows their interest in each other to be developed to the point of preparation for marriage.

Getting Acquainted.—The element of chase which has so large a place in animal courtship shows itself in human courtship primarily in the process by which the individual who takes the more active part wins the attention of the other. What we call flirtation is a mild form of courting and adolescents are always potentially ready to enter upon the exciting experience of courting or being courted. Certainly the normal adolescent boy or girl finds the opposite sex the most interesting thing in the world and needs little opportunity to start courting. The daydreams of adolescent girls have been studied more carefully than those of boys. We find, as we would expect, that in their daydreaming girls are for the most part reveling in pleasant imaginings that have to do with either love or social prestige. Even the second type of daydream is likely to be more or less related to thoughts of the other sex, since the coveted success is either the starting point of winning a boy's regard or the imaginary delight is exhibited before the applauding male.[2]

We have no reason to suppose that the boy is less given to concentration on the subject of girls and courting when he indulges in daydreams, but he less often plays with his imagination because of his more active life. Being free to engage more openly than the girl in aggressive courtship he does not need to hide his interests

---

[2] Pruette, L., " What's Happening in the Daydreams of the Adolescent Girl," *J. Soc. Hyg.*, October, 1924, pp. 419–424.

in fiction, as must the girl, of whom social convention expects a more passive part in courtship.

It is the woman's part to attract the attention of the male and in this sense she is often the instigator of the courtship. Here is rooted the enormous control that fashion has over the dress of the woman, particularly the young woman. Those who know the working girl bear testimony to the fact that she will endure a great deal of physical discomfort and sometimes actual privation in order to have the necessary funds to spend on clothes that give her a fair chance in competing with her acquaintances for the favor of a man. At least in the adolescent period the male is influenced by the dress of the girl and her conformity to the prevailing style of adornment.

Some girls become adept in winning attention and often the intense pleasure they obtain leads them to an arrested form of courtship so that they do not pass from the first stages and to the surprise of observers they finally do not marry at all. As soon as the courtship begins to be too serious they break it off, frequently using jealousy as the means, and then without loss of time they start another experience.

A young girl of this sort was noticeable during a summer filled with flirtations because of the unusual form in which her skill showed itself. She picked up an acquaintance with a rather unattractive girl, her opposite in coloring, taste in dressing, and degree of vivacity. The flirt stuck closely to her drab friend and accepted no invitation that did not include both girls. Thus she cleverly placed herself against a background where she always excelled in contrast to the inferiority of appearance and attractiveness of the other girl. The latter was no loser since she had pleasures that would not have come to her otherwise and she felt no grievance. Whether the man-hunting girl had consciously worked out her program or fallen into it more or less by accident, she clung to it tenaciously because it so well served her double purpose of exciting the ardor of men and preventing the development of their courtship beyond the point where it gave her a sense of dominance.

Winning the attention of the candidate for courtship is only the first part of the girl's rôle; she must also incite pursuit. If she is the leading spirit in the affair it is usually necessary for her to conceal this fact lest the man lose interest and turn aside. He craves dominance and the social stage is set for him to have the leading part. It may be only in appearance that he is in the foremost position, but while this situation complicates the girl's courting, it also tends to make her more skilled in the art of retreat that subtly beckons.

The girl must also know the opportune time for the ending of the pursuit by becoming " the steady," the favored one from among those who were competing for the lover's attention. If she surrenders too soon the courtship runs risk of anticlimax, indeed the man not infrequently loses his zest as a wooer and in time the relationship breaks off. It is equally true that if he is kept too long on the hooks of indecision he may become discouraged and turn his eyes elsewhere so that he is captured by a rival. Commonly held to be a matter of intuition, it must really be observation and thought which enables the girl to know just when to bring the courtship to its climax.

There cannot be courtship without social conditions that make it possible. As many observers have pointed out, the working classes are most hampered. Often the girl cannot invite her friend to her own home on account of its crowded condition or its poverty. Students of this problem criticize the regulations of parks and other public places that would naturally be used for courtship if there were no prohibitions. Indeed these regulations are exceedingly difficult to enforce because there is such great temptation on the part of the young to evade them and it is difficult even for the police to draw the line between what is proper and what is not allowed. When one notices the way many adults who have left their courting days behind them react to any expression of attraction between young people one doubts whether, as Emerson once said, "All the world loves a lover."

The menace of the automobile is, in part at least, due to the inability of a multitude of city workers to get a reasonable chance for courtship. The great isolation that the automobile permits both makes it a favored choice for courting and leads, as does nothing else, to the incitement of vice. Not only does the automobile provide privacy, it also brings about anonymity. Thus there is temptation to exploit the girl who is not consciously accepting danger but only embracing an opportunity, as she supposes, for legitimate courtship. Society must take a reasonable attitude toward courtship and our churches, particularly those that serve young people who live in congested quarters, should more frequently than they do provide opportunity for courtship.

The advantage that the owner of an automobile has explains in part the stealing of automobiles, many of which are later returned to their owners or left where they are likely to be found by the police. The newspapers from time to time record the tragic end of a joy ride which was taken in a stolen machine and since these disastrous endings must be a small proportion of the total number of such adventures there can be little doubt that the desire for courtship is one of the motives for the borrowing of automobiles without permission. College officials, for example, know that individuals who would not ordinarily appropriate another's property have not hesitated to go off in an automobile which they have surreptitiously taken from somebody else's garage, as a means of getting girls to join a party obviously planned for flirtation or courtship.

Courtship during the period of pursuit is notorious for its financial temptation. The man often spends beyond his resources in order that he may win or hold the interest of the girl. He is expected to treat her, as a rule, although there is an increasing disposition, which should be encouraged, for the girl to insist upon paying her own way. The income of the two is so nearly equal in many cases that the man is no better able than the girl to finance all the entertainments that they are likely to attend. A young girl sometimes breaks off an association with a young man in whom she had been interested, because he is too sensible to spend beyond his means or in such a way as to hamper his business or educational progress. Such a girl indicts the man for niggardliness when an actual investigation has proven that the man was supporting a relative, paying up his college expenses, or in some other way exercising the judgment or generosity that prophesied well for his stability as a future marriage partner.

The woman likewise is tempted to spend too much money on dress. The judgment of a man, particularly in the late adolescent period, is exceedingly superficial and he is far more likely to be interested in a girl who overspends, if she outdresses her competitors, than in one who has the good sense not to live beyond her earnings.

It is impossible to consider modern courtship without frankly handling the problem of petting. Petting is a revival of customs of the past which have permitted great freedom in courtship and stands in contrast with the conventional régime of the recent period of chaperonage. To some extent it is nothing new, except that it is a familiarity more commonly allowed than in the last few generations, when it was countenanced only after courtship had passed out of its first stages and was close to actual marriage.

The exacting girl of high standards finds herself today, according to her own testimony, face to face with a serious dilemma. If she permits the freedom a man usually expects she loses self-respect and is unhappy. If, on the other hand, she maintains her customary behavior she is said to be aloof and uninteresting and is quickly dropped. Just how far this is a serious problem in the actual courtship of our youth one cannot know. It must be a problem of some size or it would not be brought up so often in conference by the modern girl.

In considering a situation which admittedly contains risk we must appreciate its origin. The increased frankness of men and women, their more open courtship, their greater sophistication and the larger freedom of their period would naturally issue in a situation involving risk. The mischievous element in petting must not blind us to the impossibility of forcing the behavior of young men and women in their courtship back to the more restrained conventions of a decade ago. Moreover, it must be frankly confessed that the change is not so great as it appears, since it is in part only a more open expression of what was largely prevalent in courtship in the past. Parents who realize the seriousness of this problem will prepare their children for the ordeal of adolescence before it comes. The parents of the boy need to give most attention to teaching the safeguarding of the newer freedom in modern courtship.

The liberties sometimes permitted in what are known as petting parties carry a danger not generally recognized, although its seriousness is realized by those who are familiar with its actual consequences. In spite of the apparent knowledge of the sophisticated modern girl, concrete cases demonstrate that she is far less able to protect herself than is usually supposed. Her ignorance is startling for she assumes the attitude of one thoroughly informed regarding matters of sex.

A recent case which resulted in the pregnancy and hurried marriage of a college graduate forcefully illustrates the situation. Such terms as birth control were mere abstractions in this girl's vocabulary and she asserted that the majority of her college mates like herself attempted to convey the impression that they were very knowing regarding physical sex when as a matter of fact they were both curious and ignorant. Anyone who knows the effort the modern girl makes to get information concerning sex realizes that men are often deceived when they assume that their partner in petting is well informed and able to protect herself from serious risk. Some boys know no more than their girl friends, although like them they think themselves well informed, as is occasionally revealed by a study of cases of illegitimacy. There is often just enough knowledge to give a sense of false security in intimacies that would not be permitted if their risk were clearly understood.

Courtship As a Test.—There is necessarily, even when it is unconscious, an element of make-believe in courtship. One who is trying to impress his personality upon another is led to some deception. All highly emotional experiences make it hard for literal fact to emerge from the coloring of heightened susceptibilities, but courtship stands out as the most liable of all human experiences to take on the atmosphere of fiction. In the grip of so powerful an emotion as comes when courtship settles into what is popularly called love it is impossible even for the person concerned to know what is genuine and what is exaggerated, for this emotional experience has the power to magnify the self and give a substance to the finer qualities of the personality that was absent previously.

All the changes that come with the intense affection expressed in courtship cannot therefore be charged up to the dramatic or the deceptive element of courtship. It seems almost out of the question for these two highly wrought individuals to be frank with one another; yet in order that there shall be a reasonable amount of real knowledge that can serve as a basis for determining the wisdom

8

of marriage, courtship sooner or later takes on a testing function and the fictitious is partially separated from the qualities that are characteristic of the person.

This provision for the getting acquainted of the two persons in a way that will give them some clue as to the advisability of going on with their marriage plans or finally separating before they take that step is one of the most important functions of modern courtship. That it may accomplish its purpose the courtship must be of sufficient duration to permit the emotional attitudes to settle themselves somewhat. On the other hand, a very long courtship tends to exaggerate differences and little by little, there being no final commitment, a schism occurs and the marriage is repeatedly postponed until it does not occur at all.

If courtship elates the two individuals enamoured of one another they must have an opportunity to come down from their super-level and see life without distortion. This can seldom be entirely brought about during courtship and herein are to be found the dangers that underlie the transition from courtship to marriage. The sharp break that for some individuals occurs so early in matrimony between the spirit of courtship and the actualities of marriage brings out the fact that each experience must be understood in relation to the other.

The Development of Courtship.—Considering courtship as it has to do with society we find that it contains three distinct processes when it has a normal development. It stimulates sex attraction even though the physical element be absent from consciousness. There is also a sublimation of this sex element and in this way the physical side of the attraction is largely kept from consciousness. As a consequence we have an idealization which is the most remarkable part of courtship and which makes this particular human relationship the favored topic of the literary artist. Human nature never reaches greater heights of unselfishness or appreciation of another's character, so far as the emotions are concerned, although most persons happily married realize that they tread higher ranges of experience, but without such intense emotional upheaval.

Anticlimax is the obvious danger ever-present in courtship. A common statement gives emphasis to this fact. "Man," it is said, "thinks of courtship as a means to an end; woman, as an end in itself." In so far as there is this difference between men and women, it is doubtful whether it is based on inherited peculiarities that accompany sex; it is rather that the woman clings to the courtship because marriage so seldom gives her the social opportunity to transfer her interests satisfactorily. The man as a competitor in the world of affairs is forced not only to make a quick departure from the intense emotional relation of courtship, but to concentrate his interests in dealing with the obligations he cannot escape.

It follows, therefore, that the woman is more likely to sense the anticlimax when the days of courtship are ended by the beginning of marriage responsibilities. Perhaps she blames the man's ambition in his business or even imputes to a lack of sincere affection the change which she meets with dismay. The conventional pictures of literature and small talk encourage this attitude in a woman by building up within her the impression that as soon as a man's courtship fervor begins to wane, her power is dwindling and the most interesting period of her life is ended; in the same way she has also been led to think that when practical interests have a large place in married life and the emotional tone of courtship and the honeymoon is lowered, the marriage has slipped from its original high plane of poetic idealism and henceforth must travel on the lower level of material advantage. It may take some years for the woman to come to the realization that her conception of higher and lower was a sentimental mixing of terms due to her immaturity of judgment, since the relationship of the young couple is of greatest social value when it ceases to be predominantly self-centered.

We have reason to suppose that the modern girl has a better understanding of the true situation than had her mother. If there is to be wholesome married life the courtship must pass on and change its spirit by becoming a part of the calmer and more satisfying experiences of happy married life. Many a woman who does not see this at first soon discovers it; others suffer acutely in their futile attempt to continue courtship beyond its season.

It would be an advantage for the comfortable development of the marriage relation if this necessary transformation from courtship to marriage fellowship were more commonly appreciated

by men so that they could more satisfactorily do their part to help
the young bride look forward rather than backward as she feels
the emotions of courtship ebbing away. It is false counsel to advise
a young man to keep the spirit of courtship, for the new relationship makes the old incompatible, but it is good judgment on the
part of every man to make his wife feel that she is not taken too
much for granted and treated with an irritating certainty which
was never present during courtship. It is well for both husband
and wife, as a means of protecting themselves from too matter-of-
fact a contact, for each to have a degree of privacy of thought
and action as well as the opportunity for self-expression that was
natural during courtship. One of the baneful results of marriage
is a transfusion of both personalities that is so complete as to sink
their association to a humdrum level.

The Wedding.—The wedding may well be considered the
ceremony that either ends courtship or commences marriage, for
it does both. It is usually to a large extent a family observance
and so many considerations enter into its performance that the
prospective bride and groom are seldom entirely free to arrange it
according to their choice. There are decided advantages in a
simple wedding since it frees the bride from fatigue and worry
and the groom from nervous embarrassment just at the critical
starting-point of their new life together; for people who are not
wealthy the wedding should also be inexpensive, for financial difficulties are only too likely to cause strain during the early part of
married life when the cost of equipping a new home is coupled
with lack of skill in the technique of household budgeting.

The only risk connected with the simpler wedding is that the
bride may be sensitive to the conventions which make the wedding
in itself so important in a woman's life, and in later years will
regret the simplicity of the occasion. The present movement
toward a greater equality of the sexes is influencing the wedding
ceremony in a far more significant way than the omission of the
bride's promise to obey her husband.

The wedding is taking a more reasonable place in the matrimonial program, and it is this perhaps that explains the tendency,
which apparently is on the increase, for the young people to cut
themselves away from all the difficulties of the wedding ceremony

COURTSHIP 117

as a family social event by quietly slipping to some other locality
and getting married with the utmost simplicity. Although the
press reports this as an elopement it is, of course, nothing of the
sort, but an effort to avoid the ordeal of the wedding which in
times past was thought of as the great climax of a woman's career,
and in our more normal period is considered merely the legalizing
of a relationship which points forward, rather than an event of
great significance in itself.

Honeymoon.—The honeymoon is a distinctly modern invention and one of the most advantageous of all that have to do with
marriage. Its actual purpose is to give the newly married a pro-
pitious start in their new relationship with an opportunity to
transfer safely from the atmosphere of courtship to the realities
of marriage. This is the easier done if travel, a new environment
or something that removes them from their wonted associations
accompanies the change of status. The honeymoon, because it
does constitute a transition from courtship attitudes to those of
marriage, has a decided significance that may color the entire
after-life of the married couple. It is here that anticlimax is felt
by the woman who lingers as long as possible in the delights
of courtship.

The honeymoon program sometimes in itself menaces the
wholesome start of marriage. The wedding may leave one or both
life partners tired, nervous and supersensitive. The travel that
conventionally goes with the honeymoon may be unduly prolonged
so that it results in excessive fatigue. There may be also financial
worry on the part of the man, for people who, like railroad ticket-
agents, know the honeymoon program of persons in moderate
circumstances tell us that frequently trips are undertaken that
are too expensive, and sometimes have to be shortened at the last
moment because of a shortage of funds. In contrast with the mistakes of such couples we have the opposite risk of the wealthy who
extend the honeymoon to great lengths or give it an abnormal testing by some such experience as a cruise around the world in a
yacht which tears the two people from their accustomed environment for too long a time, depriving them of their usual pleasures
and at the same time forcing them to depend exclusively on each

other for companionship until the association becomes monotonous and irritating.

Familiarity with the origin of family difficulties of a serious character teaches one that a considerable percentage of separations start during the honeymoon experience. This is often due to the nervousness and fatigue of one or both members of the newly founded family. Incidents and remarks that would otherwise receive little attention are magnified out of all proportion by the almost hysterical individual and from that moment a wedge enters the union and gradually forces asunder the couple.

How far such a honeymoon experience goes is well illustrated by a case reported by Morton Prince. XYZ had her feelings hurt seriously on the first night of her honeymoon. It happened that her husband went down into the hotel lobby where he met some political acquaintance and became greatly interested in a political discussion. Strange as it may seem, he forgot his waiting bride and when a few hours later he returned to her and explained what had happened she was not only terribly hurt but also angry and determined, to use her own words, that she " would be hanged if " she would show any response to his affection. The result was that she became a victim of a neurotic dissociation which completely ruined her marriage by producing a state of long-lasting asexuality.[3]

Kinds of Honeymoon.—There are various kinds of honeymoon, but the conventional short travel trip is exceedingly common. Anyone who goes about much is familiar with the couple who start their journey with a send-off from their friends that advertises what perhaps needs no announcement since the self-consciousness of the young couple would in itself attract attention. The honeymooners soon become aware of the interest of curious fellow-travelers and all in all they have a bad beginning for the kind of transition into marriage their interests demand. It would be difficult to suggest a substitute for this sort of wedding trip, but it would be a great advantage if it became a matter of wedding ethics to allow the bridal couple to slip off quietly without the horseplay that is always annoying and sometimes goes to dangerous lengths.

It is encouraging to notice the growth of the unconventional

[3] Prince, " The Unconscious," p. 436.

honeymoon. The automobile trip escapes all the ostentatiousness
of the usual steamboat or railroad journey. There is some tendency
also toward camping trips and for those qualified to enjoy a semi-
primitive life such a honeymoon is ideal. An owner of a cottage
beautifully located in the mountain section of one of our eastern
states advertises his most attractive summer place for honeymooners
and it is constantly occupied by the type of people who appreciate
wild nature. Bridal couples who have a touch of the vagabond
spirit are quite likely in these days to take a walking trip for their
honeymoon. Anything that avoids publicity is an advantage, for
experience in dealing with family difficulties reveals the frequency
of wedding-journey strain as the primary cause of estrangement
in couples that were destined otherwise to a happy married life.
The honeymoon is not a trip for the pleasure of traveling; it is a
social convention which has come about as a means of providing
favorable conditions for the transition from courtship to wedlock.
It has its serious side as a preparation for successful marriage.

CHAPTER VIII

FAMILY INCOMPATIBILITIES

Beginning the Home.—The most critical period of marriage, as a rule, is its beginning. No undertaking in life is so influenced in its later course by the conditions of its start as is marriage. There are various reasons for this. The happenings at the commencement of married life are embedded in the emotions in a way that magnifies their importance out of all proportion to the meaning they would have under ordinary circumstances; subsequent events also are apt to take on a coloring due to the memories of the first days of matrimony. The more fatigued, worried or self-conscious either husband or wife is when passing into marriage through the gateway of the wedding, the greater is the risk of emotional stress with its rapid fluctuations and inconsistencies.

Even when no strong emotional undercurrent exists, the early days of married life are particularly significant, for immediately there commences an attempt to reorganize the lives of the two persons who were previously adjusted to different circumstances and other individuals. Even if the courtship has been unusually long and frank the new relationship completely changes the interaction of the two personalities and forces a different state of intimacy.

It must not be thought from this that there is a definite procedure through which husband and wife pass in the readjusting process of the honeymoon. Human nature does not operate by a fixed rule. Some individuals slide with little difficulty into the new relationship. Others have considerable trouble, but once they come to their new understanding all goes well and they remember with a smile their serious efforts to meet problems that as they look backward appear so trivial. Still others appear most fortunate in their ease of adjustment, but the passing of time reveals that they were really only extending courtship into marriage and postponing the inevitable disillusionment. When they finally settle down in grim earnest to meet the problems of living together it grows increasingly clear that they can not be happy together. Then there are some who at once discover the folly of their marriage, their unfitness for one another, and a cleavage begins immediately and widens with time. Whatever the situation at the beginning of marriage, the current starts flowing toward or away from a successful family life.

Instruction as to marriage problems cannot prevent this necessary process of adjustment, but a previous understanding of possible difficulties does help to make the transition easier and its dangers fewer. The greater risk of committing some costly mistake falls upon those who have no insight into the testing they are receiving in their attempt to find happiness together.

Attempting too Much.—There is a disposition among moralists in writing or talking about family failures to dismiss the problem of adjustment by charging all difficulties to selfishness or deceit. Judgments of this kind even when they justly catalog the faults of character of married persons add nothing that helps in the understanding of a family situation or that protects individuals from wrecking at the start their hope of matrimonial success. What we do need is concrete studies of individuals entering marriage, their reactions and later happiness or unhappiness. Such information is at present meagre, and what we have is more a product of unhappy than of happy homes.

A mistake often made in the first steps of home-making, perhaps more common among those who achieve happiness than among those who fail, is the blunder of taking too seriously some part of the new experience. It is more often the bride who comes to grief by too much concern. She has heard much of the need of changing her habits and committing herself thoroughly to the matrimonial venture. Driven by love and influenced by her emotional state of mind, she cuts herself off from all her old ways, interests, friends and relatives, and ties herself utterly to her new experiences. After a time she finds that she has thrown overboard too much, but not until she has lost associations that she ought to have retained or interests that would have kept her from a morbid concentration upon her home. She regrets the friends she has dismissed, who now have departed from her life because they have been so carelessly treated and have been actually given to understand that they are no longer a very essential part of her world. After a little she looks back to what she threw away, blames the marriage and assumes that married life requires this breakage. It is well to consider a matrimonial undertaking as a long trip that needs a program which one can find satisfying not merely at the start but for the whole journey.

Fair it is to charge thoughtless indifference to the new duties of home-making to selfishness, but not the over-conscientious regard which may be equally destructive of family satisfaction. The wife that begins home life with too much concern for the housekeeping portion of her new undertaking provides a good illustration of the risks of attempting too much. She sets her heart upon proving herself and is therefore easily hurt by any suggestion of criticism or failure of recognition. The graver danger is that in fulfillment of her program she takes over too much of the home load and her husband accepts her sacrifice as a matter of course and thus hurts his own development and at the same time injures her by making her temporary spurt a routine.

Advantage of Preparation.—It is a decided advantage for any girl, whatever her social situation, and even if her home duties are limited to light housekeeping, to have had definite preparation for marriage and home-making. Young women who have received in their school career instruction in well-conducted home economics courses prove the advantage of such training by the greater ease with which they assume their new task. At present, however, many girls leave the high school with practically no instruction that can help them in the marriage career most of them will eventually choose and to which nearly all look forward. It is doubtful whether a high school training that does next to nothing to prepare for marriage and family responsibilities can be socially justified even for those girls who are planning to continue their education in college.

Every girl in the high school should be given some insight into the problems that marriage brings, for such instruction is a practical and economical way of lifting the standards of the home. Since there are many girls who do not enter high school there is need also of similar courses, more elementary in character, in the grammar school.

The adolescent girl is not, of course, ready for such instruction as can properly be given the matured person about to marry, but the value of such courses as can be taught in the high school is clearly demonstrated. Public school training that seriously attempts to prepare the girl for the obligations of living, and especially of living in a home, must include studies now listed under home economics. A place for such courses can easily be found by simply pushing aside such required subjects as geometry that came into the curriculum in the days of meager educational resources and continue because of the power of inertia and tradition.

If mothers were willing to help train their daughters the work of the schools would be most happily supplemented in many cases, for the average home in its normal procedure has opportunities for practical training of the greatest value. It is true that it is often easier for the mother to do the work herself or to farm out to the daughter definite routine tasks in a way that reduces to the smallest proportion their educational value by allowing no opportunity for personal initiative and no sense of self-chosen responsibility.

No child can be expected to begin at the level of efficiency attained by the mother after years of experience. From the mother's point of view the child may not keep house well. Expenses may run up, dishes be broken and the house get cluttered, but all this would be a necessary part of the learning process. It is certainly better for the girl who is likely sometime to become a bride to have some experience in the well-established home of her mother than to have everything to learn in the first days of marriage when she is forced to carry so heavy a load of new responsibilities.

Many mothers will answer this suggestion with the statement that their daughters are not interested in housekeeping and cannot be induced to try their hand at actual management of the home. This is a confession on the part of the mother of her own failure in the bringing up of her daughter, and her blunder usually goes back to the very early years when the child wishing to play house and "help" her mother in the different household operations was denied the privilege because she was so great a bother. The mother's refusal to allow the child to invest her interest in the work of the home led to the daughter's later indifference, which in time to come is bound to make unnecessarily difficult the early married life of the daughter and her husband. A mother does not do her duty by merely teaching the child to follow directions; household management involves the ability to form accurate judgments and make careful decisions based on the practical knowledge that comes only from first-hand experience gained without the hampering protection of ever-present supervision.

Those who know the working girl employed in factories, stores and offices have a decided conviction that the business girl is not so well trained for actual homekeeping when she enters marriage as was her mother. Unless the mother makes a special effort to train the child this is the result to be expected when life presents so many interests that compete against those related to future home-making. The fact that so many mothers have neither the patience nor desire to help their daughters get practical homekeeping experience makes it all the more imperative that the school do more than it does at present. It is well to remember also that many mothers are so inefficient as wives and housekeepers that they can not give their children good training, and what they do is more likely to handicap the young bride than to help her.

The boy is less prepared than the girl for the obligations of home-making, and if we want better homes we must not leave his training out of the program. He also needs specific instruction and practical experience both at school and at home. It is especially important that he be given a chance to practice the financing of a home so that he may have an idea of his future wife's budget problems. Our traditional idea that a man does his part in earning the family income is deceptive. If only one earns, both spend, and there cannot be the best sort of coöperation in expenditure unless the husband understands to some degree the financial side of home-keeping. It is also desirable in these days when good homes are more and more products of coöperative housekeeping that would have been ridiculed two decades ago, that the husband have some experience in the tasks of everyday housekeeping, especially such essentials as cooking. Wives become sick, go to hospitals, require help at the time of childbirth, even take over part- or full-time jobs, and the tendency for men to help somewhat in the housework under such circumstances is already more prevalent than is generally supposed. Boys enjoy opportunities to cook and, if given a chance to learn, in later life never regret their knowledge, indeed are more likely to be boastful of their ability along this line than in their ordinary occupation.

Disillusionment.—The illusive element in all human experience has been commented upon by philosophers since the days of the Greek thinkers, but marriage has been singled out by them as the most vivid illustration of the inevitable disappointment that comes to one who is forced to bring his hope of happiness in contact with the given facts of actual life. Poetry, fiction, and most especially the small talk of the sophisticated adult who prides himself upon his practicality, is replete with the idea that disappointment in marriage is something axiomatic.

Much of this is the product of a sensible interpretation of common happenings. Men and women do enter marriage with expectations of perfect happiness furnished by an imagination that, driven by the powerful flow of emotions and unrestrained by experience, pictures a state of bliss that nothing human could satisfy. Disillusionment in such cases is bound to come, not as the result of a serious deception in the relationship itself but simply because fancy must at last surrender to fact. Such experiences occur constantly as the individual travels forward from childhood and tries in one way and another to fulfill his cravings. The happy husband and wife look back upon these earlier adjustments with a tender sympathy but with no sense of having been betrayed by false hopes. The fact is that more was gained by the ordeal than was lost.

This transition from love-making to marriage does hold an element of danger and becomes for some married couples a cause of psychological incompatibility. The appeal of courtship for some persons lies almost wholly in its fantasy. They insist upon remaining in an atmosphere that gives them the luxury of the daydream. If the husband or wife becomes the instrument by which such a person is brought back to reality or even pushed toward it, at once upon the head of the ill-fated partner in matrimony falls the blame for having spoiled marriage. The daydreamer who has carried on from childhood the habit of castle-building is the kind of person who cannot make the adjustment from courtship to family responsibility required by wholesome marriage. Any attempt to bring the family life into accord with actual circumstances is resented and the other member of the matrimonial alliance is chided with bitterness for lack of affection.

It is necessary in such cases to notice that any other relationship involving responsibility and adjustment to obligations would have revealed the character-defect just as did marriage. Marriage tempts such persons because courtship offers an exceptional chance for the daydreamer's revels, and they accept marriage as a means of prolonging this delightful experience. These daydreamers detect the ordeal awaiting them in other relationships and either refuse to enter or else try to protect themselves from the rude awakening which they always dread. Marriage is not justly charged with having misled the type of person whose whole life is a pilgrimage in deceit.

The woman who declares that marriage offers nothing except the pleasures of courtship and of the wedding confesses her inability to pass into a mature family relationship, and her statement that marriage is a failure is actually a confession of an infantile character that forbids a genuine trial of marriage.

Marriage is by its nature a testing undertaking, for those who are trying to escape adult responsibilities and those who are unable to pass the examination are naturally more likely to blame their partners than to accept criticism for their own failure. Thus it comes about that family life is at times marked almost at its beginning by the unwillingness of husband or wife to accept a normal, sincere commitment to the tasks of married life.

It is equally true that the opposite fault shows itself in family life. All the idealism and thought of another's welfare that some individuals ever experience in any large way appears in courtship. After marriage these persons flatten out and settle down to a Main Street humdrum that blankets all the hopes of their finer-grained spouse. Protest against making marriage a deadening routine is not evidence of a daydreamer's hostility to the meeting of life squarely, but of a discernment of the tragedy of allowing the finer attitudes of early marriage to evaporate.

A wife or husband who sees that the family life has sunk through the other's indifference into an endless round of toil or social dissipation has a just cause for feeling cheated. It is difficult to become reconciled to the draining of any experience of all its human values, but impossible to see a relationship that opens with the promise characteristic of the beginning of marriage fade into dull or even coarse routine without profound resentment. Here also is born a psychological incompatibility. Courtship can at times stir into temporary flame what appears to be noble passion, but due to thinness of personality the fire soon dies down. Even if the attitude was genuine during courtship it appears wilful deceit to the other member of the new family who feels victimized by the marriage partner's pretenses.

Sometimes an incompatibility is caused by one of the married couple discovering that he or she has been consciously deceived by the other. This may be in regard to something comparatively trivial, which in spite of its unimportance comes to have a separating influence. For example, in one case the family difficulty originated from the wife's discovery that her husband chewed tobacco and had secretly continued the habit throughout courtship. It was a disquieting thought that there had been a determined effort to hide from her something that he knew she would not approve. How far could he be trusted in other matters? She reacted at once to the suggestion of suspicion and for a time it seemed as if her married life would come to a quick end. Pride probably saved her from a public confession of failure but she never developed genuine confidence in her husband.

If the husband or wife becomes careless in dress or in any other habits there is danger of the mate's becoming irritated and disappointed. What starts as a feeling of disapproval and occasional embarrassment grows by constant association until it finally turns to shame and anger. Perhaps the more careful and ambitious member of the household develops the idea that the bad ways of the other are an obstacle to success for both of them and then hate sets in. Family disasters of this type are not the result of the common transition from courtship, with its element of acting, to the serious tasks of marriage, but rather the product of a moral letting down of character which the more efficient individual resents.

A Stimulus of Disagreeable Thoughts.—It is a common psychological experience for one person to stir up disagreeable ideas in the mind of another. Even plants and animals come to have the power of suggesting the unpleasant to those who in childhood had some unhappy experience with a particular plant or animal. Perhaps certain flowers bring always a spontaneous feeling of repulsion. This is even more frequent with reference to definite foods, especially when they bring back memory of some illness connected with them. We have habitual likes and dislikes that appear at once when the appropriate stimulus acts upon us. It may be that a person with a certain color of hair or a definite mannerism in walking or talking starts disagreeable feelings in the consciousness of one with whom he comes into contact.

The mental mechanism holds in the close contact of home life and in this way one individual is said to get on the nerves of another. This is a type of complex-reaction that grows rapidly in continuous association and often the originator of the emotional recoil is utterly oblivious to the influence he generates. At first the feeling of repulsion may have gathered about some one characteristic of the other member of the family, later spreading until the entire personality stimulates the victim adversely.

Mrs. L, the wife of a doctor, has left her home and is planning to get a divorce. Her marriage was for spite. She became angry over a note incorrectly interpreted, written by the young man to whom she was engaged, turned from him and a few months later married a doctor with whom she had meanwhile become acquainted. At first the marriage appeared successful but after a year trouble began to brew. She complained of habits that annoyed although she had to admit they were rather trivial and balanced by other qualities most desirable. The real situation immediately appeared when she told of her first engagement, her regret that she foolishly broke it off, and declared that the habits of her husband that annoyed her always suggested her first lover since they were just opposite to his ways. Clearly her husband had become an innocent victim of her regrets by stimulating thoughts that she found painful.

Becoming an Obstacle.—Another social situation that leads to family incompatibility comes about when the husband or wife seems to the other an obstacle to ambition. The following case illustrates a problem of this kind.

Miss K, the youngest and most spoiled of several children, recently became pregnant. The father of her offspring was a young college student who had still one year of study before graduation. He was as much surprised as the girl when he learned of her predicament and before he could adjust himself to the position in which he was placed the girl's mother entered the discussion with demands that he marry at once. It is probable that he recognized this as his duty; in fact there was no reason to suppose that the idea of marriage was not attractive to both young people. The mother of the girl, however, displayed the same emotionalism that was the cause of her having had some serious difficulty with each one of her children. The young man was dragged to the church pastor, threatened with various penalties if he did not consent to immediate marriage; indeed greater mismanagement could hardly be conceived.

While this was developing I had been asked by one of the relatives who could view the problem without emotion to give counsel. I pointed out the need of winning the sympathy and stressing the sense of honor of the young husband-to-be so that his quick change of plans might not seem something forced upon him by outside pressure as a form of retaliation. The girl confessed at once that she was the more responsible party in the events that led to her conception. Since she had been given no help whatever by her mother I decided that the latter was the really responsible person. The mother refused to coöperate in any tactful handling of her future son-in-law but rather enjoyed to the full the opportunity to upbraid both of the young people, especially the man.

The college student was hurled into the marriage ceremony in a most insulting manner and soon trouble began between the newly married couple. What I prophesied as the most likely thing if the girl's mother continued her dominance soon occurred. The young husband had of course immediately left college " so that he might support his family," to quote the mother, although it would have been entirely feasible for him to have completed his remaining year. He found work in a few months that made it necessary for him to leave the country and soon he was safe where he could not be brought back for desertion. Were he to return he would discover that he could easily become legally free for his wife, a few months after the birth of her child, became pregnant a second time and the offender was one whom she knew only a few hours and never saw a second time.

It is easy to see that in such a case as this the young man, forced out of college into a course of action incited by the desire for revenge rather than by any serious effort to help work out a difficult situation for the best welfare of both young people, would have a sense of grievance and would think of his wife as an obstacle to his ambition. Even assuming that he was justly punished for his unconventional behavior, it is certain that using the girl as an instrument of punishment could only result in developing in him the feeling that she had spoiled his life. By the process of time through constant suggestion she became to him the obstacle between him and happiness. Successful marriage was impossible.

Persuading a young college girl to leave her education uncompleted for marriage is always a venturesome experiment. Even when the marriage turns out well, as it fortunately often does, there is a shade of regret that hampers the fellowship of husband and wife. The wife frequently feels that another year or two of delay to enable her to get her degree would have been far wiser. If the hazard created by this short-circuiting of educational preparation were more generally understood, the right sort of man would seldom urge it.

There is greater danger when the man's plans are disrupted by a premature marriage than when this happens to the woman, since in the case of the man this more often means the thwarting of his career. It is, for example, a serious handicap that a couple takes over at marriage if the man leaves college or drops a line of business or moves from some advantageous environment in order to marry. At the time this sacrifice may seem normal, if it contributes to the happiness of the bride, but in after years when it is plain that financial success has been flouted at the time when it was almost within reach, the sacrifice seems foolish and becomes a source of deep regret.

There are myriad ways by which one member of a household comes to be an obstacle to the happiness of the other so that chronic dissatisfaction follows. If there were greater frankness, especially in the first months of marriage, so that this feeling of being hampered would be confessed and talked over freely, many situations that go from bad to worse could be handled rationally at the start, thereby only cementing affection the harder. It is surprising how difficult such confidential discussions are in the relationship of marriage. In business and professional enterprises there is a far greater freedom in squarely facing the beginning of an incompatibility than there is in most homes.

Incompatibility the Result of Exploitation.—The tendency of either husband or wife to exploit the other is one of the most common and perplexing of marriage difficulties. We can assume that from the start of the homemaking one is a little more sacrificing and affectionate than the other. Being part of the new experience of pleasant intimacy, this is rather pleasant for both and it runs rapidly on until on one side there is a strong desire to sacrifice and on the other a great willingness to accept the sacrifice. If this lasts for any length of time—and once started it often persists throughout life—the resultant family situation is distinctly bad for both. It has come about naturally enough, but it acts more and more against the family welfare. If it does not last, when the movement swings back to something more normal there may be on the part of the person who received the sacrifice the feeling that the other's affection has weakened. Experience shows that it is the woman rather than the man that is apt to be too prone to sacrifice. It is therefore the man who suffers most from the fact that he becomes the exploiter. The one who gives, develops, though not so far as judgment is concerned; the other becomes unfair and selfish, even childish.

Resentment at Transferred Mother-love.—Another difficulty which has to be frankly faced occurs in greater or less degree in most marriages. Few men realize that a woman's affection has at least two emotions, tied together when she marries a man but sooner or later separated when she becomes a mother. One is the wife-attitude and one is the mother-attitude. When she first marries she thinks of her husband in a double way. He is her husband: he is also her child. With the coming of a baby into the family group the two attitudes are immediately divided even though the wife did not herself anticipate this. Once the division has taken place things can never be as they were before. Another interest has come into the life of the young woman which in some ways rivals her earlier affection; her mother attitude will now be bestowed where it properly belongs, on the child. It is not uncommon for the husband to react against this change, feeling that his wife has ceased to care for him in the intense way that she did. Then the man will make remarks that show that although he is fond of the child, its coming means for him that he must take second place.

In some women the mother attitude may seem more powerful than the wife attitude; in others the reverse appears true. But the two attitudes do not compete with each other. They were bound together in the beginning when there was no child to receive the mother affection, and now that there are two distinct objects for the two kinds of affection one attitude has been separated from the other. Whether one is stronger than the other does not matter; the husband must take what is his. If women are deeper in their affection as mothers than as wives no advantage comes from denying this. Whichever way the balance swings the family life can go on smoothly as long as the husband cherishes no hurt feelings.

To some extent the same dual affection occurs also in the man. This seems to be getting to be more true as man's love of offspring is increasing. For a long time woman has cared for the children more than has the man, but fatherhood is rapidly catching up. Occasionally it happens that a wife feels hurt by the removal of her husband's father-affection from her to their children, not realizing that she is trying to force the man to keep together things that are naturally separated—affection for mate and child.

Jealousy.—The great enemy of love is jealousy. When jealousy creeps into the home love packs up and gets ready to depart, for it cannot thrive under the perpetual tyranny of a jealous spouse. Yet nearly all jealousy is unfounded. It is the culmination of childish habits that have never been cast aside as the jealous person found it easier to conceal them than to go through the painful process of uprooting them.

Babies demand the exclusive attention of their mother; two-year-olds have been known to slap fiercely at the little baby brother or sister that has taken from them the position of supreme importance in the household; even the child of five is apt to feel pangs of jealousy on hearing the first wail of a newborn infant in the home and realizing that the name and prerogatives of "Baby" are to descend to another. Children tend to be jealous of a brother or sister who receives praise, toys or privileges that seem more desirable than the ones given to them.

Most of us outgrow our infantile habit of giving way to jealousy but a few people allow the habit to grow stronger with the passing of years because they suffer from a deep sense of inferiority and cannot accustom themselves to the idea that they merit as good treatment as others; therefore they fear lest they be given only what they would measure out as their own deserts. These people who are driven into jealousy by their inferiority complex are not necessarily inferior in any way to those with whom they compare themselves, but their lack of self-confidence keeps them ever on the watch for fancied slights and opportunities to indulge in an emotional storm of jealousy.

During courtship the jealous person holds in check his suspicions and tries to act like other adults, but once the marriage knot is firmly tied he goes back to his old ways with a slump, for now he seems bent on making up for the difficult self-control he had to exercise while winning a mate. He may dig up trivial occurrences of the courtship that were supposedly forgotten by both young people and rehearse them until he has worked himself into a jealous rage. At the slightest suggestion of rivalry in the affection of the mate, whether from parent-in-law, work or social activities, he may bury himself in the depths of bitter jealousy. The other member of the marriage partnership hardly dares to look at the opposite sex, much less show any of the courtesy convention demands; but it makes little difference what is done, jealousy can easily feed itself, and the home life is poisoned by unfounded suspicions.

Jealousy that is not a hangover from childhood may be caused by social suggestions. Literature, scenes from the moving-pictures, and the chatter of one's friends make jealousy seem the normal reaction to certain stereotyped situations, thus precluding the unemotional talking over of circumstances whose wrong interpretation causes hard feelings in both young people. The person whose jealous trend is not of long standing can free himself of the inclination before it becomes an integral part of his disposition if he has the courage and determination to carry out a long and difficult process of readjustment and can obtain the needed advice from one who understands the mechanism of this vexing adult behavior-problem.

Relatives-in-law.—Relatives, and particularly mothers-in-law, are notoriously troublesome to the newly married. Even the savages by their taboos may have registered their realization of the problems in family life caused by unwise mothers-in-law. It is a common observation that some of our marriage failures originate in the too great interference of the mother-in-law or the over-dependence of the newly wedded man or woman upon the mother.

The difficulty must be considered in its larger and more significant aspects. The mother-in-law has become a symbol of the natural obstacles that must be met by the new family in its effort to establish itself as an independent unit, free from the surveillance of either of the parent-families. The marriage of their child means to parents a breaking away from long-accustomed relationships usually maintained since childhood, while for the young married couple it brings about a new alliance which automatically includes considerable intimacy and therefore has to set earlier associations at arm's length. It is not strange that the mother-in-law, husband and wife all find a degree of difficulty in establishing the new status.

By far the most strain is felt by the mother-in-law. Not only must she give up her precedence in affection to another, but she must have the insight to see when her help is really needed and when it is far wiser to let the young couple work out their own matrimonial salvation. Her ever-present temptation is to attempt to give the young people the benefit of her experience on every possible occasion, forgetting how hard it is for anyone to profit from the experience of another and how necessary it is that the new home get firmly established on its own initiative.

Recent psychology has explained the inner protest many mothers make against their son or daughter becoming independent of early home ties. There are mothers whose whole policy has been that of repressing the personality of their children. They have made use of the strong affection between mother and offspring as a method of holding their child in a subserviency which we are wont to call a mother-fixation. This program of keeping the child dependent has become a settled conspiracy against his maturing to the point of self-reliance and what we think of as typical mother-in-law behavior is merely the continuation of a life-long policy.

The dominance of the mother is likely to be resented after marriage even when it has been accepted by the child as a matter of course up to this time. It is received with instinctive hostility by the child-in-law, who, unfettered by previous subordination, easily sees the significance of the interference and struggles against it immediately. The contest is accepted by both parties to it as a real trial of strength and in its heat there is risk of a tension developing between the married couple, whose interests are not altogether on the same side; this tension may increase until it forms the basis of a permanent separation of interest between the young folks.

It is not hard to indict the mother-in-law but the fact is that social conventions are in part responsible for her attitude. In the recent past and even yet in a multitude of cases, in certain sections and in the class of persons who are inadequately trained for life it is customary for the mother to concentrate upon her children and develop no serious interests outside her home. This is the program expected of the mother; its acceptance is held to be the mark of an ideal home.

The consequence is that as her children leave her the mother finds herself suddenly stripped of many of the habitual activities that have become by repetition the very substance of her life. Without children to assist, plan for and protect her career seems all at once like a ship that has dropped its anchor. As she has gone on in life she has never taken out any insurance in the form of out-of-the-home interests and the escape of each child leaves her with a greater void. The educated woman of the present time sees the cause of this disaster more clearly than did her mother and she is much more likely to welcome her child's maturity than to try to prevent it. The mother of only one or two children runs a greater risk of encroaching upon their proper field of development but if she faces her problem intelligently and with knowledge of its cause she also may succeed in managing her rôle without bitterness in herself or damage to her child.

This is much the same problem that the man meets who finds himself forced to give up the control of his business to a younger successor. If the older man has no strong interests outside his business, it has become a proverb that he will fade quickly upon retirement. The mother-in-law's problem is therefore not something primarily belonging to women, but the difficult adjustment that awaits the man or woman who has lived too narrow a life. The mother's solution is complicated by the affection that has developed along with her habit of caring for her child.

Fathers occasionally find the transference of a child, especially a daughter, to another home as severe a testing as do mothers and thus the father-in-law problem originates. We find aunts, sisters, brothers and foster parents also testifying by their reactions that the protest against the breaking away from home-ties to the beginning of a new home-circle is a human weakness rather than a fault characteristic only of mothers-in-law.

It would be easier to make a gradual adjustment satisfactory to each member of the tragic triangular contest if only the son- or daughter-in-law were more patient, cool and sympathetic. Jealousy flares up quickly and there is a sharp resentment that all ties with the former home are not instantly cut. It seems like criticism of the marriage itself; actually it is proof of a fondness for home-life that sooner or later without inner wrenching of spirit can be transferred from the old to the new family.

Ruth's commitment is not to be expected of every individual who enters matrimony, for it is too much to ask of all who have enjoyed a home-life rich in their parents' fellowship that they start marriage with the rigorous declaration, " Entreat me not to leave thee and to return from following after thee; for whither thou goest, I will go; and where thou lodgest I will lodge; thy people shall be my people and thy God, my God." It is well to notice that this high resolve was spoken to a mother-in-law and expresses the conviction of the author that an ideal understanding is possible between those who are relatives-in-law.

The commonness of the in-law incompatibility must not mislead one into supposing that the relationship is inherently mischievous. Although the association is a searching test of the wholesomeness of character we have every reason to suppose that the greater proportion of those who pass through it meet their trial with success.

CHAPTER IX

DIVORCE AND DESERTION

Modern Life and Divorce.—The trend in modern life toward an increase in divorce is unmistakable. Although the record of this country is particularly bad with reference to the number of divorces granted, the influences that are stimulating the divorce rate are world-wide phenomena and issue forth from the environment of modern man and woman rather than from social conditions distinctly American. The forces that tend to bring about divorce are in some countries checked from expression by repressive legislation or the influence of the churches that hold to a sacramental interpretation of marriage and refuse to recognize the right of divorce. There is, indeed, unmistakable evidence in all progressive civilized countries of the working of social influences that favor divorce. It is, however, the American situation in which we are interested.

The History of Divorce in the United States.—As has been previously stated, the American colonies differed with reference to the granting of divorces. Although we find variations in the New England colonies, the general trend was in harmony with the teachings of early Protestantism; marriage was made a civil contract and the right of legal divorce became a logical deduction. The Southern colonies, on the other hand, under the influence of the teaching of the Church of England, moved in the opposite direction, and absolute divorce was not recognized. The statute books of these southern colonies are void of any reference to the subject of divorce restriction.[1] The middle colonies also were conservative in their attitude toward divorce, their sentiment being more in sympathy with the practice of the southern colonies than with the liberal policy of their New England neighbors.

During the latter half of the nineteenth century not only was there a sharp rise in the divorce rate in America, but also a multi-

---

[1] Howard, G. E., "A History of Matrimonial Institutions," vol. II, p. 367.

plying and still more liberal legislation covering the legal grounds for divorce. Sectional differences in regard to divorce still exist, the high divorce rate of New England, the Middle Western States, the Pacific States and the Rocky Mountain States contrasting markedly with the low rate of the Southern States.

Statistics of Divorce.—The United States Government has made four investigations of the American situation with reference to marriage and divorce. The first, conducted by the former Department of Labor, covered the twenty-year period from 1867 to 1886; the other three, made by the Bureau of the Census, reported the twenty-year period 1887 to 1906, the calendar year 1916 and the calendar year 1922.

The total number of divorces reported for 1922 was 148,815 as compared with the record of 112,036 for 1916, but the latter report was incomplete, lacking returns from ninety-five counties. A comparison of the two reports shows an apparent increase of divorces amounting to 36,779, or 32.8 per cent. If we exclude the divorces reported for 1922 from the ninety-five counties that do not appear in the report for 1916, amounting to 1799, the increase in divorces granted in 1922 over 1916 is 34,980 divorces or 31.2 per cent. An increase in the number of divorces reported appears in each geographic division, in the District of Columbia and in forty of the forty-seven States which permit divorces. The lowest rate of increase was 23.8 for the Mountain division and the highest, 43.3 for the South Atlantic group of States. The comparison of the several States reveals that Idaho had the lowest rate of increase, 5.6, and Colorado the highest, 94.7. Both North Dakota and Washington State show a large decrease in the number of divorces granted, but in the case of the latter State the report was influenced by changes in the divorce law which reduced the number of divorces during 1922; at the time of the 1916 report divorces became effective when granted, while in 1921 a change was made in the law so that divorces do not become effective until six months after the interlocutory decree is granted.

The report of the Government makes a statistical comparison between the situation in 1922 and 1916 in the following table:

TABLE III.[2]

Divorces reported, with numerical and percentage increase, for divisions and States: 1922 and 1916.

[A minus sign (−) denotes decrease]

Division and State	Divorces reported			Increase: 1922 [a] over 1916	
	1922		1916	Number	Per cent
	Total number	Number in area reporting in 1916			
UNITED STATES............	148,815	147,016	112,036	34,980	31.2
GEOGRAPHIC DIVISIONS:					
New England...............	7,192	7,191	5,739	1,452	25.3
Middle Atlantic...........	13,112	13,090	9,418	3,672	39.0
East North Central........	37,951	37,907	28,837	9,070	31.5
West North Central........	21,408	21,393	16,412	4,981	30.3
South Atlantic.............	11,069	10,516	7,336	3,180	43.3
East South Central.........	12,881	12,382	9,939	2,443	24.6
West South Central........	23,859	23,274	17,287	5,987	34.6
Mountain..................	7,412	7,363	5,947	1,416	23.8
Pacific...................	13,931	13,900	11,121	2,779	25.0
NEW ENGLAND:					
Maine.....................	1,143	1,143	702	441	62.8
New Hampshire............	604	604	698	−94	−13.5
Vermont...................	369	368	419	−51	−12.2
Massachusetts.............	3,227	3,227	2,336	891	38.1
Rhode Island..............	819	819	623	196	31.5
Connecticut...............	1,030	1,030	961	69	7.2
MIDDLE ATLANTIC:					
New York.................	4,137	4,115	3,269	846	25.9
New Jersey................	2,082	2,082	1,169	913	78.1
Pennsylvania..............	6,893	6,893	4,980	1,913	38.4
EAST NORTH CENTRAL:					
Ohio......................	10,181	10,181	7,607	2,574	33.8
Indiana...................	7,110	7,070	5,636	1,434	25.4
Illinois...................	11,057	11,053	8,546	2,507	29.3
Michigan..................	7,570	7,570	5,327	2,243	42.1
Wisconsin.................	2,033	2,033	1,721	312	18.1
WEST NORTH CENTRAL:					
Minnesota.................	2,587	2,587	1,956	631	32.3
Iowa......................	3,862	3,862	3,309	553	16.7
Missouri..................	8,344	8,329	5,791	2,538	43.8
North Dakota.............	336	336	478	−142	−29.7
South Dakota.............	560	560	585	−25	−4.3
Nebraska.................	2,280	2,280	1,675	605	36.1
Kansas...................	3,439	3,439	2,618	821	31.4

a Exclusive of 1,799 divorces reported in 1922 for 95 counties not reporting in 1916.

TABLE III.[2]—*Continued*.

Divorces reported, with numerical and percentage increase, for divisions and States: 1922 and 1916.

[A minus sign (−) denotes decrease]

Division and State	Divorces reported			Increase: 1922 [a] over 1916	
	1922		1916	Number	Per cent
	Total number	Number in area reporting in 1916			
SOUTH ATLANTIC:					
Delaware................	224	224	210	14	6.7
Maryland................	1,426	1,426	1,003	423	42.2
District of Columbia........	161	161	47	114	†
Virginia.................	2,413	2,257	1,886	371	19.7
West Virginia.............	1,467	1,340	789	551	69.8
North Carolina............	1,317	1,176	668	508	76.0
South Carolina*...........	....	....	....	....	....
Georgia.................	1,833	1,719	1,399	320	22.9
Florida.................	2,228	2,213	1,334	879	65.9
EAST SOUTH CENTRAL:					
Kentucky................	4,041	3,922	2,981	941	31.6
Tennessee...............	3,901	3,795	2,800	995	35.5
Alabama................	2,620	2,535	2,265	270	11.9
Mississippi..............	2,319	2,130	1,893	237	12.5
WEST SOUTH CENTRAL:					
Arkansas................	4,038	3,996	3,747	249	6.6
Louisiana...............	1,727	1,616	1,343	273	20.3
Oklahoma...............	5,567	5,567	3,693	1,874	50.7
Texas..................	12,527	12,095	8,504	3,591	42.2
MOUNTAIN:					
Montana................	1,206	1,206	1,484	−278	−18.7
Idaho..................	844	842	797	45	5.6
Wyoming................	508	484	296	188	63.5
Colorado................	2,075	2,066	1,061	1,005	94.7
New Mexico..............	473	459	387	72	18.6
Arizona.................	677	677	613	64	10.4
Utah...................	603	603	661	−58	−8.8
Nevada.................	1,026	1,026	648	378	58.3
PACIFIC:					
Washington..............	2,182	2,182	3,448	−1,266	−36.7
Oregon.................	2,522	2,491	2,100	391	18.6
California...............	9,227	9,227	5,573	3,654	65.6

a Exclusive of 1,799 divorces reported in 1922 for 95 counties not reporting in 1916.
† Per cent not shown, base being less than 100.
* All laws permitting divorce were repealed in 1878.
  [2] " Marriage and Divorce, 1922," Government Printing Office, p. 10.

It is apparent that no satisfactory comparison can be made between the numbers of divorces reported for the various periods studied by the United States Government unless the increase in the number of divorces be interpreted in the light of the changes in population. This comparison has been made by the investigation of the Federal Government and reveals that for more than half a century, expiring in 1922, the growth of divorce has been greater than the growth of population. This appears in the following table:

TABLE IV.[3]

Year	Number of divorces per 100,000		Population to one divorce	Married population to one divorce a
	Total population	Married population		
1922†.................	136	330	734	303
1916†.................	113	281	884	356
1906†.................	84	231	1,185	433
1900*.................	73	200	1,363	500
1890*.................	53	148	1,881	676
1880*.................	39	107	2,551	935
1870*.................	28	81	3,517	1,233

a For 1870 and 1880 the married population was estimated, while for 1890 the married population of Indian Territory and Indian reservations specially enumerated was estimated.
† The figures for 1922 are based upon estimated population, and those for 1916 and 1906 upon estimated population exclusive of population of counties for which divorce returns were lacking.
* The figures for the census years 1870, 1880, 1890, and 1900, respectively, are based upon the average annual number of divorces for the 5-year period of which the census year is the median.

That these detailed comparisons between the reports of 1916 and 1922 show the increase in divorces in relation to the changes of population appears in Table V.

Study of the comparison between the reports for 1916 and 1922 brings out the fact that the divorce rates for the States show greater variations than do those for the geographic divisions. The variation between the States is to be explained, as the report states, by such influences as differences in color or race composition of the population, differences in the proportion of foreign-born and in the countries from which they came, the relative strength of the prevailing Churches, especially that of the Roman Catholic Church, differences in the laws regulating divorces, and in the practices of

[3] *Ibid.*, p. 11.

TABLE V.[4]

Divorce rates, based on total population, on married population, on population to one divorce, and on married population to one divorce, for divisions and States: 1922 and 1916.

[The populations on which the rates are computed are estimated.]

Division and State	Number of divorces per 100,000—				Population to one divorce		Married population to one divorce	
	Total population		Married population					
	1922	1916a	1922	1916a	1922	1916a	1922	1916a
UNITED STATES....	136	113	330	281	734	884	303	356
GEOGRAPHIC DIVISIONS:								
New England........	94	81	231	201	1,060	1,236	433	499
Middle Atlantic......	57	45	137	109	1,756	2,243	729	915
East North Central...	170	142	392	335	588	703	255	298
West North Central..	168	135	403	334	597	743	248	300
South Atlantic......	77	59	198	156	1,303	1,704	504	640
East South Central...	143	119	362	310	700	843	276	323
West South Central...	225	183	566	477	445	545	177	210
Mountain...........	211	200	521	497	475	499	192	201
Pacific.............	235	220	530	517	425	455	189	194
NEW ENGLAND:								
Maine.............	148	93	344	217	678	1,081	291	462
New Hampshire.....	135	159	320	378	739	628	313	265
Vermont...........	105	120	245	276	955	835	409	362
Massachusetts.......	81	64	202	161	1,233	1,574	494	621
Rhode Island........	132	107	330	272	757	934	303	367
Connecticut.........	71	75	172	184	1,407	1,337	581	543
MIDDLE ATLANTIC:								
New York...........	39	33	92	81	2,589	3,012	1,087	1,236
New Jersey..........	63	40	148	96	1,592	2,509	674	1,044
Pennsylvania........	77	60	188	149	1,304	1,675	531	673
EAST NORTH CENTRAL:								
Ohio................	169	141	382	324	591	710	262	308
Indiana.............	238	199	525	450	420	502	190	222
Illinois.............	165	139	386	334	606	722	259	300
Michigan...........	195	159	443	366	514	631	226	273
Wisconsin...........	75	68	186	174	1,332	1,467	537	574
WEST NORTH CENTRAL:								
Minnesota..........	105	86	270	231	954	1,163	370	433
Iowa...............	158	141	368	341	634	707	272	294
Missouri............	243	173	559	413	411	577	179	242
North Dakota.......	51	77	141	218	1,979	1,301	708	459
South Dakota.......	86	95	221	250	1,161	1,056	453	400
Nebraska...........	172	133	416	330	580	752	241	303
Kansas.............	192	150	443	356	520	665	225	281

a Exclusive of population of counties for which divorce returns were lacking.

TABLE V.[4]—*Continued.*

Divorce rates, based on total population, on married population, on population to one divorce, and on married population to one divorce, for divisions and States: 1922 and 1916.

[The populations on which the rates are computed are estimated]

Division and State	Number of divorces per 100,000—				Population to one divorce		Married population to one divorce	
	Total population		Married population					
	1922	1916a	1922	1916a	1922	1916a	1922	1916a
SOUTH ATLANTIC:								
Delaware..........	98	97	224	230	1,019	1,026	446	435
Maryland..........	96	72	231	180	1,044	1,390	433	555
District of Columbia..	37	12	85	29	2,718	8,493	1,177	3,411
Virginia...........	102	90	266	243	983	1,113	376	411
West Virginia........	96	67	244	173	1,040	1,490	409	576
North Carolina......	50	30	136	85	2,012	3,284	733	1,173
South Carolina†......	....	....	....	....	....	....	....	....
Georgia............	62	55	160	148	1,620	1,804	626	678
Florida............	218	152	515	375	460	656	194	267
EAST SOUTH CENTRAL:								
Kentucky..........	165	130	407	331	606	767	246	302
Tennessee..........	164	127	408	326	609	787	245	306
Alabama..........	109	103	287	277	917	969	348	360
Mississippi.........	130	112	332	299	772	893	301	335
WEST SOUTH CENTRAL:								
Arkansas..........	225	224	560	578	445	446	179	173
Louisiana..........	94	82	244	223	1,063	1,218	410	449
Oklahoma..........	262	195	647	491	382	513	155	204
Texas.............	258	201	649	525	388	496	154	191
MOUNTAIN:								
Montana..........	203	305	497	775	492	328	201	129
Idaho.............	184	233	455	517	544	429	220	193
Wyoming..........	246	177	587	448	407	565	170	223
Colorado...........	213	122	502	292	470	819	199	342
New Mexico........	128	122	342	324	780	818	293	309
Arizona...........	184	213	465	549	543	469	215	182
Utah..............	129	157	336	420	778	638	297	238
Nevada............	1,325	820	3,289	2,008	75	122	30	50
PACIFIC:								
Washington........	155	270	350	643	647	371	286	155
Oregon............	311	286	689	671	322	350	145	149
California..........	250	183	563	428	401	547	178	234

a Exclusive of population of counties for which divorce returns were lacking.
† All laws permitting divorce were repealed in 1878.

[4] *Ibid.*, p. 12.

the courts having jurisdiction over the granting of divorce and in inter-State migration for the purpose of obtaining divorces by taking advantage of the laws of the more liberal States.

The Federal report summarizes this difference between the States as follows:

The divorce rates for States show much wider variations than do those for geographic divisions. The number of divorces per 100,000 total population varied, in 1922, from 37 in the District of Columbia and 39 in New York to 1325 in Nevada, while in 1916 the variation was from 12 in the district of Columbia and 30 in North Carolina to 820 in Nevada. Similarly, the number of divorces per 100,000 married population varied, in 1922, from 85 in the District of Columbia and 92 in New York to 3289 in Nevada, and in 1916 from 29 in the District of Columbia and 81 in New York to 2008 in Nevada. The population to one divorce ranged, in 1922, from 2718 in the District of Columbia and 2589 in New York to 75 in Nevada, while in 1916 the range was from 8493 in the District of Columbia and 3284 in North Carolina to 122 in Nevada. There was, likewise, a wide range in the married population to one divorce—from 1177 in the District of Columbia and 1087 in New York to 30 in Nevada in 1922, and from 3411 in the District of Columbia and 1236 in New York to 50 in Nevada in 1916. It will be noted that in the case of each rate, in 1922, the District of Columbia was lowest, New York next lowest, and Nevada highest. In 1916, in the case of each rate, the District of Columbia was lowest and Nevada highest, with New York next lowest as to number of divorces per 100,000 married population and as to married population to one divorce, and with North Carolina next lowest as to number of divorces per 100,000 population and as to population to one divorce.[5]

Since the Southern Atlantic States are the most conservative in their divorce policy, the report of conditions in Florida and Mississippi, made by Dr. R. M. Harper, statistician and geographer of the State of Florida, is most interesting. The results of Doctor Harper's study appear in the April, 1926, issue of *Eugenical News.* The divorce situation in Florida is portrayed by Doctor Harper in the following table:

TABLE VI.[6]

1923–24	Per cent of population		Rate of marriages to divorces
	Marrying	Divorcing	
United States......................	2.2	0.30	7.1
Florida...........................	3.0	0.42	7.1
Ten city counties	3.0	0.57	5.2
Rest of State	3.0	0.27	11.1

[5] *Ibid.,* p. 13.
[6] *Loc. cit.,* p. 55.

Concerning Mississippi, the investigator states:

Only one-fourth of the couples divorcing in Mississippi had children, averaging not quite two per couple, or less than half a child for each divorce as compared with 2.2 adults and 2.2 children in the average Mississippi family in 1920.[7]

Comparison of Husband and Wife with Reference to the Granting of Divorce.

—There has been little change in the proportion of divorces granted to husbands and wives from 1887 to 1922, as appears in the table that follows:

TABLE VII.[8]

Year	Total number	Divorces			
		Granted to husband		Granted to wife	
		Number	Per cent	Number	Per cent
1922.................	a147,775	47,359	32.0	100,416	68.0
1916.................	†108,702	33,809	31.1	74,893	68.9
1906.................	72,062	23,455	32.5	48,607	67.5
1896.................	42,937	14,448	33.6	28,489	66.4
1887 to 1906.........	945,625	316,149	33.4	629,476	66.6
1897 to 1906.........	593,362	195,547	33.0	397,815	67.0
1887 to 1896.........	352,263	120,602	34.2	231,661	65.8

a Exclusive of 1,040 cases of divorce for which no detailed statistics were reported.
† Exclusive of 3,334 cases of divorce for which no detailed statistics were reported.

During the thirty-six years covered by this study, less than one-third of the divorces granted were obtained by husbands and more than two-thirds by wives. The difference is largely due to the fact that the wife has given her by law a larger number of legal grounds for divorce. For example, in 1922 non-support or neglect to provide was not a legal ground for divorce on the part of the husband except in Utah, although a frequent cause for divorce on the part of the wife. Even grounds for divorce that apply equally to husband and wife, from their character, as appears in the case of cruelty, are more common offenses among men than women. It must be remembered also that the social consequences of certain charges made the basis for divorce carried more weight for the woman than for the man, as is true of adultery. In some circles, therefore, the

[7] *Ibid.*
[8] "Marriage and Divorce, 1922," Government Printing Office, p. 14.
10

social code demands that the man assume the burden of guilt, at
least as far as legal procedure is concerned, and the husband in
response to this convention at times protects the character of his
wife by taking the blame when he is entirely innocent. This masculine code has a definite influence on the granting of more divorces to
women than men.

The Grounds for Divorce.—Anyone familiar with the divorce
trial realizes that the legal ground given for divorce is often not
the true cause. The reason advanced for the giving of the divorce
necessarily is influenced by the law of the State; the real root of the
family discord may be one not recognized as a sufficient ground for
divorce by the courts, so it becomes necessary to make the plea on the
basis of some ground that falls within the statute. It is also true
that there is sometimes a disposition on the part of both husband
and wife to protect their future by having the complaining party
charge a less severe cause for the divorce than what both know to
be the real reason.

The following table gives the legal grounds for divorce as
reported in 1922:

TABLE VIII.[9]

| Cause | Divorces, distributed by cause: 1922 | | | | | |
| | Total | | Granted to husband | | Granted to wife | |
	Number	Per cent distribution	Number	Per cent distribution	Number	Per cent distribution
All causes..........	a147,775	100.0	47,359	100.0	100,416	100.0
Adultery...............	16,053	10.9	8,333	17.6	7,720	7.7
Cruelty................	51,030	34.5	11,818	25.0	39,212	39.0
Desertion.............	48,507	32.8	20,979	44.3	27,528	27.4
Drunkenness..........	1,536	1.0	120	0.3	1,416	1.4
Neglect to provide.......	6,212	4.2	......	....	6,212	6.2
Combinations of preced-ing causes†...........	12,849	8.7	2,182	4.6	10,667	10.6
All other causes*........	11,588	7.8	3,927	8.3	7,661	7.6

a Exclusive of 1,040 cases of divorce for which no detailed statistics were reported.
† See explanatory text, p. 15.
* Includes cause unknown.
    [9] *Ibid.*, p. 16.

In a comparison of different States as to the frequency of any definite cause for divorce appearing in statistics, great caution must be observed; even when the same term is used by different States as a ground for divorce, the statutory definition or the legal interpretation with reference to a given cause may so vary as to make any statistical statement with reference to the frequency of the cause studied misleading. There are also cases where the legal ground for divorce as it appears on the court records is itself a result of a family situation too subtle to come under the range of any legal term, but which is nevertheless the actual cause of the divorce.

We can catalogue the reasons for divorce under the legal grounds, the moral causes or the social situation. It is, however, only when we study the divorce problem as an interaction of two personalities, expressing itself in a definite social situation within the family, that we can gain any considerable scientific insight into the influences that lead toward divorce. Divorce is a conscious recognition of marriage failure and, like any other maladjustment, has as its fundamental cause character defects or bad social environment or both.

A comparison of the record of 1922 with that of other periods appears in Table IX.

Social Restlessness and Divorce.—If the analysis of a definite divorce leads to an explanation of its cause by revealing the interplay of personality and environment, investigation of the increase in divorce characteristic of the modern trend emphasizes the significance of modern society itself as the operating cause: what is to be its ultimate influence is beyond prophecy, but at present modern civilization is stimulating the increase of divorce. A large number of modern men and women express in all sorts of ways a tendency toward social instability as a result of rapid changes in modes of living. The pulsations of life move swiftly, thoughts are discarded, conventions superseded, thrilling experiences not previously dreamed of are provided, former habits loosened, and the formation of new habits accelerated by the momentum of present-day civilization. Marriage is one of the most delicate and sensitive of human relationships, and it would be strange indeed if it did not reflect

TABLE IX.[10]

Comparison is made in this table of the percentages just presented for 1922 with those shown by former reports for the years 1916, 1906, and 1896, for the 20-year period 1887–1906, and for the 10-year periods 1897–1906 and 1887–1896.

Cause	Per cent distribution of divorces by cause						
	1922	1916	1906	1896	1887 to 1906	1897 to 1906	1887 to 1896
	Total						
All causes.......	100.0	100.0	100.0	100.0	100.0	100.0	100.0
Adultery............	10.9	11.5	15.3	16.6	16.3	15.5	17.5
Cruelty.............	34.5	28.3	24.3	21.3	21.8	23.0	19.8
Desertion...........	32.8	36.8	38.0	38.9	38.9	38.7	39.1
Drunkenness........	1.0	3.4	3.9	3.7	3.9	3.9	3.9
Neglect to provide....	4.2	4.7	3.9	3.6	3.7	3.9	3.3
Combinations of preceding causes *a*	8.7	8.6	8.9	9.5	9.4	9.0	10.0
All other causes†	7.8	6.8	5.8	6.4	6.1	6.0	6.4
	Granted to husband						
All causes.......	100.0	100.0	100.0	100.0	100.0	100.0	100.0
Adultery............	17.6	20.3	27.2	29.0	28.7	27.5	30.8
Cruelty.............	25.0	17.4	13.3	9.9	10.5	11.8	8.4
Desertion...........	44.3	50.0	49.1	49.2	49.4	49.8	48.9
Drunkenness........	0.3	0.8	1.0	1.1	1.1	1.1	1.1
Neglect to provide....	.....	.....	.....	*	*	*	*
Combinations of preceding causes *a*	4.6	4.3	4.2	4.8	4.5	4.3	4.8
All other causes†	8.3	7.2	5.2	6.1	5.7	5.5	6.0
	Granted to wife						
All causes.......	100.0	100.0	100.0	100.0	100.0	100.0	100.0
Adultery............	7.7	7.5	9.6	10.3	10.0	9.6	10.6
Cruelty.............	39.0	33.2	29.6	27.0	27.5	28.5	25.8
Desertion...........	27.4	30.8	32.7	33.7	33.6	33.3	34.0
Drunkenness........	1.4	4.5	5.3	5.1	5.3	5.2	5.3
Neglect to provide....	6.2	6.9	5.7	5.5	5.5	5.8	4.9
Combinations of preceding causes *a*	10.6	10.5	11.1	11.8	11.8	11.3	12.7
All other causes †	7.6	6.5	6.1	6.6	6.4	6.2	6.6

a See explanatory text, p. 15.
† Includes cause unknown.
* Less than one-tenth of 1 per cent.

[10] *Ibid.*

the general unrest of our times.) The life comradeship of a man and woman, to be successful, requires the development both of qualities of personality and of spiritual ties less easily established now than in the slower-moving civilization.

A careful investigation recently made regarding divorces granted in Suffolk County (about 90 per cent. of which is the city of Boston) from January, 1900, through December, 1921, shows the effect of the World War upon the increase of divorces within that county. A remarkable increase of divorces appears for the years 1919, 1920 and 1921. A corresponding investigation of marriages discloses that there is no proportionate increase in marriages for these three years nor for the few years immediately preceding; there is a slight increase, temporarily, in marriages for the year 1917, but not of a character to explain the increase of divorces from 1920–1921. The author also rules out an explanation of the rise in divorces based upon industrial conditions. He concludes that what seems to be the only reasonable deduction as the essential cause of this phenomenal increase in divorces was the disrupting influence of the World War; this great conflict was both an expression of the general restlessness which is the bitter fruit of contemporary civilization, and, itself, a source of social discontent. All parts of life felt its upheaval. Nowhere was its effect more clearly registered in disturbing and uprooting influences than in the family.[11]

Divorce and Parenthood.—Compared with the period 1887–1906, the proportion of cases of divorce in families with children had decreased in 1922 from about two-fifths to slightly over one-third. In the three Government investigations, 1887–1906, 1916 and 1922, children were reported more frequently in divorces granted women than in the case of divorces granted men. (The explanation suggested for this is that where there are children the court is more likely in case of divorce to give them into the care of the mother, and because of this the father is less likely to seek divorce than the mother, since he would run risk of losing his children.) The statistical statement follows:

[11] Hexter, M. B., "Social Consequences of Business Cycles," Ch. VI.

TABLE X.[12]

Year and class with respect to children	Divorces				
	Total number	Granted to husband		Granted to wife	
		Number	Per cent	Number	Per cent
1922 All cases...............	a147,775	47,359	32.0	100,416	68.0
Reporting children............	50,315	12,796	25.4	37,519	74.6
Reporting no children..........	82,819	29,562	35.7	53,257	64.3
Not reporting as to children.....	14,641	5,001	34.2	9,640	65.8
1916 All cases...............	†108,702	33,809	31.1	74,893	68.9
Reporting children............	41,009	9,403	22.9	31,606	77.1
Reporting no children..........	56,651	19,837	35.0	36,814	65.0
Not reporting as to children.....	11,042	4,569	41.4	6,473	58.6
1887 to 1906 All cases...............	945,625	316,149	33.4	629,476	66.6
Reporting children............	376,694	82,207	22.1	294,487	77.9
Reporting no children	380,608	148,504	39.0	232,104	61.0
Not reporting as to children	188,323	85,438	45.4	102,885	54.6

a Exclusive of 1,040 cases of divorce for which no detailed statistics were reported.
† Exclusive of 3,334 cases of divorce for which no detailed statistics were reported.

Divorce a Product of Family Incompatibility.—Divorce is the climax of family difficulties. It follows that an adequate treatment of the problem of divorce involves a study of family life in all its social aspects. In a previous chapter appears a discussion of some of the outstanding family situations that lead to incompatibility; elsewhere, the author discusses from a different point of view the social causes of divorce.[13] It is important to interpret the divorce situation with an understanding of the entire social situation of the modern family in order to escape the fallacy of attempting to deal with divorce as something that exists by itself, an exhibition merely of personal faults unrelated to social conditions that influence character. The family does not live its life in a social vacuum, and

[12] "Marriage and Divorce, 1922," Government Printing Office, p. 32.
[13] "Education and Social Problems," pp. 162–175.

when a marriage undertaken with the promise of happiness ends in the tragedy of divorce, a just summons for investigation as to cause includes society as well as the individuals concerned.

Divorce Legislation.—Although the evils resulting from the diversity of the legislation of the various states in regard to divorce may have been exaggerated, there is general agreement as to the desirability of greater uniformity. At first advocates of divorce reform pleaded for a Federal law, a program which required for its success the passage of a Constitutional amendment. Because of the practical difficulties involved in getting this amendment, later effort has been directed towards procuring greater uniformity in the laws of the separate states. Progress is undoubtedly being made, and the general trend seems to be toward greater uniformity among the states respecting the essential features of divorce legislation.

There does not appear to be the amount of moving from one state to another having more lax divorce regulations that one would expect of persons seeking matrimonial release, but there is undoubtedly interstate migration for such a purpose. Apparently there are practical considerations which hamper the movement of those who find the getting of a divorce in their own state difficult. The differences in the legal grounds for divorce in the various states do not, according to Wilcox, influence materially the number of divorces granted, but affect chiefly the choice of the ground upon which the divorce is sought.[14]

The contrast between the divorce rates of the different sections of the nation is not a mere expression of variation in legislation. Even if we had a Federal law or if the statutes of all the states were essentially the same, we should still have variation because of unlike conditions in the different parts of the country.

Legislation that encourages divorce is of course a social menace, but drastic legislation has its dangers also. Some advocates of divorce reform undoubtedly seek stringent legislation, but their solution of the divorce problem, if it were attainable, would prove mischievous and intolerable. The friend of the family will remember that it is not the legal opportunity for the getting of divorce, or the desire for such separation, but the family situation that seeks court relief which constitutes the heart of the divorce problem.

[14] " Divorce Problems," pp. 37–38.

Howard has well said, " For the wise reformer who would elevate and protect the family, the centre of the problem is marriage and not divorce." [15]

Without question legislation influences divorce. We need the best laws that can be written to conserve family welfare, but any attempt to solve the divorce problem by the mere passing of new laws will be futile. The American divorce record is, from a social point of view, startling and, when one translates it into the disappointment and suffering of individual men and women, pathetic; but its real significance is the revelation it gives of social forces at work that are making marriage success difficult, or—and this side of the problem must not be overlooked—the growing intolerance of low marriage standards or vicious conditions within the home circle. An increase in happy, wholesome marriages is the only permanent solution of our divorce problem, for the divorce is only a product of the family's reflection of widespread social conditions that make matrimonial comradeship between modern men and women more difficult than once it was. Divorce, like crime, is forceful evidence that our civilization is developing to a point of strain where there is special need of strengthening the weakness disclosed by using our social resources to encourage sane ways of living.

Divorce and Marriage Legislation.—There may not have been in recent years too much discussion concerning laws proposed to decrease divorce, but there certainly has been too little attention given to the question of marriage legislation. Although it is not possible to trace with any degree of exactness the influence of our marriage laws upon our divorce rate, there can be no doubt that one of the effective ways of legislating against divorce is by the enactment of more uniform and better marriage laws than we now have. The states of the Union show great diversity in their marriage laws. It is of course to be expected that because of the varying social conditions of the different states and sections the same regulations of marriage should not prevail everywhere, but there is far greater variation than can be socially justified.[16] As is the practice with so

---

[15] Howard, *op. cit.*, vol. iii, p. 223.
[16] Hall and Brooke, " American Marriage Laws and Their Social Aspects."

much of the legislation passed in this country, such laws as we have are frequently administered by officials in a lax way. Marriage laws are even disregarded to the point of permitting illegal marriages. One investigation disclosed that more than half of 240 marriage licenses issued had been granted illegally.[17]

A great deal of the variation between the states with reference to marriage legislation does not reflect the social conditions, but merely expresses lack of understanding or indifference in regard to the social consequences of discordant marriage legislation. Conditions which permit couples married legally in good faith in one state to become, by merely crossing the state line, guilty of crime and their children bastards, owe their existence to the fact that they echo prejudice or traditions of a haphazard and accidental origin.

In many of our states there is need of legislation to lift the minimum age of marriage, and the trend fortunately is in that direction. This tendency, which shows itself from time to time as state laws are changed, is encouraged without question by the political influence of modern women. Although the student of the family will welcome an increase of scientific information regarding the problems connected with the minimum marriage age, such knowledge as we now have justifies the position that the marriage of the socially immature child, even when physically developed, is undesirable and should be prevented as far as it can be eliminated by law. The statutes of the various states regarding the minimum marriageable age of girls, including laws passed at regular sessions of the legislatures meeting in 1919, are summarized by Hooker.[18] There is need also of laws requiring a medical certification for marriage. Wisconsin was one of the first states to pass such a law and its practical value seems clearly demonstrated by a recent study of its results. The law has acted as an educational instrument leading to public discussion and a much wider appreciation of the risks of venereal disease, the need of early discovery of infection and thorough treatment by a reputable physician.[19] The law has led men who are planning to marry to make sure of their fitness before applying for a marriage license. In some cases

---

[17] Richmond and Hall, " Child Marriages," p. 72.
[18] " The Laws of Sex," pp. 155–169.
[19] Hall, F. S., " Medical Certification for Marriage."

examination has led to the discovery of disease which has postponed marriage.

The Wisconsin law, however, has not been a complete success. Some of the examinations have been merely routine and the statements issued by the physicians have been, so far as protection from venereal disease is concerned, valueless. The fee permitted doctors for the examination has been inadequate and it does not appear that the medical profession has heartily coöperated in the carrying out of the law.

Although too much may easily be expected of laws requiring medical certification for marriage, it represents a step in the right direction and has an educational influence in elevating the idea of marriage along other lines than those that have merely to do with physical welfare.

Common Law Marriages.—There is need of legislation abolishing common law marriages. Common law marriage means to most people the living together of a man and woman in adultery, but where such marriages are recognized as valid by the state, the individuals concerned are as much married as those who, having obtained their license to marry according to law, have celebrated their union by a church wedding. To create a binding common law marriage most courts require " present consent followed by cohabitation " or an assumption of the marital relationship. This means entering marriage by the pathway of fornication. Common law marriage is defended as necessary to protect from illegitimacy the children born of such a union; some also insist that the abolishment of such marriages would strike away one of the rights of the individual.

The common law union debases conventional marriage and encourages deceit and vice. The state certainly has the moral obligation of protecting the institution of matrimony from exploitation by the indifferent and by those who wish to enter marriage under cover because for some reason they wish to escape the responsibilities of a publicly acclaimed union, although as a matter of fact the couples living together in common law marriage do not usually regard themselves as married and generally do not intend to live together permanently.

The matrimonial anarchy produced by recognition of the com-

TABLE XI.[20]

State	Per verba de praesenti		Per verba de futuro cum copula	Presumption of, from cohabitation after removal of impediment
	Without Cohabitation	Followed by cohabitation		
Alabama	Invalid (c)	Valid (c)	Invalid (c)	Yes (c)
Alaska	Invalid (s)	Invalid (s)	Invalid (s)	Yes (s)
Arizona	Invalid (s)	Invalid (s)	Invalid (s)	No (s)
Arkansas	Invalid (c)	Invalid (c)	Invalid (c)	No (c)
California	Invalid (s)	Invalid (s)	Invalid (s)	No (s)
Colorado	Invalid (c)	Valid (c)	Invalid (c)	Yes
Connecticut	Invalid (c)	Invalid (c)	Invalid (c)	No (c)
Delaware	Invalid (c)	Invalid (c)	Invalid (c)	No (c)
District of Columbia	Doubtful (n)	Doubtful (n)	Invalid (n)	Doubtful (n)
Florida	Doubtful (n)	Valid (c)	Invalid (n)	Yes (n)
Georgia	Doubtful (c)	Valid (c)	Doubtful (c)	Yes (c)
Hawaii	Invalid (n)	Valid (c)	Invalid (n)	Yes (n)
Idaho	Invalid (s)	Valid (s)	Invalid (s)	Yes (c)
Illinois	Invalid (s)	Invalid (s)	Invalid (s)	No (s)
Indiana	Doubtful (n)	Valid (c)	Invalid (n)	Yes (c)
Iowa	Invalid (n)	Valid (c)	Invalid (n)	Yes (s)
Kansas	Doubtful (n)	Valid (c)	Invalid (n)	Yes (c)
Kentucky	Invalid (s)	Invalid (s)	Invalid (s)	No (s)
Louisiana	Invalid (s)	Invalid (s)	Invalid (s)	No (s)
Maine	Invalid (n)	Invalid (n)	Invalid (n)	No (n)
Maryland	Invalid (c)	Invalid (c)	Invalid (c)	No (c)
Massachusetts	Invalid (c)	Invalid (c)	Invalid (c)	No (c)
Michigan	Invalid (c)	Valid (c)	Invalid (c)	Yes (c)
Minnesota	Valid (c)	Valid (c)	Doubtful (n)	Yes (c)
Mississippi	Valid (s)	Valid (s)	Doubtful (n)	Yes (n)
Missouri	Invalid (s)	Invalid (s)	Invalid (s)	No (s)
Montana	Invalid (s)	Valid (s)	Invalid (s)	Yes (n)
Nebraska	Invalid (s)	Invalid (s)	Invalid (s)	No (s)
Nevada	Doubtful (n)	Valid (c)	Invalid (n)	Yes (c)
New Hampshire	Invalid (c)	Invalid (c)	Invalid (c)	No (c)
New Jersey	Doubtful (n)	Valid (c)	Invalid (n)	Yes (c)
New Mexico	Doubtful (n)	Valid (n)	Invalid (n)	Yes (n)
New York	Valid (c)	Valid (c)	Invalid (c)	Yes (c)
North Carolina	Invalid (s)	Invalid (s)	Invalid (s)	No (s)
North Dakota	Invalid (s)	Invalid (s)	Invalid (s)	No (s)
Ohio	Doubtful (n)	Valid (c)	Invalid (n)	Yes (c)
Oklahoma	Doubtful (n)	Valid (c)	Invalid (n)	Doubtful (c)
Oregon	Doubtful (c)	Valid (n)	Invalid (n)	Doubtful (n)
Pennsylvania	Doubtful (c)	Valid (c)	Invalid (c)	Yes (c)
Philippine Islands	Invalid (s)	Invalid (s)	Invalid (s)	No (s)
Porto Rico	Invalid (s)	Invalid (s)	Invalid (s)	No (s)
Rhode Island	Doubtful (n)	Valid (n)	Doubtful (c)	Doubtful (n)
South Carolina	Doubtful (c)	Valid (c)	Doubtful (c)	Yes (c)
South Dakota	Invalid (s)	Valid (s)	Invalid (s)	Doubtful (n)
Tennessee	Invalid (c)	Invalid (c)	Invalid (c)	No (c)
Texas	Invalid (c)	Valid (c)	Invalid (c)	Yes (c)
Utah	Invalid (s)	Invalid (s)	Invalid (s)	No (c)
Vermont	Invalid (c)	Invalid (c)	Invalid (c)	No (c)
Virginia	Invalid (s)	Invalid (s)	Invalid (s)	No (s)
Washington	Invalid (s)	Invalid (s)	Invalid (s)	No (s)
West Virginia	Invalid (s)	Invalid (s)	Invalid (s)	No (s)
Wisconsin	Invalid (s)	Invalid (s)	Invalid (s)	No (s)
Wyoming	Doubtful (n)	Valid (n)	Invalid (n)	Yes (n)

(c) By court decision. (s) By Statute. (n) No decision on the question.

[20] Koegel, "Common Law Marriage," *The Family*, November, 1923, p. 175.

mon law marriage as valid appears plainly in Table XI, which shows the legal situation as it is at present in the United States. In interpreting this table it is necessary to remember that there are two ways of entering a common law marriage, one by present consent to become husband and wife, *per verba de praesenti,* and the other by an agreement to become husband and wife at some future time followed by carnal intercourse, *per verba de futuro.*

Alimony and Divorce.—Modern economic conditions as they affect women show their influence in the attitude of some of our judges in regard to the granting of alimony. In a recent decision Judge Strong of the Appellate Division of the New York Supreme Court is quoted by the press as having said, " Everything considered, I believe alimony should be discontinued because it keeps certain women lazy, gratifies their revenge, makes men miserable and serves no good ends." A woman's right to financial support from her husband when she has successfully divorced him has been taken for granted so long that we have assumed its justice as a matter of course.

Alimony in the first place was an attempt to give protection to the woman who left her husband and under the handicap of her sex tried to make her own way in the world. In those days when matrimony was the only vocation for women, it seemed fair that the woman driven from her husband's protection by his misdeeds should receive from him maintenance in proportion to his income as a substitute for the support which he promised her at marriage and which she was now losing through no fault of her own.

In the early history of the American colonies it was so difficult for either man or wife to be self-supporting without the help of the other that couples who separated were sometimes publicly commanded to take up again their life together, lest either of them become a burden on the community. Often the man was ordered to live with his wife or else give her a definite sum of money, or a certain number of pounds of tobacco or bushels of corn and wheat per year for her maintenance.

Since those days women have gone into competition with men in every kind of industry, and matrimony is no longer ordinarily entered upon as a means of support. We have countless women in this country who can earn more than their husbands. It is even true at times that a wife can find employment when her husband cannot.

So long as women were social dependents with no means of support except wifehood, alimony was not only just but a public necessity. No woman, however cruelly treated, would attempt to get a divorce if this left her financially stranded, a candidate for the almshouse. Without the possibility of alimony the right of divorce was a mere farce.

The possibility of obtaining alimony if her marriage venture fails is without doubt in the mind of many a woman who is enticed into matrimony by economic ambition. To such a woman divorce may come to mean freedom from the limitations of marriage without the sacrifice of the financial advantages she sought in marrying. The court decree may furnish her with an allowance that permits an indulgence in personal luxuries beyond what she enjoyed as wife. The opportunity to get alimony easily becomes under such circumstances a stimulus to divorce.

Even when the divorce is sought without mercenary motive, the very fact that the court orders the husband to give a stated sum to his wife when they have separated for some trivial reason makes later reconciliation difficult. Encouraged perhaps by a type of lawyer who fattens on the profits of divorce cases, the wife who left in a fit of anger may refuse to meet her husband half way in an effort to forget the past and get a second start on the road toward marriage happiness. If the prospects of alimony were ruled out, the professional divorce lawyer would often be less keen in urging a divorce, knowing that even were the decree granted, it would not be followed by a series of payments to the wife, a substantial part of which he could expect to fall eventually into his own hands in the form of fees charged for his services.

Family Desertion.—Divorce and desertion are family problems that have much in common. On account of this likeness desertion is commonly called "the poor man's divorce." Although this statement correctly brings out the fact that desertion among the poorer classes is often a substitute for divorce, it is misleading in so far as it conveys the impression that these two forms of family disintegration are the same, except that one is confined exclusively to people of a lower economic status. Desertion is one type of family disintegration, divorce is another; the wealthy, the professional classes and those socially well established turn for various reasons, when family life becomes unsatisfactory, to the divorce court for relief, while the more mobile unskilled worker, or the individual whose occupation provides great economic freedom, cuts himself away from family difficulties by merely leaving the home and disappearing. There are many reasons why the well-to-do should prefer the use of the legal method of getting free from marital difficulties. In addition to the other social advantages of divorce, it is the customary way of getting freedom in their class and, therefore, in accord with the proprieties. In the professional class divorce frequently carries with it social risks from which the individuals shrink, but to attempt to escape these by family desertion would be ruinous; in some cases it would mean throwing away a professional reputation and giving up all hope of a second start in one's vocation. Here also the class code does not include family desertion as a proper means of getting rid of marital difficulties.

There are many motives that tempt the poor in family unhappiness to desert rather than to have the court cut the matrimonial ties. It is, of course, in this country the man who generally deserts. Apparently under other social conditions the woman rather than the man may be tempted to leave the family, for I am told by Miss Asa Matsuoka, a Japanese graduate student, that it is the woman rather than the man who more often deserts in Japan.

A study of the conscious motives that lead men in the poorer classes to leave their families discloses the fact that desertion is not just an easier and cheaper way of ending matrimony than is offered by divorce. Often the husband seeks not so much to get rid of the family as to become free from an economic burden, from conditions of work that seem intolerable or from unemployment that appears hopeless; then the family is not so much repudiated as left behind. The man is consciously seeking not so much a permanent separation from his family as a brief spell of relief from the heavy load he has been carrying or an opportunity to start afresh. To be sure, rationalization is as often found in the motives that lead to desertion as in other lines of conduct where the reasons built into consciousness conceal the deeper desires that bring about the behavior. It is easy for the desertion that starts as a temporary expediency to become a permanent separation, and in many of these cases the men drift into a complete and final severance of family ties rather than deliberately breaking from the family with a definite decision to seek a divorce.

It is easy for the unskilled or factory worker to pack up and leave a family situation which has become troublesome. Indeed, this procedure is often the line of least resistance, for it seems, and often actually is, easier to go than to stay. Wanderlust and the desire for travel are at times contributory motives, and they may even constitute occasionally the chief cause of desertion. It is this type of desertion that has led the social worker to call desertion "the poor man's vacation from his family," rather than a divorce.

Where the desertion results from a family incompatibility which in some other class would be likely to end in a divorce, it is easy to understand why so many men prefer leaving their family to the legal method of separation through the divorce court. They are familiar with desertion, for it is frequent enough in their class to be a matter of common knowledge, and they have little understanding of court procedure, particularly when they are immigrants who are perhaps suspicious of any process that has to do with our legal machinery; moreover, if they have religious scruples against divorce they find desertion less antagonizing to their conscience.

Desertion brings out clearly the greater instability of family life in the city as compared with our villages and country places. In addition to the greater difficulty of holding together the family in the city, urban life encourages desertion by its greater mobility, the ease with which one can disappear; the city-dweller has fewer of the face-to-face associations that tend to check the feelings of anonymity and irresponsibility which encourage family desertion.

The earlier treatment of the deserting husband by our social agencies stressed the law. Largely as a result of their effort, legislation with reference to non-support and desertion has been passed by many of our states. Now that our courts are better prepared to deal adequately with the deserter, the tendency has been to make use of the law only as a last resort. Increasingly it is becoming clear that little headway can be made against the tendency among the poor in our cities to desert their families unless each case is treated as a home problem, complex in character and requiring diagnosis and sympathetic treatment. If rehabilitation of family life is desirable, haling the deserter into court and bringing in the wife as complainant is all too apt to become a hopeless obstacle in the way of any later attempt to reëstablish the family life.

Desertion, like divorce, is an expression of the instability of modern family life and it can be more successfully attacked by efforts to reënforce the family and to procure social conditions that will minister to its health than by regarding desertion as a crime that deserves just punishment. The statistics of family desertion seem to demonstrate that the family agencies at present are making little headway against it, and there is no hope of substantial progress in dealing with this particular product of family instability until greater and more practical effort is made to conserve home life.

CHAPTER X

THE BROKEN FAMILY AND ITS SOCIAL RESULTS

Social Consequences of Divorce.—There are relationships that we break, even when they have led to considerable intimacy, with little consequence; sometimes we feel relief that the association has finally come to an end, sometimes we have a mild regret that it ever started. The family, from its makeup, is an intimacy that cannot issue in a breakdown without untoward results. The effect of a given divorce on the lives of the different persons concerned varies in accord with the circumstances, such as the amount of attention the divorce has received and the attitude of neighbors and relatives toward it, the religious background of those formerly united by family ties, the living conditons that are endured or enjoyed after the decree of separation.

It is thought by many that a divorce has little significance for the husband and wife in cases where there are no children or when the children have grown up. This assumption, however, cannot be maintained by anyone familiar with the results of some of our divorces, even when the marriage has been childless. Some of these reactions are indeed morbid, but if the divorce trial has received sensational publicity or if one of the parties concerned is particularly sensitive, or if the road that led to marriage was especially bright with promise, thus making the anti-climax of divorce all the more disappointing, the dissolution of marriage injects bitterness into the personality and at times creates anti-social attitudes. It is doubtful whether any couples who have started marriage with genuine affection are left after their divorce free from scar. Those who seek marriage from purely sexual motives, using sexual in its narrowest meaning, void of the psychic element which idealizes and spiritualizes the more mature attraction, escape most lightly the consequences of divorce.

There are those also—and they must not be forgotten, though they are in a minority—who look back upon the divorce procedure, for which they were themselves responsible, with deep regret; since divorce as well as marriage can be entered upon without due con-

11   161

sideration, under the sway of a fleeting emotion. The conscientious lawyer, who is called upon to give counsel to a husband or wife that is seeking a divorce while under the spell of a temporary fit of anger or resentment or in the midst of an unfinished quarrel, knows how easily reconciliation can be brought about in a number of cases if the effort is tactfully made. It sometimes happens, even while the trial for divorce is proceeding, that the contestants settle their differences, and not always with the assistance of their attorneys. The divorce sought without serious deliberation, in a momentary mood or for superficial reasons, may entirely change the personality and discolor the outlook upon life.

Although divorce may mar adults, it is the children of divorcées that suffer most. The truth of this is generally recognized, for everybody regards a divorce procedure where children are involved as much more serious than one in which husband and wife are the only interested parties. It is, of course, true that some divorces are obtained primarily because the wife realizes that the welfare of the children demands separation from the intolerable conditions of the home as it exists, but in contrast with this are the greater number of parents who for the sake of their children are willing to continue a marriage situation which, were the problem of concern only to themselves, they would at once take to the courts. Recently, for example, a woman obtained a divorce for which she had waited thirty years, believing it better for the children to have a father than for her to get the relief which she was justified in seeking; therefore she carried her family burden until her youngest child was well established, when she at once went to the court.

It is impossible to unravel the social factors that influence developing character with a precision that shows how far a home broken by divorce is responsible for delinquency and other forms of youthful failure. We also do not know to what extent the child who has suffered by his parents' divorce receives hurt that carries over into his adult experience and becomes a cause of unhappiness or failure in later life. Although the conditions that influence the life of a child who has grown up in a home broken by divorce are too complicated to be expressed satisfactorily in statistics, there can be no doubt that the divorce of their parents is for many children a real social handicap.

Social workers who deal with juvenile delinquency find divorce or separation constantly recurring, either as the chief cause or as a contributing cause of the child's difficulty. In view of this fact the state fails in its obligations to child life if it does not attempt, through legislation, to conserve marriage and faithfully safeguard the interests of children in all divorce litigation by the wisest laws it can frame.

The consequences of family desertion are similar to those of divorce, but in the case of the former it is more difficult to trace the causal influence. This comes about because the majority of families deserted have so many unfavorable conditions that work against the welfare of the family group. The poverty that may have preceded the desertion or resulted from it, inefficient housekeeping, bad housing, a vicious neighborhood, intermittent schooling, or the unfavorable reputation of the family may make it impossible to estimate how much social harm comes to the children from the desertion directly and how much their career is warped by other bad influences.

Families Broken by Death.—No greater tragedy can come to a family than the death of the father or mother, for added to the grief at the parting of the life of the parent beloved, there is in the case of children a broken family of the most serious kind.

Although the surviving parent may double his efforts in his endeavor to make good the loss suffered by the children, in spite of all he or she does, the family circle is at once stripped of its normal atmosphere and the home functions as a broken instrument. There is general agreement that the family that has lost its mother encounters greater trials than if it is the father who has died, for hers is the larger contribution. The father who is left to care for little children because of the death of the mother faces a very difficult problem and one increasingly hard to solve. A generation ago, an unmarried relative offered the commonest and best solution and in cases where there were none to be called upon a housekeeper could usually be had. The new economic opportunities for women have greatly changed this situation; relatives are far less likely to feel it their duty to assume a task that all recognize to be a severe test of character, and efficient housekeepers, at least for men with moderate incomes, are even more scarce than sacrificing relatives.

As a rule, widowers find the only solution of their problem to be a re-marriage, but although this gives them an immediate way out of their predicament it is likely to create perplexities that do not exist in the normal unbroken family.

Naturally the man hesitates to remarry and experiments, if he possibly can, with other solutions. His delay in the effort to rebuild a home life heightens the risk involved in bringing a new wife into the household; the children may have been hurt during the period of transition, indeed, the recognition of this fact may be the compelling reason why the father has finally remarried. At any rate, the children have grown older and are more likely, unless they are still very young, to sense the difference between the new régime and the old, which memory idealizes. The burden the new mother assumes is apt to be one which the most courageous woman would instinctively shrink from accepting. As a consequence the broken family is repaired, but not cemented into an affectionate unity. If the new wife brings her own children into the family circle, complications are multiplied. In spite of all the hazards incident to such a rebuilding of the home life, many foster-mothers succeed wonderfully and the children suffer nothing that human skill and good purposes in such circumstances can prevent.

The difficulties of widowers deserve more attention than they now receive from social organizations that attempt to serve the family. Such organizations at present find it easier to help women who have lost their husbands than men who have lost their wives. This is partly due to the fact that these societies have had more experience with the widowed mother's problem, but in some measure it is the result of not sensing the fulness of the man's problem.

It is not at all surprising that we find children who have lost their mothers or fathers by death, and who have not been given satisfactory home life by the successful re-marriage of their remaining parent, so often drifting toward some sort of delinquency; their unsuccessful social adjustment bears tribute to the social values of the normal family and reveals in a striking way the misfortunes that must come to children whose family life is mutilated by death.

If the children have been committed to an orphan asylum because of the loss of both parents or the inability of the one remaining to keep the family together, they disclose how lacking the most efficient institution is in such qualities as children need for their wholesome development, and which spontaneously appear in the affectionate and sensible home. It is not strange that the best practice in dealing with children who must be given foster care is their careful placing out in some home where they will receive the individual attention and sympathy without which a child's character cannot thrive. As a permanent method of dealing with normal children, the orphan asylum, in spite of conscientious and expert management, is archaic. The Children's Home at best is only a substitute for a home.

The Mother Who Works Outside the Home.—Many homes whose mothers are employed outside have conditions resembling those in the homes where death has removed the mother. A considerable part of the child's life, if supervised at all, is under the influence of someone else than the mother. Even when at home, the mother is likely to be too tired to deal wisely with her children or to give them a normal expression of mother-love; she may be so busy with the physical tasks of housekeeping that she cannot find time to pay them the necessary attention. She is denied the amount of association necessary for the getting of a good understanding of their normal behavior. It is not uncommon for the children, especially the older ones, to act quite differently while the mother is at home than when they are under the control of her substitute.

The working mother also frequently has to depend on her older children for the care of those younger, and this in itself constitutes an abnormal relationship between the children; the younger ones react with an antagonism to the discipline inflicted by their older brothers and sisters which they would not feel if the punishment or restrictions were imposed by one of the parents. Undoubtedly this becomes at times the original source of hostility to authority which later pushes the youth straight into some kind of delinquency. It is also not good for most older children to have the power and responsibility that fall upon them when they act as a substitute for the mother. On the other hand there are cases, as all social workers know, in which the conscientious boy or girl of 'teens age

treats his younger brothers or sisters with consideration and judgment far beyond his years.

The home life broken by the absence of the mother at work
runs risk of injuring the school career of the child since he is
liable to be kept at home to help with the household tasks; the
amount of work put upon him out of school hours may over-tire
him and prevent him from obtaining the necessary vitalizing recreation. As a consequence of absence or fatigue or little time for
study, or apathy because of the dulness of his life, he does not do
as good work at school as his intellectual capacity warrants.

A recent investigation discloses that the children of wage-
earning mothers, in comparison with all the children of the city,
not only show too large a proportion of children in the elementary
grades, but a startling proportion in the lowest grades. The following table summarizes the findings of this survey.

TABLE XII.[1]

*Retardation among children of wage-earning mothers compared with all children
in elementary grades of Philadelphia Public Schools.*

	Per cent below normal grade for age			
School grade	Children of wage-earning mothers in			All pupils in Philadelphia public schools
	Public and parochial schools	Public school	Parochial school	
All elementary grades.	41.2	38.7	44.3	25.4
First..............	25.0	18.6	31.1	10.7
Second............	25.9	19.7	34.0	20.3
Third.............	47.8	40.0	54.9	29.0
Fourth............	51.1	49.4	54.0	35.2
Fifth.............	56.7	57.3	55.7	36.3
Sixth.............	50.0	54.9	43.6	34.0
Seventh...........	33.3	28.3	45.0	21.6
Eighth............	25.0	26.3	23.5	16.5

Religious Discord in the Family.—It is a common observation that marriages of couples brought up under the influence of
religions that are widely separated assume an extra hazard. We

[1] *Philadelphia Board of Education, School District of Philadelphia,
Statistical Report of the Department of Instruction, Table 54,* Distribution
in the Grades by Ages of All Pupils in Actual Attendance October 8, 1919.

do not at present know just how influential religious differences in childhood are in breaking down the unity of family life. A recent investigation made by one of my students of some sixty families that represented marriages of mixed religion, and that were in difficulties of one sort or another great enough to bring them to the attention of a social agency, did not yield any definite conclusion with reference to the question, how far religious differences operate against successful family life. The study made clear, however, the fact that most of the families were hampered by the differences in religious traditions, so that their unlike faiths were at least contributing causes to the family problem. It was also evident that the interference of relatives who wished the household committed to one of the two churches represented was at times the origin of trouble. The couples studied represented marriages of individuals brought up under the dominance of the fundamentally different religious traditions of the Roman Catholic Church, the Jewish Synagogue, and the Protestant denominations. One experienced in dealing with family discord of religious origin knows that a home where one of the parents is a strong adherent to the Christian Science faith and the other is violently opposed to it produces a most tumultuous type of family discord.

Since morality and idealism are almost universally rooted in religious faith, the home broken by religious dissension can become particularly mischievous in its influence upon the developing character of its young children. Not only do they run risk of losing all respect for religion, but their impressions of moral anarchy as a result of the clashing of their parents' early teaching may rob them of all ethical substance. When they mature, even if through prudence they outwardly observe ethical conventions, they are liable to be without convictions and to express in personal behavior low standards of conduct.

Differences of Race and Culture.—The marriage of couples representing two fundamentally different races, even when happy for the individuals concerned, creates social difficulties of the most serious sort for the family, and, in the case of the marriage of a white and black in this country, results in tragedy for the child which makes normal development impossible. The child soon realizes that each parent is outside the fellowship and traditions of the group to which the other belongs. Although by color of skin and social conventions the child may find himself forced to remain within the racial group to which the negro parent belongs, the influence of the white parent may be predominant in the home and because of this the child in his attitudes and outlook upon life may be fully committed to the Caucasian group. Under such circumstances only the strongest individual can free himself from a deep sense of social inferiority. From a strictly social point of view the intermarriage of individuals of races whose differences stand in such sharp contrast as those of negroes and whites and American and Japanese represents in the United States a matrimonial handicap from which all but the bravest or most thoughtless persons would shrink.

The career of the immigrant in America illustrates the difficulties of a family adjusted to one culture adapting itself to widely different social conditions. The problem created is not merely that which we see in the immigrant who has recently arrived and cannot speak English. The helplessness of the foreigner who speaks another language than ours and has been accustomed to a very unlike social environment may attract our attention because of his need of assistance, but often the adult who has been with us five, ten or fifteen years and who speaks English and wears American clothes, is, in spite of appearance, so linked in habit and attitude to his former experience as to make him almost as badly adjusted to American civilization as he was the day he landed on our shores.

The tug between the old and the new is bound to show itself to some extent in the atmosphere of the immigrant home. It is, however, the gulf that develops all too commonly between the parents and children that constitutes the graver social problem.

Although the child, to all outward appearance, has become thoroughly American, it is seldom that he has received no injury in his social development because of the antagonistic contact between the culture of his home and that of the school and community life. At school he has been taught one thing and at home another until he finds it difficult to commit himself absolutely to either one of his contending environments. Perhaps he changes his name to one more American in sound and ridicules the customs to which the parents attempt to adhere. What he does brings great pain to his parents and his regret for their suffering makes him react excessively, even to such an extent that he either denounces things American or stifles his conscience and smothers affection in his determination to escape the marks of his parents' culture. Inconsistency of conduct is the more natural since the immigrant of the second generation finds it almost impossible to hold steadfastly either to his sympathies for American life or to his affectionate regard for the ways of his parents.

If he marries a woman who has been brought up in a home consistently American the new family is certain to be overshadowed by the tragic conflict of his original family circle. In his attitude toward his wife he is apt to be inconsistent, at times acting in an intolerant manner under the influence of his parents' tradition, at other times over-generous in his desire to be characteristically American. It is difficult for him not to show the same division which has been built into his personality in his dealings with his own children. As he senses their difficulties he feels anew the discord which he suffered in his father's home.

It takes little imagination to picture the handicap of the child of the immigrant who is thus tossed about by two antagonistic emotional currents and to realize why he figures so prominently in the records of the juvenile court. One must not forget in judging his difficulties that he is fortunate if he never has occasion to resent the reaction, at least as he interprets it, of the American portion of his community, an irritation from which he suffers in addition to his family situation.

Moral Separation Between Parents.—Separation within the family caused by differences of moral standards becomes a serious obstacle to the wholesome development of children; a moral discord creates a deep cleavage. The parent that resents the vicious conduct and bad reputation of the other parent, who has brought disgrace to the home, is constantly trying to protect the child from following in the evil footsteps. The attempt to save the child from the influence of the bad parent is almost certain to be overdone and by its very excess to attract the attention and perhaps the interest of the young child. The parent who realizes that he is being held up as a horrible example may do his best to combat the teaching of the other parent who is striving to undermine his influence with his

own children. In spite of bad conduct he may have the more
appealing personality and knowledge of this fact intensifies the
resentment of the righteous parent.

Sooner or later the child as he grows up is certain to receive
from some source in his life outside the home disapproval or suspicion which is born of his parent's fault in those cases where the
family disgrace is publicly known; in other cases where the
parent's misdoings have been successfully concealed, he is likely
to have fear of their possible discovery or to feel that he is not quite
honest in keeping from his friends something that might influence
their conduct toward him. One young woman in this predicament
was forced by her conscience to tell the man to whom she was
engaged to be married, shortly before the wedding, of her father's
theft, his disappearance, and her adoption by an aunt with the
change of her name. Although the confession was received most
generously by her lover, her tension and remorse and her ques-
tioning whether she had a right to marry became at least contributing causes to a mental condition of which there had been no
premonition, but which required her commitment for a considerable period to an insane hospital.

Absent Husbands.—There are many homes from which husbands because of the nature of their business frequently and for
long periods are absent. Although this does not by any means
constitute in most cases a broken family, it is occasionally the first
cause of a family catastrophe. To a certain extent family conditions are similar to those where the husband has died. The children are excessively under the influence of the mother and lack
the comradeship and insight of the father at times when they are
forced to meet a crisis while the father happens to be away. The
father, as a result of his lack of comradeship, may not understand
his children sufficiently to influence them wisely, while they in
turn may miss the intimacy necessary for their affection. If his
home-comings are usually marked by punishment inflicted on the
children at the request of the wife for their conduct during his
absence, he at once becomes to them an intermittent police official
whom they may fear but cannot love.

The traveling father, if he faces his handicap squarely, can
offset much of the loss due to his absences by corresponding

with his children, by generous comradeship at those times when he is at home, and by interesting his children in his own travel and experiences. Carpenter, for instance, whose popular travel letters emphasize the fact that he spent a large portion of each year in foreign countries, used to take one after another of his children with him on his trips as soon as they were old enough. When some such program is followed, not only do the children look forward, during his absence, to the father's return, but they will become intimate and confidential immediately after his arrival.

Automobile Migrants.—A real home requires permanent settlement. This is well illustrated by the family life of the gypsy, which, even when strongly knit together, has been necessarily meagre. A wandering family cannot establish the community contacts that form part of the substance of a normal home. In these days we have a new type of gypsy family life in the automobile migrants.

These families, found in greatest abundance in the Far West and the South, and especially in Florida, wander about in their cheap cars, frequently, like the gypsies of old, receiving enough from the generous people whom they meet to keep them on their way.

In different parts of the country, and particularly in Western cities, are found camping places, both public and private, for these migratory families. They are not, of course, all the same in their characteristics or in the motives of their going about. Some travel in expensive cars, splendidly equipped, because they enjoy the life better than conventional travel, while others take to the car because only so have they hope of satisfying their wanderlust. In 1923 there were in Camp A, the municipal auto camp of Los Angeles, 6193 different cars; and during the year nearly a thousand cars were turned away because of lack of space, yet in that time more than 20,000 camped in the parks of Los Angeles.

There are all sorts of motives behind the wanderer: restlessness, response to advertising, the lure of the romance of the West and South, expectations of a new start in life, the desire to improve or find health, craving for frontier experience, longing to be rid of conventional habits of life, and pure love of automobile travel.

It has become the conviction of social workers familiar with this type of wanderers, that the problem they present is with us permanently. If so, we have a new but serious family instability. Many of the migrants have children who, as they travel from place to place with their parents, are denied not only proper schooling but normal family experience. It is interesting to conjecture what will be the effect of this migratory life upon the social character of the developing child. It is not to be expected that such individuals upon maturity will find it easy to settle down and maintain normal home life. They are no more likely to take root than the tramp. The children of these auto parties are frequently exploited and suffer not only along lines of health and education but at times also morally. The following extracts from the reports of two Western social agencies show how the welfare of the children can be endangered:

> If a family stays long enough for the Compulsory Education Department to get after them, they move on. The children develop a wanderlust and restlessness . . . are much excited at the prospect of moving on to a new place and plainly show the love of adventure which a roving life . . . .presents. They work along with their parents in the fields gathering cotton, and walnuts, picking berries and fruit. They are considered an asset. . . . It is not infrequent that the parents tell us they could not "make a go of it" without the help of their children. . . . We have been morally certain that couples were not married, and that some of the children did not belong to the group, but had been picked up in some unexplainable manner and were being used to provide meal tickets.[2]

War and Family Demoralization.—The social upheaval that accompanies war and the restlessness and disorganization that follow it upset family stability; indeed, no social institution can more justly indict war than can the family. War snatches from home the breadwinner, affords opportunity through the absence of fathers for children to drift into delinquency, gives to countless husbands who finally return home restlessness and wanderlust; it brings to both men and women temptations that lead them to deviate from former moral standards, it stimulates and brings to expression neurotic tendencies that might not have developed to the point of hurting the family had there not been the stress of war.

Modern warfare by its slaughter of males produces, as it has

---

[2] Buffington, "Automobile Migrants," *The Family*, July, 1925, p. 151.

in certain parts of Europe, a preponderance of women and removes from many of them a chance for marriage—a situation which puts additional burden upon the influences that attempt to maintain and elevate the standards of sex morality. It stimulates fatalistic attitudes toward life which lessen the sense of family responsibility. In short, nowhere does the strain of war show itself more quickly or act more disastrously than in the family. During the war when the minds of the people are concentrated on the conflict and the general excitement makes sane thinking difficult, the havoc suffered by the family is not keenly felt, but once the war is over its effects appear. Children are not spared; not only are they robbed of their parents in those cases where the fathers die on the battlefield and their mothers succumb to worry and disease, but also their mortality rate, especially that of the younger ones, increases; the older children, and the infants who survive, may carry the mark of their experiences in their lessened physical vitality, while an attack is made upon their welfare from another direction by the removal or ignoring of laws regarding child labor.

Parental Status and Delinquency.—Although we cannot in so complicated a matter as youthful delinquency analyze the causes so as to give a precise statistical statement, investigations have been made that yield interesting results and emphasize the influence of the home. The study of fifty consecutive cases of delinquent boys, carried on by the research department of the Los Angeles schools, under the specific direction of Willis W. Clarke, showed the following situation.

TABLE XIII.[3]

Parental status of the fifty delinquent boys

	Nos.	Per cent
Parents living together..................................	30	60
Father dead, child with mother..........................	5	10
Mother dead, child with father..........................	5	10
Both parents dead.......................................	4	8
Parents separated or divorced...........................	6	12
TOTAL	50	100

This table shows that 40 per cent of the cases studied came from broken homes.

[3] Cordes, "A Study of Fifty Delinquent Boys," *Journal of Applied Sociology*, May, 1923, p. 273.

The results of a larger study are statistically expressed as follows:

TABLE XIV.[4]
Parental conditions of delinquent boys in State industrial schools
Totals for thirty-one States

Parental condition	Number of delinquents	Per cent of distribution
Parents living together	3,663	48.2
Mother dead	975	12.8
Father dead	1,362	17.9
Total one parent dead	2,337	30.7
Both parents dead	429	5.7
Parents divorced, separated or deserted	802	10.6
Other abnormal	280	3.7
Unknown	87	1.1
Total	7,598	100.0
Total Normal	3,663	48.2
Total Abnormal	3,848	50.7
Unknown	87	1.1
Total	7,598	100.0
Having step-mother	197	5.2
Having step-father	334	8.9
Total having one step-parent	531	14.1

Here again the broken home contributed to delinquency in fully one-half of the cases.

A more recent study regarding conditions in New York institutions for delinquent boys shows 45 per cent to come from homes with abnormal marital relations. This is reported in Table XV.

Although delinquency is one way of measuring the harmful results of a broken home, it is not the only way. Children may be made unhappy or injured for life by the mischievous influence of the broken home, especially during their period of development, and still not become delinquent or in any way show traits that

[4] Shideler, E. H., "The Delinquent Boy," *Journal American Institute Criminal Law and Criminology,* vol. viii, p. 713.

TABLE XV.[5]

Giving the marital relations of parents of delinquent boys at four institutions; and comparing them with similar data obtained on New York City public school children (Slawson) and on New York State employed boys (Burdge); and inserting estimates for the unselected population based on the 1910 United States Census (Shideler).

Marital relations of parents	N. Y. House of Refuge		State Agr. & Ind. School		Berk. Ind. Farm		Hawthorne School		All Inst. combined		N. Y. C. Pub. School Children		N. Y. State employed boys	Estimates for entire country based on 1910 Census
	No. in given rel.	% in given rel.	No. in given rel.	% in given rel.	No. in given rel.	% in given rel.	No. in given rel.	% in given rel.	No. in given rel.	% in given rel.	No. in given rel.	% in given rel.	% in given rel.	% in given rel.
Parents living together	304	51.0	376	59.1	27	28.1	196	61.0	903	54.8	2576	80.7		
Mother dead, father living	101	16.9	81	12.7	20	21.0	36	11.2	238	14.4	170	5.3	5.0	}16.0
Father dead, mother living	116	19.5	97	15.3	14	14.5	67	20.9	294	17.9	319	9.9	10.0	
Both parents dead	27	4.5	12	1.9	8	8.3	8	2.5	55	3.3	23	0.7		
Parents separated or divorced	48	8.1	70	11.0	27	28.1	14	4.4	159	9.6	110	3.4		3.3
Total no. of cases where marital relation is known	596	100.0	636	100.0	96	100.0	321	100.0	1649	100.0	3198	100.0		
Total abnormal marital relations	292	49.0	260	40.9	69	71.9	125	39.0	746	45.2	622	19.3		

would be catalogued statistically. The consequences of the broken home are a source of social mischief far greater than the records of juvenile offenses disclose.

Social Implications of the Broken Home.—When the home has been broken or in any way becomes unstable it must be dealt with as an individual problem. The social worker who assumes the task of helping the family soon discovers that the family dis-

[5] Slawson, "Marital Relations of Parents and Juvenile Delinquency," *Journal of Delinquency*, September, 1923, p. 280.

aster cannot often be treated in isolation. A family breakdown produces social consequences; social conditions outside the home are in large measure the forces that wreck the home.

The family life once broken is difficult to mend. The constructive policy of social service stresses preventive work, for no amount of patching home misfortunes will prevent other families from going wrong. Social strategy requires that we keep in mind the implications of family disorder and encourage every movement that makes for wise ways of living and wholesome character. We shall always have broken families to deal with, but whether we have few or many and handle those we have with much or little success is primarily determined by the soundness of society.

CHAPTER XI

MODERN CRITICISM OF THE FAMILY

Skepticism Regarding Family Life.—This is an age of social criticism, and it would be strange indeed to find no attack directed against the family. At a time when every social organization is scrutinized and subjected to critical analysis the family is, from its social importance, bound to receive hostile attention from those who question its efficiency. This criticism of the family, however, is not entirely new. Beginning with Plato, there has been a long line of hostile observers of family life who have been sensitive to the social failures of the home and who have advocated substitutes for the family or radical changes in it.

Although the family has always received its share of criticism, we find a new and characteristic aggressiveness on the part of those who at present are finding fault with it. This is a natural product of modern life. Psychology, sociology, and particularly psychiatry are revealing with increasing clearness the social consequences of family inefficiency, and as a result the modern criticism of the family has more substance than in the past, when it rested upon a less scientific foundation. The development of mental hygiene has necessarily impressed the student of human conduct with the serious injury that the personality of the growing child may receive from the mistakes committed in the home by parents. From the same source comes information with regard to the mischievous social results of an unhappy marriage or unprogressive family traditions and habits. These findings of the various sciences that deal with family and marriage failures furnish effective ammunition for the modern critic of the home.

Science has dislodged the home from its safe refuge in sentiment and has forced it to come under an impartial investigation, and the result has been a disclosure of the bad functioning of both the family and marriage, which has weakened the confidence of many in regard to the social value of these institutions. It is to be expected that the attack on the home and marriage will become

12   177

even more aggressive as new information is gathered regarding the social evils that are products of unwise home life, and as the reformer learns from actual experience how difficult it is to change unwholesome family life or to remove from the personality injury that has been received from harmful contacts within the home circle.

The recent advances in the social sciences that throw light upon human conduct make it necessary that we enlarge our ideas of family failure. From the point of view of mental hygiene, the bad home is not merely the place of low standards, poverty, obvious brutality, or discord. Family life that runs smoothly, yields a fair share of happiness to its members and outwardly shows no evidence of disturbances may contain, as we now know because of our better understanding of the problems of conduct, conditions inherently mischievous that prohibit normal personal development and distort emotional behavior to such an extent that good social character becomes impossible.

Formerly, the distinction between the good and bad homes lay on the surface and was patent to all observers. Now that science has made a beginning in its study of family life, we have to include in our list of bad homes many that in former days were considered markedly good. The problem has become complicated by our new knowledge, and the differences between the homes that function well and those that function to the detriment of personal happiness and social welfare have become more subtle. Naturally, the first phase of this change is the growing skepticism with reference to the social value of marriage and the home.

Literary Skepticism Concerning Marriage and the Home.— Modern skepticism regarding marriage and family life appears constantly in the literature of our period. Both the play and the novel reflect our widespread matrimonial restlessness and family discontent. This literary interest is in part the consequence of social conditions influencing family life, and in part an appreciation of the dramatic elements present in the situation of the modern family. Literature is always quick to see the significance of social disturbance and the opportunities it provides for artistic portrayal. The writer thus far has had a keener sense of the predicament of the modern home than has the social scientist. The novelist, with uncanny skill, has dissected every form of marriage trouble and family incompetence. He has also, to a lesser extent, used fiction to advocate marriage reform or to establish a new theory of the family. Whoever wishes to become familiar with the skepticism of modern life affecting the family or with radical theories in regard to marriage and the home must turn to literature, for nowhere else will he find this material in such abundance or expressed with such great force.

There is, of course, no uniformity of attitude or general agreement as to necessary reforms among the multitude of writers who have used the novel to discuss family problems. The most common element in this material, which is so varied in both content and form, is the portrayal of the failure of the family as an institution in its effort to satisfy human desire. As one would naturally suppose, the novelist is more skilful in his criticism of family life than he is when he presents suggestions for reform.

The description and analysis of marriage difficulties provides an easier task for the writer than the presentation of a program for the reconstruction of the family. The novelist is, of course, not to be criticized because he makes a better critic than reformer, for the interpretation of human experience offers more dramatic opportunity than the effort to direct human behavior. Nevertheless, the student of the family who turns to modern literature for assistance in finding clear pathways through present family difficulties into a more satisfactory home life is bound to be disappointed. What modern literature does give is a realization of the great variety of unhappy home life in our modern social world and the different ways in which family troubles come about.

Any attempt to estimate justly the significance of this literary presentation of the tragedies of marriage and the home must take into account the temperament of the writer. The literary artist is apt to be a person who is super-sensitive to the faults and irritations of the family experience. He is also, because of his gift, a person who has a vivid appreciation of the ideal and an intolerance in dealing with the hard circumstances of every-day realities. He obtains personal relief from what is, by his portrayal of what he would wish to have true. What becomes for him a means of releasing his emotions acts to the reader as a stimulus and to some extent encourages matrimonial restlessness and impatience in dealing with the problems of the modern home.

It is well also for the modern student of the family who turns to literature for insight into the matrimonial restlessness of today to remember that the writer himself is sometimes a victim of personal experiences, and that he finds emotional relief in generalizing regarding home conditions on the basis of the happenings of his own childhood or the dissatisfactions that have come to him through marriage or parenthood.

In the literature that is characteristic of our times, we also find a greater and franker attention given to problems of sex, especially as they have to do with matrimonial happiness. This feature in the recent novels also reflects changes in our social culture. As the taboo with reference to sex has largely broken down, and as science has come to have a larger understanding of the significance of sex as an influence upon human behavior, literature has naturally tended toward greater and more conscious use of sex as a motive in literary creation.

In its efforts to make use of the material newly furnished by science which reveals the social significance of sex, modern fiction more than any other influence has lessened the power of taboo and has made it possible for the student of the family, in his discussion of home problems, to deal justly with sex as a causal influence in both marriage and family experience. Among the contemporary novelists representative of the group of writers who have shown unusual skill in dissecting family experience and uncovering the incompatibilities and tragedies of the home, are Robert Herrick, W. L. George, Sinclair Lewis, Sherwood Anderson and D. H. Lawrence. Another popular literary form for the expression of present-day skepticism regarding the home and marriage is the short story, especially among the younger writers, who are naturally most sensitive to the prevailing criticism of the family.

Family Skepticism and the Newspaper.—Much of the popular every-day skepticism of our times with reference to the family obtains expression in the newspaper. The newspaper editor knows that a large proportion of his readers are keenly interested in divorce trials of a scandalous nature, in family tragedies and in any unusual and sensational statements regarding the home, and in so far as it is the policy of his particular paper to cater to this type of interest he makes use of such news material. Some newspapers may be justly said to specialize in sex appeal and family scandals, and that they have a correct understanding of popular taste is proven by their tremendous circulation.

It must not be thought strange that so many readers of newspapers are interested in stories that have to do with family disasters and marriage failures. That this interest is not something new developed by the press is clear to anybody who has intimate knowledge of the content of much of village gossip. Family tragedies have news value, especially for those with untrained minds who read newspapers primarily to satisfy their curiosity in regard to all sorts of tragedies, scandals and sports. Readers with wider interests do not want their newspaper to be exclusively devoted to such material, but most of them, on the other hand, do not want it entirely left out, for they also are interested in sensational happenings, particularly those that have to do with marriage and the family.

It is impossible to estimate how much practical influence the newspaper's discussion of family difficulties has in building up suspicious and critical attitudes toward marriage and the home. Doubtless the critic of the newspaper would be liable to exaggerate the practical effect of current newspaper policies as a source of suggestion hostile to wholesome family life. It would be a mistake, however, to suppose that the sensational newspaper's playing up of family disasters is of no practical importance as a source of influences that affect family life. One of the most mischievous effects of this exploiting of family tragedy is that it makes the reader so familiar with family breakdowns that such experiences come to seem almost normal; he is much too apt to forget that successful family life contains no news value.

The editorial policy of newspapers is almost always friendly to the family as an institution. Even the most sensational newspaper, which appears to the prejudiced critic as entirely made up of suggestions harmful to the family, contains articles, editorials and news items that are constructive and helpful. Moreover it is easy to forget that the reason why the reader delights in following the divorce trial of some wealthy couple is not so much because he is interested in the family situation as a scandal, as because he covets the opportunity of coming in contact through the press with the experiences of people whom he envies because they have the riches he cannot have. In other words, the reader's interest in such papers is often due to his eagerness to make use of the opportunity to share the life of those who have greater advantages, rather than to his curiosity regarding the family tragedy itself.

In any case it is hopeless to ask the press not to print material that its readers crave. If any reform is to be had it must come primarily by educational influences that will lift the level of interest of the mass of readers. Meanwhile the newspaper that is filled with family scandals appears as a constant reminder of the seriousness of the task of improving family standards.

Socialism and the Family.—Many socialistic thinkers are critical in their attitude towards the family and some are antagonistic to the family as an institution. Socialists are no more in perfect accord with reference to their attitude toward the family than they are regarding other matters that appear in their discussions. These differences of opinion make it impossible to define with exactness the attitude of socialism with reference to the family. To many Socialists the family represents an institution that conserves private property rights and protects the exploitations which they consider inherent in our present capitalistic system. Believing as they do that the family retards social progress and perpetuates the dominance of capitalism, they attack the family as an obstacle which prevents the development of a more wholesome social state.

Some socialistic writers are not hostile to the family as an institution but merely to its patriarchal form. They regard the dominance of man which lingers still in the average home as one of the most mischievous influences in modern life. They demand not only for the wife but for the children as well a social status which will make possible the fullest expression of independent personality. They insist upon absolute social equality for women. Since they find in the family as it now exists conditions that hamper the self-expression of women, they insist that reform must start with the home.

Some of the Socialists who are more radical in their attitude toward the family look forward to what they regard as a free marriage. By free marriage they mean making matrimony a personal matter, not to be regulated by the state and not requiring court action for its dissolution. From this point of view mating is a purely private affair. Men and women are to be permitted to enter marriage by mere volition and to separate by the same procedure. Even though it might be wise for public convenience to have their marriage registered, it would not be the business of the state to interfere with the marriage or to make it in any way difficult for the couples to separate.

Some of the socialistic advocates of this freer type of marriage recognize that it is not so simple as it seems, and they make a serious effort to face the problems involved and to offer solutions for them. For example, it is clear that with the coming of children to a couple who have been attempting the free marriage based upon agreement which some of the Socialists advocate, arises a very complicated problem. No longer is the maintenance of the family of significance only for the adults since the dependent child more than either parent has need of the home. In cases where the child is concerned it becomes evident that the state must assume some obligation for the child's protection. Some writers propose to meet this problem by permitting the state to take over responsibility for the child's maintenance, and in practice it is conceded that this will represent more regulation on the part of the state than is in accord with an absolutely free matrimonial alliance.

Socialistic writers also face the fact that the freer type of marriage would encourage the irresponsible, selfish attitude toward matrimony which now shows itself in the tendency of some to use the divorce as a means of having repeated matrimonial alliances, none of which are entered upon with any sense of serious obligation either to the matrimonial partner or to society itself. It is admitted that human nature will need better discipline and higher ideals than many people now have if any scheme of free marriage is to prevail without injuring the personality and lowering public standards of conduct.

What the socialistic writer who wishes to establish a theory of free marriage does not always fully recognize is the fact that the values that have come to be regarded as highest in marriage comradeship would be for many submerged and impossible of attainment by the emphasis upon sex that would surely follow the establishment of a free-marriage program.   Granting as we must that a considerable number of those now married obtain a very limited appreciation of the satisfactions made possible by the permanent commitment of affection in the union of marriage, any social scheme that encourages looking upon matrimony as a merely temporary venture that concerns only the two forming the association will make it all the more difficult for the great majority of persons to achieve the higher joys of monogamous marriage, or even to realize that such values exist.   Under the free-marriage régime the general tendency would be to make marriage a mere sex experience or a matter of convenience.   The losses that would result are so obvious that the program of free marriage is never likely in America to advance beyond a purely theoretical discussion to the point where it would reveal its social unsoundness by the testing of practical experience.

Emotional Radicalism.—There are attacks upon marriage and the home which find expression in writing, addresses and conversation that are both radical and emotional.   The constant attendant at forums is familiar with the questions and statements that members of the audience inject at any opportunity without reference to the topic under discussion, which express an emotional radicalism that seldom has any positive program for social reconstruction.   As some tirade against industry in order to give vent to personal discontent and tension, so others inveigh against the family as a means of escape from inner unhappiness.

This type of radicalism must not be mistaken for that which is essentially intellectual and represents genuine, impersonal doubts of the adaptability of the orthodox home to modern life.   The emotional type of radical, though he may wear the cloak of the Socialist or the serious critic, is actually reacting against family tragedy or matrimonial unrest.   His attack is self-projection and is to be considered a confession, unconsciously made, rather than a skepticism that deserves serious consideration.   Radicalism of this sort constitutes a problem for the psychiatrist, not the sociologist.

Faults of Family Life.—A considerable part of the criticism directed against the family comes not from those who are skeptical with reference to the family as an institution but from social workers and mental hygienists who from their practical experience have discovered how imperfectly the family does its social task and how great is the social cost of this lack of efficiency. Without question many of our most troublesome social evils are the product of the family's failure to do what is reasonably to be expected of it as a primary social institution.

It is necessary that the believers in family life face squarely these criticisms that come out of the experience of those who deal with the results of harmful home influences. Nevertheless it is only fair when studying such problems to recognize that they are caused by faults that more essentially belong to personalities than to the family as an institution; even if we had no family we should still contend with these common problems that are charged against bad family training, merely because children in their first contact with adults, whatever the form of the association, are liable to be molded by the unfortunate impressions which come from human weakness as well as to receive the more favorable stimulations that come out of the attitudes of wholesome character.

One of the practical criticisms directed against the home, which is to a large extent deserved, is the charge that it is responsible for many of the prejudices of present-day society that make people unhappy and slow down progress. The child of course has no means by which he can discriminate between the reasonable judgment of his parents and the attitude that represents mere emotion and unfounded opinion made up of pure prejudice. It is even true that the child is more likely to respond to the prejudices than to the better judgments of the parents since the former are expressed with an intensity that attracts his attention.

The worst thing about such teaching may be that the child's mind will be closed by the opinion that he receives from his parents, so that in later life he will not correct his mistaken judgment, but will as a parent once again attempt to pass over to his children false and unjust feelings and beliefs. A large part of our educational energy is lost in the effort to correct the mistaken ideas that have been pressed upon children by parents who are narrow in their sympathies and enslaved by the weaknesses that they have had built into their own personalities in childhood. It would be unquestionably a great relief to society if young life could pass through its critical period when social attitudes are first made, without receiving the injuries which come from contact with prejudices. But this improvement can come only by the slow growth of social tolerance and understanding which will drive prejudice more and more from the large place it now maintains in average human nature.

The family is blamed also for instilling into the life of little children false standards, particularly regarding the values of life. This criticism of the family must also be respected by those who are willing to face facts, for there is evidence of its weight. It is only fair to remind the critics of the family that false standards are as often reflected from the life outside the family as they are originated within the home itself. It is true that many adults who live unhappily, or who miss the joys of living made possible by the resources at their command, are the victims of early, low family standards.

The greatest danger for the child comes from the perverted attitudes of parents with reference to money and love. Where the family teaching makes the getting of wealth everything, it is difficult for the child to carry into life a personality unscarred by materialistic cravings. Wrong ideas regarding love are even more harmful, because they spoil the child's character at a deeper level. A home that is destitute of genuine affection, or that never achieves any appreciation of the higher satisfactions of love, gives the child a slim chance to prepare for successful adult living.

The egotistic family is also condemned by those who realize the harm it brings to the child's character and to society itself. The bad effects of egotistic family life are easier to see in the rural and village environment where primary contact reveals how quickly and how seriously the child may be hurt by a home where the limited associations inherent in country life magnify family rivalry until it destroys everything that makes for sane living. Family competition and hostility may even go so far as to become fixed as a family feud that, going on from generation to generation, becomes a menace to the whole community. Even if the contest is not carried on by the rifle as so often it has been in the past among the mountaineers of the South, it nevertheless shows itself in ways that hurt the community in personal, political, or commercial bitterness. In some New England communities, for example, hostility between families robs the community of all its social vitality, and becomes a curse to the children who come under its influence.

A widespread criticism of the family is that it makes for selfishness. This is a common indictment of the home because observers trying to see the family as it is so frequently discover that individual homes are in every way possible encouraging selfishness in their children. So much has been said about the over-indulgent parent that one would suppose that any intelligent father or mother would be guarded against the danger of making children selfish. The fact is otherwise. One cannot know many families without being convinced that a proportion of them are guilty of encouraging in their children selfishness by their mismanagement of child life. This is in part due to their difficulty in seeing the mistakes they make in handling their children.

The affection of the parents in such cases cannot be made a defense. It is the business of affection to be understanding, to appreciate its own dangers and to guard the child from injury. Obviously, parents who have had hard circumstances in their early life, or who have acquired sudden wealth, or who are too concentrated upon their life work, run greatest risk of being over-indulgent.

Another criticism of the family made by the experienced social worker is its responsibility for many of the jealousies of life. There can be no doubt that the charge made against the home as a chief originator of jealousy is justified in the light of the facts, for the analysis of concrete cases of jealousy shows how frequently the mismanagement of children by parents starts the development of chronic jealousy. The partial parent who discriminates against one child in favor of another is especially likely to hurt the personality of a young child by starting a habit of jealousy that in the adult years becomes a menace to good adjustment. The growth of jealousy is only another illustration of the enormous power parents have over their children, an influence that becomes good or bad according to the character of the parents.

Another fault that is often found with the home by its critics is its deadening effect upon young life. It must be confessed that the parent who has had his life flattened out as he has gone into adulthood is apt to attempt to crush the joyfulness out of childhood and the romance out of youth. It is unfortunate that so many adults achieve maturity only at the expense of becoming dull and turning life into a monotonous routine, but the home itself is more often the victim of such circumstances than their cause.

The prosaic character of the home life is the consequence of tendencies in individuals and society that rob living of its vitality and reduce experience to an uninteresting grind. The going on in life has its losses as well as its gains, and nowhere do we find a better illustration of the power of experience to destroy than in those persons who have lost all the zest of living as they have grown older. This criticism of the home reveals one of the most common and inevitable incompatibilities between the youth and the adult. Fortunately the child and the young man or woman have vitality enough to withstand a considerable pressure from those who, having lost their flair for living, have become the enemies of all who find life filled with meaning. Since the child cannot be his own parent, there is no way in which he can be protected from the danger of being crushed by his older associates, other than by efforts to conserve in the adult social vitality and spontaneity.

Another criticism made against the family is the social determination which is built upon family reputation and which limits young people or gives them special advantages in ways distinctly unjust. It is true that family influence has much too large a place in deciding the opportunities of the individual. No young person is socially judged apart from his family connections, and the unfairness of this appears particularly in the two extreme types of families: those that have a bad reputation and those that are regarded as highly successful. In education, in business, in politics and especially in marriage opportunities, the practical influence of the reputation of the home into which the person happens to be born shows itself in ways that give some people advantages they do not deserve, while others are denied their fair deserts.

With the decrease in the functions of the family there is likely to go also a corresponding lessening of the tyranny of family reputation. The trend at present is unmistakably in this direction. Family connections do not count as once they did and in business especially, at the present time, there are striking examples which demonstrate that real ability can push forward in spite of family prejudices and that it is becoming increasingly difficult for persons to keep the positions that they obtain in business on the mere basis of family pull without real fitness. Even in marriage selection the tendency seems to be away from the influence that family connections once had.

In spite of the fact that family reputation can be so easily exaggerated, there is need of realizing that there is a genuine basis for taking seriously the influence of family life in any judgment to be passed upon personality. Unfortunately the classification of good and bad families which we so often make is most fallacious. Nevertheless no influence operates upon the personality more powerfully than the home life, and if we have accurate knowledge of the character of the family, we at least positively know some of the stimulations to which the personality was exposed, and it is reasonable to infer that in most cases the personality has developed in harmony with the early impressions it received.

Criticism of the family made by those who attempt to help unadjusted individuals is a plea not for its abolishment but for its socialization and improvement. Family life can do great harm because it has the power of accomplishing great good. It is necessary to check up as accurately as possible the actual effects of family life, not to attack it, but in order to make it a more successful social institution.

Need of Family Balance.—Criticisms of the family show us that we must not expect too much of the institution. Even home life should be taken in moderation. A good many of the faults of family life originate primarily in the lack of proportion. Human nature needs the family, but it is just as true that it is hurt by excessive family control. In the past the family has been an obstacle to progress because it has been too dominant. In our times the family by the intense competition it has received is protected from the risk of doing too much. The ultimate effect of this change will be to show that much of the criticism of the family has been directed against faults due to an exaggeration of family influence rather than against the failure of the institution itself.

Good family life is that type of home which furnishes what is needed by its members at a definite time and place. As social conditions change, the task of the family also changes. In our times human experience has been enormously enriched by the results of science and invention. As a consequence much that was expected of the rural family, to a lesser extent of the urban family, in the past we now have from other agencies than the home; and what seems to us the good influence of the home of the past was really due to the relative emptiness of the life of that period.

Those who regret that the family today does not have the command it once had over human behavior are asking for the advantages of modern culture built upon all the resources of applied science and at the same time the kind of home that flourished when living conditions were very much more simple. The demand for the home of the past amid the opportunities of the modern world is a hopeless request. Even if it could be proven that the former home life was better adapted to the needs of human nature, it would make no difference. The home of the past can only be brought back by wiping out the accumulated resources that are making modern life possible.

Criticism of the family reveals, however, that the institution has been too faulty to make good use of the opportunities it had when it commanded a larger influence than it does at present. If the quantity of influence of the present-day family is less than that of the past, it nevertheless has real need of an increase of efficiency since to meet its obligations it must compete with other agencies that are ever ready to take over what the family cannot do, or to exploit those persons who come from families that have been unsuccessful in meeting their obligations.

Family Strategy.—The conscientious parent needs to study the strategy of his position. Many of the faults of the home would be corrected if parents only realized that it is their business to direct the stimuli that play upon the personality of the child, rather than to attempt the futile effort to provide for the child all the experiences that he needs for his development. It is an unwise home that attempts to monopolize the child or even to limit him during his period of growth by permitting him to have as little experience as possible outside the family circle. Much of the criticism brought against the home as a training place for the young results from a misinterpretation of parental functions and a too narrow home program. Every father and mother need to make a conscious effort to supplement their influence upon the young child and bring him under the stimulations of other people who from time to time can give to the child what the parents lack, or at least novel impressions of contact with another personality.

Parents have a large opportunity in the choice of visitors; in bringing to the home friends they should keep in mind not only their own pleasure, but the advantages that come to the child from receiving contact with guests. As far as possible the child should be permitted to enter into the conversation and experiences made possible by visitations. Ambition, insight, tolerance, interest and a host of other social virtues can be stimulated by the child's meeting family friends. Biography gives constant illustration of the deep impressions children have received by coming in contact with men and women whom their parents have invited to visit in the home.

It is also an unwise policy for parents to neglect the opportunities of the community. A shut-in family is just as bad as a shut-in personality, and the parents must protect the children from an excessive concentration of family life by directing them to the stimulating experiences offered by the community life. Fairs, picnics, church festivals, lectures and concerts must not be thought of merely as a means of entertainment, for they are never primarily that for the young child. Intensely interesting as they usually are to the younger members of the family, they are exceedingly stimulating and their effects upon personality are necessarily lasting. They offer the parent opportunity to furnish the child with experiences not possible within the home itself. In our times the radio offers resources of contact undreamed of in times past, but here especially there is great need of the parent's discriminating direction of the child's interest.

The boy and girl whose parents open up chances to come in contact with modern industrial life are exceedingly fortunate. The parents should at least permit the child to become familiar with their own work, but valuable as this is for fellowship between parents and child, it is not by itself a satisfactory program. The child will be greatly interested in all sorts of industrial experiences if only they are provided early. Today a town child may easily visit factories and different sorts of business, while the rural child can be brought in contact with the various kinds of farming experience and if a little effort is made to help the child interpret what he sees, his opportunities will be both enjoyable and impressive.

It is a great mistake to ignore the girl as so many parents do and assume that only boys need to come in contact with business life. In our time the business world cannot be maintained upon a sex basis. Good preparation for life requires from both the boy and girl, whether in village, city or country, personal experience with as many forms of industry as possible.

Most children, even when they are over-protected by the home, come in contact perhaps by accident with persons who have experienced circumstances and culture that differ from those of their home. For example, the child's first contact with representatives of other races and nationalities very unlike that type of personality which from his family association he has come to think of as standard is generally most significant. Such happenings give the parent a splendid opportunity to build up democratic sympathy, social justice and tolerance.

Sometimes parents, in their efforts to decrease the curiosity of the child or because of their fear that he will suffer from associating with an individual who is very different from his usual companions, show an intolerant attitude that is not even a fair expression of their general feeling. If such a policy protects the child, though even in this it often fails because it increases the child's curiosity, it also hardens the child's sympathies and in the end this may prove more harmful than any influence that would have come from the contact itself. The mother must be especially careful that she does not narrow the child's association by her personal limitations. She is easily tempted to try to put upon her daughter the restrictions of sex-consciousness and social handicaps that she herself, as a well-behaved girl of her period, had to expect.

Art as an Antidote to Family Narrowness.—Influences from outside the home that would help to correct the faults that are bound to occur in any individual family are not confined to associations with people. There is another realm of influence of very great importance that no parent can wisely neglect, represented by art. Fortunately art in some form is available for any home, but the child cannot find, as a rule, entrance into artistic experience and appreciation without the guidance and encouragement of the parents.   Poetry, natural beauty, literature, music, and if possible painting, architecture, and sculpture should be introduced to the child not once but again and again until the taste of the child is necessarily stimulated.   Of course, here as elsewhere, judgment is necessary, for the parents must not force upon the child that for which he has no interest until he develops a hostility toward what his parents are providing instead of the appreciation that they seek.   Love of beauty is a growth, an inner development, which cannot be built into a child's soul mechanically or by pressure; it responds, however, to a favorable opportunity for normal flowering.

13

CHAPTER XII

FAMILY ADJUSTMENT

Family Life Unstable.—Although, as we have seen, people persist in thinking of the family as a static institution, it is never that, but like all social organizations is always changing in its attempt to adapt itself to a social environment ever in flux. Students of the family are agreed that the family as an institution changes, but even yet in the discussion of family life there is too great a disposition to treat the individual home as an organization of persons who, living in close contact, assume each his proper rôle in an ordered way that suggests play-acting rather than the actual facts of every-day life. The family as a group experience is even less stable than the family as an institution. Indeed it is the unstable character of the specific family that forces the institution to change. Family habits are broken and family traditions supplanted by the individual members of homes until a new set is established and the institution takes a different form.

The home is much more than merely an arena where human nature expresses itself in conduct characteristic of intimate association. It is also a centre where persons act upon one another. This has been well expressed by Professor Burgess, who insists that science can not make substantial progress in its effort to understand the home unless the family is regarded as a unity of interacting persons.[1]

The Family Arena.—A family is a group life into which each member enters with a function to perform which is his alone; he also has some idea of what he expects from his contacts with the others. Each member of the group is in a reciprocal relationship with every other member, but nothing is fixed or permanent. The interplay of personalities is constantly shifting. The rôle assumed by each one is in perpetual variation and the more progressive and vital the family, the more frequent and profound are the changes.

---

[1] "The Family as a Unity of Interacting Personalities," *Family*, March, 1926.

No day passes without new home adjustments, new attitudes on the part of every member in his reaction to each of the others. The family provides a centre of interest which forces all its constituent persons to pay heed to one another's doings and desires and makes it impossible for them to be indifferent to its kaleidoscopic experiences.

Sense of Family Permanency.—Although the family is in constant change, it has for each member a sense of permanency, for it becomes a focal point where the same kind of relationships are always in interaction. Each person contributes something to the common fund of experiences which constitute the character of the individual home; if he assumes complete indifference and gives nothing to the general possessions of the group he becomes an alien member and is soon regarded by the others as the family problem. Each person draws, or at least attempts to draw, from the association satisfactions, and when he feels that he is not successful the family life becomes to him disappointing and irritating. These satisfactions may come, as is so often true of the mother, from giving to the others and doing for them rather than in getting from them, but, however obtained, it is these experiences that provide the gratifications of the home experience.

It is this holding of the different persons in an intimate contact which calls forth the peculiar interactions of home life that constitutes the essence of the family. Any group of people living together would react upon each other. The home intensifies such responses and gives them added meaning because of the closeness of the contact and the attitudes each person takes towards the group life.

Belonging to a home seems different and has more significance than boarding or lodging with others just because the family from the early experiences of childhood calls forth interactions from the deeper levels of personality. Social pressure from tradition and contemporary conduct helps construct an attitude towards family happenings which makes all the interactions within the home appear distinctive.

Clashing of Interests.—There must be this sense of contact in a peculiar relationship or there can not be a family, but this by no means demands a harmonious adjustment. No family can escape the clashings of conflicting interests, desires and judgments. Even the most despotic type of family, dominated by a wilful father whose word is law, is free from disturbances only on the surface. The secret inner life at least opposes the authority of the tyrant, and this mass of concealed reactions of the submerged individuals is as truly interaction as open insolence and rebellion would be.

The family as a social experience is always in the process of being changed and being formed. Even when each individual has a clear concept of his special rôle in the circle, the clash of purposes is to some extent inevitable. No rôle can be assumed by any member without awakening in each of the others an idea of the proper way it should be played, and these ideas are as different as the unlike social backgrounds of the various persons.

The mother-rôle, for example, means one thing to the mother, something else to the husband, and a somewhat different thing to each child. Indeed it is still more complicated. The child, A, perhaps views the mother as having as her obligation the rôle of the ideal mother; he has an equally clear notion how she should and how she does actually act her part in relation to himself and also, if there are other children, how she should and how she actually does deal with them. A, in his reaction to his mother, is influenced by all these attitudes and any others that may be called forth by his thoughts of the mother-rôle. As the boy grows and enters new experiences and enlarges his knowledge of people, all his various attitudes towards mother, father and other relations change.

There can not be a final adjustment of the interacting personalities within the family, for the positions of all in their contacts with the others are constantly in a process of alteration. Each also senses the variations in the others' thought of him, and the relationships are still further entangled by the responses A makes to the changes he notices in B, the reasons he gives for them and the actual motives behind B's new attitudes towards A, which B may or may not correctly interpret.

Family Inequalities.—The causal influences that flow from each person within the home and move upon all the others are in constant interplay. Each individual becomes a stimulus to the others, bringing forth response and molding character. The relationships are not, however, of equal significance. Every element that reveals the differences between the persons shows in the causal contacts of their interaction. The ages, dispositions, habits, opportunities, successes, failures of one as compared with another show in the responses of one to the personality of the other. If a family has become fairly well adjusted to its interacting situation, the mere coming of another child destroys the equilibrium already achieved, and a new process of adjustment begins at once. The rôle of the first-born is different, and his reactions to the parents and theirs to him must change because he now constitutes only a part instead of the whole child-life of that particular home.

If we regard the ideal home as that in which each individual has an equal chance to develop and express his personality, we need to recognize that this is difficult to accomplish, and in full measure even impossible. The opportunity of any child would be changed by transferring him, if this were possible, from the place of the first-born to that of second or third, just as in the larger social life outside the home one individual begins a career of dominance and by his success lessens the self-assertion of others. It is the task of the parent to seek to distribute to all the children opportunities for equal self-expression, and this from the first demands of parents that they treat the children differently, since one may require encouragement and another the checking of efforts to accomplish his purposes.

Nor do the parents in their relation to the children and to each other escape the risk of becoming too dominant or too subservient. The new status of women with their increased freedom and greater realization of their desires for self-expression loads onto the modern home a much greater burden at this point than was true when men had the advantage of social dominance, and generally were ascendant in family life.

Our modern education by its stress on self-expression sharpens and reveals to the child his cravings for achievement, and adds complications to the always difficult problem of preventing the more dominant members of the group from using the opportunities provided by family association to hurt the others.

Conditions that Influence Family Association.—An analysis of a family situation, however admirably done as a case study, always bears to the changing home experience much the same relation that a photograph does to the living person. We can by painstaking investigation obtain a clear-cut description of home conditions at a given time, but our study is no sooner finished than new developments begin.

One of the influences that is constantly showing itself in the home is the effect of ages. The mere growing up of children and the growing older of parents modifies the family behavior and demands of all new adjustments in their inter-related conduct.

It is, of course, literally impossible for any parent to give two children of different ages the same treatment or to provide each with the same environment. The difference in age produces an essential unlikeness in their home experience. The older child and the younger child as a rule react upon each other in ways characteristic of their age rôles. If the positions of the children in their associations are the reverse of what their ages would suggest, the fact that the older is subservient adds all the more significance to the dominance of the other so that the influence of the age difference does not disappear.

A child is prone to criticize his parents for dealing with his brothers and sisters differently from the way they treat him. Putting aside the variations in dispositions, the mere age differences would lead parents to handle the children in ways that would invoke comparisons. A child, for example, who has an older brother has been influenced by the relationship to an extent that forces his parents to recognize this fact and give him somewhat different treatment than his brother at the same age, for the latter had no older brother's contacts to modify his conduct.

In judging the variations of parents in dealing with their brothers and sisters, children are not only unable to appreciate the distinctions that must be made by a wise parent, but their memories carry too much emotional reaction to their own former experiences to make them safe critics. A definite prohibition that led to considerable emotional protest on the part of the child is remembered, and if the parent in his program of management of a brother or sister appears more lenient, much feeling arises for there is no realization of the differing circumstances which may fully justify what seems to be a change of policy.

It is often minor experiences, easily forgotten by the parent, that attach to themselves most emotion in the child's memory. The child reacts to an experience not in proportion to its actual importance but according to the way he felt at the time, and this feeling is the product of all the conditions that influenced his responses. The purely subjective elements of such an occurrence have much to do with the child's attitude, but it is a rare parent that senses this and a rarer child that can be made to appreciate it.

The family that contains growing children is always in the process of adjustment to the interactions that contain an age element. The children in their contacts are in frequent strain, both conscious and unconscious; one child is attempting to arise from the limitations set by another because of advantage in age and the older is endeavoring to continue the former status or at least is finding difficulty in accepting the fact that the other is demanding more opportunity for self-determination. It is folly in so complex a situation to separate family life into hard and fast types and assume that there is the one-child and the two-child and the three-child home, each with definite characteristics.

Out of any family life there comes, through the interactions, a concrete situation which in spite of change may at least for a time have fairly discernible features, but the family life that emerges is no automatic product of a one-child or a two-child home. For example, a child may shut himself from his brother's or sister's interferences and may be protected in his social isolation so as to have in abundance the mischievous results that are associated with the only-child status. On the other hand a one-child home does not necessarily or inevitably produce a spoiled child whose disposition reveals the evils of lack of competition and contact. The risks of the one-child home are certainly great, but a wise parent who senses the dangers may bring a lone child to maturity with all the traits of a well-developed personality.

The effect of age upon the parents is a matter too important to be forgotten. Parents are altered by their going on in years, and this is reflected in their interactions with their children. Grandparents are prone to react in characteristic ways, not just because they are grandparents but because their age-attitudes show in their dealings with children as in their other reactions to life. Children detect the difference in parents as they change through the adding on of years, and they respond in accord with their personal feelings. It is not just that the parents are older but rather that they are older and also modified more by the addition of life experiences. Here as elsewhere the exact differences are too concrete and individual to be satisfactorily generalized. One parent grows closer to child experience as he gets older; another goes farther away. One gets greater insight, while another becomes the more blinded by prejudices and less able to adjust to changing circumstances as he increases his years of living.

Competition and Distinction.—The inner life of a family group is like the broader life outside, a place where rivalry and even conflict is constantly expressed. The large family has as its asset the opportunity it naturally provides for the various children to get a taste of the competition of later life and a realization of the necessity for coöperation. This valuable preparation for later living the one-child home cannot itself give, and unless it utilizes substitutes the child is emotionally retarded in his development.

In the incessant interplay of personal desires and the contests that arise between the egoistic strivings of the various members of a family, as they clash with one another, achievement and distinction are constantly demanding readjustments. No member of the family wins honor or gets a new means of pleasure or a greater advantage in play, business, school, or social intimacies without thus at once affecting his family position, his attitude toward the other members and their responses to him. In the same way dishonor, losses or failure on the part of one person changes at once the entire situation of the home and influences every member.

The reactions to all such experiences will differ among the individuals according to the personality which they have developed; in the quality or the amount of their responses appears the evidence of their dispositions and their own social experiences. In pitting one child against another in order to stimulate, or in contrasting one child's failure with the other's successes, well-meaning parents at times ruin all chance of wholesome family associations and make the less distinguished child bitter and self-contained.

It is not true, however, that the parent has it in his power to prevent comparisons of child with child, for rivalry is bound to occur, and all that the father and mother can do is to minimize unfair competition and, if possible, give a child who runs risk of inferiority feelings a chance to find, in some field where he has success, a basis for self-respect.

The Family as a Continuous Socializing Process.—The power of the family to construct character comes from its having, at the very beginning of infancy, opportunity to set in motion influences that give the child his first social experiences. The baby, just as soon as he begins to express his impulses in activities, comes in contact with the environment of the home. He is forced into a relationship with persons who are able and determined to interfere with his behavior. It is this thwarting of his impulses that introduces him into social experience. In his attempt not to do those things that he has found productive of unpleasant social consequences, the young child finds compensation for the desires he has to check by dwelling upon his wish to please those from whom his satisfactions and affection come. His control of behavior that is frowned on by his elders is made possible by building up these compensatory wishes.[2] With the origin of the desire to do the forbidden thing, there arises also in addition to the thought of punishment the wish to win social approval and continue in a relationship of affectionate fellowship by being obedient.

By this process of building compensations for perverse cravings the child enters into a sense of the meaning of relationship and in the conflict and conquest of antagonistic motives he becomes consciously social.

The home not only begins this process of socialization for the child who experiences normal family life; it also continues the process for a long period, for most persons throughout life. The motives of right and wrong, the first social patterns of behavior, are embedded in the life at the level of early experience where family influences are predominant, but upon these foundation-experiences all the later attitudes of the personality rest. It is fortunately contrary to fact to say that the personality is necessarily con-

[2] Kempf, E. J., " Psychopathology," p. 77.

structed in harmony with these first compensatory reactions, for in that case the power of the family would become a social tyranny forbidding the possibility of progress.

It is true that, varying with the individual, each person continues through life to react to social situations somewhat in accord with these first impressions. The family contribution seldom if ever becomes merely a past experience continued as a memory, but for most people at least it remains a continuous influence and, on account of the tenacious emotions that cling to these first impressions of the home, is constantly bringing about the very same struggle between conflicting wishes that characterized in early childhood the original socializing process.

Thus the family influence as a socializing force remains present in greater or less degree for all persons, and is not permitted to become emotionally a mere happening of the past. Many of the social struggles of life, the tragedies of personality, are the product of this power of the home to keep its influence alive throughout the social career of the individual. It is not strange that attacks are made upon the family by those, often themselves reacting slavishly to family influences that they cannot shake off, who blame the home for inflicting this emotional servitude which so frequently distorts judgment and robs people of the ability to follow without misgivings mature convictions when they are contrary to the early teaching of the home. They declare that the home ties to the individual a weight of prejudice which he drags after him as he goes on in life. The home obtains its influence from the fact that it starts the socializing process, and if this were begun in some other institution the results of these first happenings in the social life of the child would show themselves in equally persistent emotional attitudes.

The home not only begins the socializing experiences of the child; it continues to contribute to his later social development, for compensatory wishes are constructed by the adult as they were by the child, and the home remains for most men and women a chief source of compensatory motives. Parents die, the other family members separate, but the home as a relationship, the home as a means of crushing individual desires and awakening social attitudes, persists. Emotionally the home never passes.

Early home influences are to a large extent transferred from their original form to a different relationship. This especially appears when we consider the usual experience of those who marry. The attitudes once developed in contact with parents pass over into the new union and upon husband or wife are affixed the emotional reactions that became habitual in early childhood. The first and second home experiences are coalesced in such a way that the inter-actions of the marriage relation seem also a continuation of the earlier responses to association with the parents. In the home where good adjustment is maintained this flowing of the emotional results of childhood into the life of the married couple becomes a great advantage since the social motives and sentiments of the first period are continued in the interactions of the second and the socializing process goes on without break or emotional disturbance.

The situation is not so good in homes where faulty adjustment prevails. In the home life of this type of family the continuation of early experiences makes present reactions more difficult. Either husband or wife—or both of them—may so cling to the first experi-ences as to attempt a duplication of the earlier life rather than a coalition of the two relationships with the second dominating; or the fixation of husband or wife on one of the parents may make the marriage-association a futile attempt to find in each other the personality of the parent toward whom, whether dead or living, the married person is continuing an infantile subjection.

Such a marriage becomes farcical, for the union is fictitious. Immediately influences arise that tend toward maturity and inde-pendence. These are resisted in the effort to maintain childhood reactions and at once the marriage interactions are a mixture of antagonistic trends. The situation is rationalized by the individual holding to his childhood submergence in the parent's personality, and any effort of his partner in matrimony to release him from his emotional chains is interpreted as self-interest, jealousy and an attack on his own loyalty to his parents. After struggle and much unhappiness some persons develop out of their predicament and the child-parent relationship becomes subordinated to the marriage association; others go on so long as the union endures, insisting that the parent's control be continued, and in order to accomplish this they frequently withdraw from the reality that makes such a pro-

gram impossible and live over in the present the wish-experiences
that were enjoyed in the period of childhood fixation.

The Home and Personality-making.—Personality is the
product that results from the influence of social contacts in molding
the hereditary equipment of the individual. In this process of
personality-making the home must necessarily have the foremost
place since it provides the most productive stimulations by intimate contacts at a time when the child's unformed personality is
supremely sensitive to his associations. By the mere accident of the
individual's having fallen ino one home rather than another personality gets its start along the lines in which it is most likely to
develop. Experience shapes the personality and the home has the
chief opportunity to furnish the experiences that set the personality for life.

The home is the factory where the greater part of a personality
is made. The method by which the family gets its power is clear
indeed. The child, so soon as he expresses in activities his fundamental reflexes, begins to receive reactions from the elders about
him and these are incorporated as stimuli in the sum-total of experience which he associates with the activity. Out of this gradually
develops, as the child has the same experience repeated many times,
a conditioning of the original reflex. In time the response or attitude of parents becomes to the child the most impressive part
of the whole experience and a definite behavior is encouraged or
repressed by the reception it has obtained from the older members
of the family. Grandma picks up the two-months-old baby every
time he cries and pets him till he falls asleep, or failing that, until
his next meal-time comes; and soon the erstwhile well-regulated,
" good " baby cries at all hours of the day, keeping Grandma danc-
ing attendance upon him until she is quite worn out, when the inter-
vention of a sterner disciplinarian gradually brings the confused
baby back into his earlier routine of a peaceful day spent in eating, sleeping and reacting to the customary stimuli of his environment, with crying once more become an unusual occurrence.

The Home and Personality Tension.—The parent in his dealings with his children is not free from the danger of using his
relationship as a means of providing for himself compensatory
satisfactions which will smother his feelings of inner tension or

remove his sense of outward social inadequacy. He does not come to his child with merely the attitude that is generally presumed to spring from a parental instinct. His contacts do not express automatic conduct that can be charged to the working of an instinct in the way that we find lower animals dealing with their offspring.

The parent's personality colors his conduct and what the child receives is not the discharges of an instinct but the reactions of a person who has himself been conditioned by social experiences and who brings into all his associations the complicated clashings of his various mechanisms and desires. The superiority and authority of the parent give him special opportunity to use his relationship with the child to extract responses that he may not obtain in his contact with his social equals.

He may crave sympathy and seek it from the child. If he believes himself badly treated by his spouse he may rehearse his grievances and win what he covets from the child. In accomplishing this purpose, which he may construe as an act of justice, a hate-attitude is engendered in the child toward the offending parent, which not only alienates the child but also gives him a positive sense of personal injury. If it is the mother who is getting even with the husband because of inner hostility or jealousy or fear, she does not find much difficulty in instilling in her offspring suspicion or hatred, but the child who gets the inoculation shows in his developing personality the serious injury he has received. His personality, fed on such deadly influences, may later bring forth fruit that will be bitter even to the mother. Whatever the final effect of the experience may be it will always remain an essential part of his emotional character.

The parent may turn to the child for relief from his sense of failure in meeting the tests of life. The forms of this reaction are many. The parent may instil enormous ambition in the child in his effort to make a vicarious compensation for his own thwarted ambitions or he may destroy all hope of the child's achievement by constructing for himself and the child a fictitious method of attaining without struggle by means of air-castle building. He may, and he more often does, create in the child the idea that the parent is a martyr to the unfair treatment of his competitors until the child in his hero-worship mistakes weakness for strength.

The parent who is himself suffering from habits he cannot control or from a consciousness of past failure may war on tendencies toward similar behavior in the child and may by his severity lessen his own emotional tension.   In such cases the excessive reaction of the parent to the child's behavior is as likely to stimulate the child toward the undesirable trait as to warn him from it.   Even when the parent successfully kills all curiosity or inclination that would have led the child toward the thing forbidden the result is unwholesome since it produces unnecessary emotional attitudes and makes the personality of the child unbalanced and unreasonable throughout life in dealing with matters in any way related, or even apparently related, to the original problem.

The important thing about all such situations, a fact that the parent finds it so difficult to comprehend, is that in all home-relationships we have not an expression of something which we can call parental or filial attributes but of individual personalities which disclose themselves in opportunities furnished by the parental or child status.

In the case of serious dislike or incompatibility between parents the personality of the child runs the greatest risk of injury.   These clashings are, as has been said in the chapter on incompatibilities, the product of deep-seated mechanisms brought about by personal experiences.   It is never merely different opinions or tastes or desires but fundamentally unlike and discordant personalities that collide.   It is just this which makes family discord so serious, especially for the child.   The individuals at odds are driven to their collisions by the momentum of their different personalities.

The sex element involved in such conflicts is too important to be ignored.   Sex relationship would naturally have a large place in difficulties between husbands and wives because, in addition to the differing responses to sex experiences which would lead to emotional separation, there is likelihood that any alienation between the married couple will show at once in their sex behavior.   The large part that psychic attitudes play in all mature sex experience gives conflict in the home power to destroy in married persons all sex response so that marital relations become distasteful.

These are facts that must not be forgotten in the discussion of divorce.   The child suffers from the dissolution of the home

made by the court, but he also suffers and frequently suffers more *The child*
if he has to live with parents that are emotionally divorced and
unable to maintain a married comradeship even though they abide
under the same roof. Persistent stimulations originating in the
chronic discord of father and mother which has spoiled all hope
of marriage fellowship are constantly received by the child until his
personality is saturated with the poison of hate and anger frequently
discharged by his parents. To forbid separation only adds greater
force to the tension in the home. Family therapeutics demands a
positive attitude in such cases and the effort to bring about understanding and reconciliation through a scientific analysis of the
causes of the difficulty; if adjustment is impossible, a frank
recognition of this fact and a humane policy of matrimonial separation is for the advantage of husband, wife and especially children,
where they form a part of the family problem.

Family Problems of the Aged.—The conditions of modern
life that are expressing themselves in changes within the family
are making more difficult the family position of the aged and
especially of those who are dependent. The smaller house, the
transformation of the family from a rural producing unit to
a group of urban consumers, the rapid and radical changes in
manners, dress and social codes are widening the gulf between
the middle-aged son or daughter and the parent who has entered
old age. Differences of ideas as to how children should be brought
up easily lead to contention and even chronic hostility. The
burden—both social and economic—of the elderly is increasingly
irksome to ambitious as well as pleasure-loving offspring.

Some of our states have had to pass laws to protect parents when
old from being neglected by the children but the problem is not
easily disposed of by legislation. For example, a pathetic case was
recently heard in a Massachusetts court. Two grown-up children,
a son and a daughter, were charged with neglecting their mother.
The son admitted that he would not take his mother into his home
for if he did his wife would at once leave him. The wife, who was
present, admitted that what her husband had said was true but
defended herself by saying that the mother was a trouble-maker.
The daughter had no home and could not support her mother from
her small wages. The son was forced to contribute to his mother's

care but what it was reasonable to ask of him was far too little to give the mother adequate assistance and finally in spite of the court the problem was not satisfactorily solved.

The sad fact that this case illustrates is that the aged family member at times is literally a burden upon the family, perhaps even so disrupting an influence as to spoil the life of the home. In some cases the effort to be just to the aged prevents giving the young children of the family the opportunities they deserve and could otherwise have. This is especially true when medical science keeps alive, but helpless, aged people who have a chronic ailment that makes them both a trial and a burden to those responsible for their care.

Another type of family situation is found when the aged family-member, by controlling the purse strings, is able to dominate the others in the home and force them to conform to standards and conditions with which they have no real sympathy. The consequences of this unnatural family experience are dishonesty, inner strain, bitterness and loss of affection on the one side and suspicion and tyranny on the other.

In so far as science lengthens life and brings a larger proportion of the population to an advanced age, the larger must this family problem of the aged become. The weakening of family ties and the development of a keener desire for self-expression, both products of present-day social conditions, must tend to make the care of the aged within the home an ever-increasing problem of family adjustment.

The Rôle of the Parent.—Thanks to the new psychology, we have a better understanding of the difficulties of the parent's rôle and a clearer conception of its temptations. Were it not for this rapidly accumulating information, the task of getting parents to meet present-day responsibilities would be most discouraging. The former view that affection and general intelligence are quite enough to produce efficient parenthood has been proven most misleading. A parent equal to the demands put upon him by his child in these days must have some realization of the mistakes he is most likely to make, and the future of the home is bound up with the popularizing of this new knowledge so that it can influence the practices of all well-meaning parents.

The authority of the parent represents a temptation. No person receives power over others—especially over children who are relatively helpless in the hands of adults—without running risk of using the situation as a means of satisfying the subjective cravings of his own personality rather than ministering to the good of the individuals under his control.

The long-established tradition that makes obedience the chief virtue of the child opens up opportunity for a most mischievous dominance of the child by the parent. When fear in any form is made the motive for forcing upon the child conduct which he accepts merely because of superior force, the strength of the child's personality is threatened. When the command goes forth constantly as a fiat of the parent requiring no explanation or sympathetic interpretation so that the child's doings are a mere blind acceptance of authority, consisting of acts that in no degree issue from his own desires, the vitality of the child as expressed in initiative and curiosity is sapped and the home becomes a place where personality is more often slaughtered than developed.

The training that produces docile obedience spoils the child's native aggressiveness and leaves him to be easily beaten in the later competitions of life by minds superior only in their inner preparation. In other cases the child rebels against the parent's influence and suffers an unnecessary conflict between affection and the needs of self-expression which may make him unsocial in his attitude toward all authority or give him a stubborn intolerance in dealing with those who later come under his power.

The authority of the parent is a responsibility rather than a privilege. It is to be used as a means of wholesome growth for the child and not as a method by which power-loving persons obtain their much-desired social luxury of rule. Until the dangers of parental authority are generally recognized the home must continue to be for many children the place where their individuality is crushed by the exploitations of adults who use children to fatten their own weaknesses.

Another risk assumed by parents, which is not so commonly understood, is that of hurting their children by affection. Love-attitudes are the normal attributes of parents but even love has its dangers. Human experience has out-travelled the instinctive

14

basis upon which the parent's attachment to his child rests and so there is no automatic corrective of excessive and unwise affection of parent and offspring such as happens so naturally among the lower animals. Where instinct governs the relationship the regard of the parent usually lasts long enough to carry the offspring through the days of physical weakness; with the growth of the helpless animal the attachment dissolves and an independent existence of the offspring automatically starts.

With humans the love-attitude may persist in such a way that the child never actually matures and comes to have a fully developed self-life, or indulgence heaped upon the child by the parent may spoil the zest of life and keep the child emotionally infantile. He may become fixed upon the parent so that he is essentially parasitic in his inner emotional cravings and cannot maintain normal relationships in business, social contacts or later family life if ever he attempts to establish a home of his own.

Parental affection is not *per se* a morbid or undesirable influence in the development of a child. It is a necessary and wholesome contribution to the growing personality but it must not be excessive in expression, narrow and selfish in its spirit and demands, or self-seeking in its unwillingness to permit the final maturity of the child and the awakening of his need of affection from others and especially in due time from a sex-mate.

Psychological literature is replete with the dangers of unrestrained and irresponsible affection of parents in their treatment of children. Many parents neither see the necessity of allowing the child's love-attitudes to widen nor understand the tragedies that result from the child's fixations.

It is the proper business of the parent to assist the child in his endeavor to wean himself from the early dependence so satisfying to the parent who enjoys his opportunity of providing son or daughter with the emotional responses of affection.

The home that denies the child affection and crushes his cravings for tender emotion robs the personality of resources for life of the greatest importance to happiness. The two extremes of too much or too little affection of parents are equally harmful and both spoil character. Parents are not required to withhold or destroy or even to weaken affection but rather to control it as it enters the child's personality as a causal influence and to encourage the widening out of the child's sympathies and love.

Home Experience Compound.—The new psychology reveals on the plane of affection more complications than were formerly appreciated. For example, we are wont in our thinking of the relationship of parent and child to regard it as one either of affection or dislike, not realizing that the reciprocal contacts are compound rather than single experiences and permit at one and the same time both love and hate attitudes. In the past we have assumed that the predominating quality of such a relationship was its exclusive characteristic when as a matter of fact both hate and love reactions have come forth from the association. This double character of intimate association is a most important factor in family life and throws much light upon marriage and home interactions.

Thus even when there is a love attachment toward father or mother the child may come to have jealous feelings also because the parent appears to rival the child successfully in his craving for complete satisfaction in fellowship with the other and favorite parent. The child loves the father but hates him for being so intimate with the mother and having such a close comradeship. Parents by too open expression of their mutual affection can stimulate these feelings in the young child, who senses more of the happenings of the home than his elders suppose. The child also easily develops a love-and-hate-attitude toward his younger brother whose recent birth has upset the family concentration upon the older child.

Love-and-hate-tendencies appear even in parents with reference to one another and their children. A parent finds himself in competition with his own child in his desire to keep the monopoly of intense affection which he formerly enjoyed in his relations with his matrimonial partner. This experience is especially characteristic of men who feel the sudden change upon the part of the wife when she gives birth to her first child. Her affection for her husband immediately changes. It does not lessen necessarily but it is no longer so nearly an exclusive experience in her life. Under such circumstances the feeling of the father for the child may be almost, or altogether, hate but in less extreme and more common

cases the father senses a double reaction which signifies that he
has elements of love and of hate in his reaction to the baby.

Parents sometimes compete with each other for the child's love,
and this rivalry of the parents may bring about reactions of hate
in spite of a love attachment. Children also show jealousy when
they are in competition with each other for a parent's affection or
fellowship or when their contest is to gain a superior relationship
in their associations with a third child.

The Advantage of New Knowledge.—The first effects of
these discoveries of the complications of family interactions have
been in some parents depression and doubt. Modern life, it is well
to remember, has created no new tendencies in home contacts; the
problems under discussion have always concerned thoughtful
parents who have had insight into the difficulties of home association. The new factor is a better understanding of the mechanisms
involved in family reactions and this gift of recent science is not
a new burden on the parent but a source of help.

Understanding the meaning of the contradictory behavior of
child or parent helps those who have practical need of dealing with
family situations. A realization of the possibility of both hate-
and-love-feelings does even more than give assistance to those who
find themselves involved in the family's heterogeneous emotional
expressions; it keeps understanding persons from reacting emotionally to a situation that may grate upon them. He who is caught
in the emotional current may not at first sense his predicament,
and this blindness on his part makes it all the more necessary that
his family colleagues calmly review his plight and assist him by
tactful, patient interpretation instead of driving him more furi-
ously along his perilous course by attacking him emotionally and
thus increasing his feeling.

The home has had so little applied science brought within its
circle that many people at first react with suspicion and fear to the
discoveries that science is beginning to make in its effort to understand the functioning of the home. Since we must live through
home experiences as they actually are and not as our wishes would
paint them we must turn to science for help in meeting the tests
of home contacts.

Understanding the facts is the first step in dealing with any problem and this is just as true and no more true of family matters than of any other kind of difficulty. Both parent and child have nothing to lose and everything to gain by the entrance of science into the territory of the home, once the stronghold of sentiment and too often the prey of prejudice and ignorance. There is no need of exaggerating the help science at present can give the home but it is imperative, if we are to have families that can function for individual and social welfare, that parents should not resent or disregard the valuable information that is now being gathered by specialists in the investigation of the interactions of the family.

CHAPTER XIII

THE PARENT AND THE CHILD

Parenthood and Childhood More Difficult.—There can be no doubt that both parenthood and childhood are becoming increasingly difficult. The reasons for this are not hard to discover since it is due to the ways of living that are characteristic of our modern life, particularly in the cities. The family, like every other social institution, has been made more complicated by the development of modern civilization, especially its rapid advance during the last decade. Many of the problems that vex parents and add to the risks of childhood are caused by the complexities of life today.

It must not be thought that these changes in the family are found only among the well-to-do or within the cities. The poorest family is involved, and urban culture is no longer confined by city walls. It is useless to look backward and attempt any revival of the simpler family life of yesterday. The family itself could not be modified unless all the circumstances of our life were altered, and as these have come as a means of more thoroughly satisfying human cravings that have been aroused by invention, discovery, organization, and mechanical and social efficiency, nothing but a deterioration of civilization can possibly reduce life to a simpler form. The family must meet its present obligations, and this means that parenthood has to accept higher responsibilities.

If parenthood has become more exacting, childhood is even more influenced by current ways of living. Although it sometimes seems on the surface as if the child's life has been lightened, what has happened is that he has been relieved of most of the irksome toil that used to fall to him and has been placed for a longer period under the stimulation of an educational system more efficient than that of the past. It is true he has more opportunity but this must not hide the fact that his adjustments to meet this new condition are more difficult than when his life was lived on a lower plane. Moreover, in the outside world of his experiences away from the home and school he has the most fascinating kinds of stimulation offered him in a quantity that is wellnigh overwhelming. Much of this that he receives through commercial recreation is precocious in its effects upon him, unregulated by standards that would conserve child welfare, and so interesting as to occupy far too much of his attention. Even the school, which is taking over more and more of his time, in spite of the highest possible motives and a desire to give him the largest self-expression compatible with the directing of his mental life, is an institution that demands complicated adjustment, and therefore does not always act in harmony with the child's needs.

His life is played upon by so many opposing forces, each attempting to impel him toward some definite goal, that he is increasingly dominated by nervous tension as troublesome for him as the complexities of life are for the adult. His mistakes may easily be more costly than those of the adult because so much of his later life is involved in his present choices; for example, if he prematurely leaves school because he finds the educational program offered him distasteful, his whole future development becomes hazardous beyond anything possible to an adult as a result of a change of occupation. So far as the child is concerned he is changing only from one kind of work to another; so far as his future is concerned he is accepting a limitation which, without heroic effort on his part, will later automatically shut him out from many of the opportunities of life.

Advantages of New Knowledge.—From the very first human thinking has naturally emphasized various forms of dualism. Much of our progress comes from reaction to the evils involved in progress already made. Many of our evils result from our not taking advantage of the new opportunities presented. This is exactly the situation with reference to the present family. Science, the creator of the modern world, has given us the complications that are loading parents and children with their present burdens. Science has thrown into our life abounding luxuries, the decrease of the working day, such recent inventions as the automobile and the radio, and makes even the poorest a sharer of enjoyments that the most wealthy and powerful in earlier times never had.

It is to this same science that we must look for the help that parent and child need in steering a safe course through the channel of modern society. Fortunately science is advancing rapidly in this realm even if it has not yet caught up with the strides of material science. From the laboratory, the clinic, the scientific observer and counselor an immense amount of valuable experience is being gathered, most pertinent for both parent and child. The task now is the bringing of this help to the average parent and making him feel that mere traditional attitudes in accord with his own child-hood experiences or in reaction against them are not sufficient for the management of his home.

The problem is nothing new for one area of experience after another has been drawn into the domain of applied science by the loosening of habits of thinking and acting built upon tradition. Agriculture presents one of the most inspiring histories of such a change; even during the last generation in sections of our own country the industry of farming has been transformed from a purely traditional occupation into one largely established upon the teaching of experimental science. Indeed in backward regions this same process of changing the farmer's attitude to conform to the more scientific era in which he lives as compared with his fore-fathers is still going on.

The fact that human relationships are more complex than those of plants or animals and always involve the emotional reac-tions of the persons concerned makes it evident that we can never ask parenthood to be scientific in the impersonal way that is char-acteristic of man in other activities. But the rigid procedure re-quired in producing a chemical compound is not needed in dealing with children. An attempt to manipulate children as if they were mere substances will not only fail but will throw discredit upon those who carry out such a program in the belief that this is follow-ing science. The scientific knowledge coming to us from physiology, psychology, sociology and psychiatry is changing very rapidly, but without great violence, our past ideas of the obligations of parents and the needs of children. Difficult as it is to connect this material and separate true conclusions from the false so as to bring to the parent what is of value in the form that will be intelligible and useful, the hope of the family absolutely depends upon this being done and there is no other possible source of help for either parent or child.

Preachments are ineffective since they only point to goals and do not provide knowledge of methods. It is the way of accomplishment that presents difficulties. Programs built upon the experience of parents under different circumstances are bound to prove hopeless when tested by the actual experience of the present day. It is most fortunate for the family and for the child that we not only have the beginning of a science of child-training, coming from various sections of scientific investigation, which has been from its origin practical in its point of view; we also have effective means of bringing this to the attention of people, and as the information accumulates and its need becomes more evident we shall develop even better means of popularizing it.

The Child the Battleground.—The statements coming from science that are of value for the parent and child cannot at present be formulated as if they represented a final attainment. It is the nature of science to be forever reaching forward, correcting its mistakes, making new discoveries, obtaining new conquests. It is merely mischievous dogmatism which leads some interpreters of our present psychological and sociological sciences to formulate their teachings with finality. We are nevertheless in possession of facts that are of the greatest value for parents, teachers and all who deal with children. Much of this material is just a more accurate understanding of the reasons for principles that, embedded in proverbs, have been commonly applied to the care of children for centuries.

Our modern science shows us that childhood is largely a battleground. It also discloses that this ordeal which every child passes through as he goes on toward maturity is most significant on account of its influence over the whole period of life. Better knowledge of heredity stresses more and more the determining influences of the social environment in producing from the hereditary possibilities those qualities of personality that are actually expressed and made permanent parts of a human being.[1] Thus the old statement that

---

[1] Jennings, H. S., "Heredity and Environment," *Scientific Monthly*, September, 1924, pp. 225–238.

"As the twig is bent the tree inclines" is getting its full significance revealed by the more exact knowledge of science.

Recent science is also disclosing the central point of difficulty in this important period of human life. It is the child's emotions that are the disturbing element, as is true in the critical problems of the adult. The emotions draw up the demands that the child makes upon his environment. He comes to his contacts with a host of desires clamoring for satisfaction; this constitutes his emotional equipment. His emotions attempt to reject those things that appear in opposition to his desires or he tries to color the meaning of discordant experiences so that the emotional satisfaction can remain undisturbed. The emotions that drive the child to look for satisfactions from his environment, or that come as the result of the clashes between what he wants and what he gets, are ever entering in conflict with the rigid facts of the child's surroundings, composed of things and other people.

This forms the basis of a perpetual conflict between the impulses of the child, the fundamental element upon which the emotions rest, and the environment, which must grant or deny the child's desires. The situation is much more complicated than such a statement suggests. The impulses that send the child to his environment and make him react emotionally to his experiences are themselves products of environmental stimulation. What happens to him makes him wish other things to happen, and the desires that appear to him to be so spontaneous are largely registrations of his social contacts under stimulations that play upon him. He is not only pushed first in one direction and then in another, but is driven strongly in several directions at once. It is just here that the parent comes to have such a determining influence since, by manipulating stimulation, he partially controls the environment from which the child gets his desires, and the parent is himself in no inconsiderable degree the child's environment. The younger the child, the more the parent means as an originating source of stimulation.

What is true of the parent is to a lesser extent true of other individuals with whom the child later comes in contact. Each one that touches his life becomes a source of reaction and stimulation. It must not be thought, however, that the people who have to do with the child merely stimulate to activity; they also have a negative influence and act as inhibitors either by the method of stimulating the child away from desired activity or by forcefully blocking his desires so that the influence of these individuals is felt by the child as a conscious pressure.

The child soon learns that there is disagreement among the adults that try to control him and still greater disagreement between the demands put upon him by adults and those of his own playmates. He is in a perpetual conflict of opposing stimulations by which he gets his development. The variations that he discovers bother him more because at first his life is a struggle for consistency. It is only when he has been trained to see the impossibility of a perfectly ordered life that he gets the compartment relief which is so characteristic of adults. The adult responds to differing sets of stimuli, passing quickly from one type of expression to another. The most consistent person practices this rapid transformation somewhat; the highly susceptible and the inherently dishonest carry the same tendency to great length. Modern life is organized for the adult in harmony with this compartment attitude, but the child does not realize this fact and thus his struggles of adjustment are intensified by his hopeless attempt to build up a consistent system of reactions.

The situation of the child reveals the futility in these days of a dominantly repressive program. It is one thing to prevent stimulations from originating; it is quite another to prevent their expression once they have started as a result of environmental contact. The impulses cannot be blocked without much greater difficulty than they can be headed off at the start. It is not only an economy but a far more effective program for the parent to make his control largely positive. In the place of undesirable activities he must if possible put others that are wholesome and can satisfy the child's desires. At every point the program must be as constructive as it can be made. This, of course, does not mean that the child is to have right of way but simply that his life must be thought of in the same way that we think of our own, as a life of expression rather than repression. Only so can the parents exercise their fundamental control in this era when our social surplus makes self-expression the normal goal.

The parent must be looking forward always to the time when the child will be obliged to make choices and meet difficulties by himself. It is impossible to give the child the preparation for life that science knows is necessary, by any rigid system of prohibitions; he must be gradually taught to choose wisely unaided. This requires patience in the parent and skill in bringing to the child opportunities for choice and at the same time revealing values so as to construct an inner self whose impulses will more and more press forward to the things that are desirable; the final end must be self-control and childhood must be thought of as a training-place for this.

The child's natural impulse to do for himself and his hostility to manipulation and coercion must be taken advantage of in working toward the goal of self-reliance. If the parent steadily keeps his eye upon his aim, the means suggest themselves in the daily experiences of the child. The more the child can do for himself without hurt to his essential good, the more opportunity must be provided by the parent and teacher for free expression. No matter what his policy, the parent must not forget that he cannot in days like ours have the amount of supervision of his child's life that was possible to his own parents and more particularly to his grandparents.

The child of today cannot have any safety in meeting the ordeal of life unless he be made inwardly safe by the policy of the parent who uses his opportunities not merely to control the child but to control him by enlisting his sympathy with the purposes of the parent. There must be an alliance of coöperation in which the parent exercises leadership rather than dominance. Under present circumstances there can be no other pathway to wholesome character. The centre of control must finally be within and we have every reason to suppose that the future development of society will make this more true than at present.

Need of Wholesome Parenthood.—Since the parent has and must continue to have the largest opportunity to influence the child unless the family life is radically changed from what has been for centuries, efficient parenthood becomes a social necessity. No society can expect to make social progress without improving the conditions of family life.   This is particularly true in the United States, where the home has been struck by the full force of modern scientific culture.   Here at least the home lags behind in its adaptability to modern conditions.

The standards of parenthood must be lifted; otherwise the opportunity that is given to the child by modern civilization will to a large extent prove detrimental rather than helpful.   Parenthood cannot be detached from the educating influences that surround the child.   The training of parents to meet their responsibilities in the light of such science as we now have is necessary to complete our educational program.   It is natural enough that the family should be the last educational influence operating upon the child to be consciously organized, since it is the most difficult.   The development of the public school and the increased emphasis placed upon it as a means of conserving wholesome social life necessarily leads backward to the home, as experience demonstrates clearly that the school cannot do its part unless it has the intelligent coöperation of the home, and particularly an understanding on the part of parents of the socially determining influences of the early years of home life.

The Risks of Parents.—Although good parents cannot be made a matter of formula, it is not hard to discover the points where parents are most liable to fail in their treatment of the child. One of the outstanding difficulties is the ever-present tendency of adults and especially parents to become impatient with a child's consciously organized, since it is the most difficult.   The develop- for life makes them over-anxious to bring him quickly to certain attainments which the parents feel are desirable, and in consequence there is the inevitable emphasis on drill as a quicker process than the slower cultivation of inner attitudes that will afford root for the practices that the parents wish. Childhood is not a passageway through which a child must be rushed that he may the more quickly reach the goals that have been placed ahead of him; it is an opportunity for nurture.   Parents waste great effort, alienate their children, and mar the lives of those whom they wish most to help, by struggling to get prematurely reactions the child must be allowed to grow into if there is to be any substance behind his behavior.

Modern child study has for all time removed the notion once common that character can be made by a molding process. In a static social life it is possible to harden the child into certain patterns by drill and punishment; in our time to make such an attempt in childhood results in either producing a child utterly unfit to live in the adult period a life successfully adapted to changing social conditions or it brings about a diametrically different kind of person than the parent was trying to produce.

Another fault of which we hear much as the result of our better knowledge of childhood is committed by the best intentioned parents; it is that of trying to hold back the child's development. As a rule this retarding process affects chiefly the emotions of the child; it appears most commonly in the form of fixation, which is a consequence of the way the child has been treated. His personality is welded into the life of the father or mother through the use of his natural affection to such an extent that he finds it difficult to develop his own individual characteristics. He leans on his parent, more frequently his mother, in much the same way he did as a little child, although constantly advancing in intellectual knowledge and accumulating his own desires. As a result not only does he often fail to meet adequately the circumstances of his life which require of him an expression of his own personality, but he is constantly torn from within by two well-organized sets of conflicting ideas. On the one side are the natural impulses to develop independence which, because of the way he has been trained, mean for him an emotional separation between himself and the parent whom he loves; and on the other side is a continuation of the parasitic habit he has established of leaning constantly upon another. Usually he finds it impossible to commit himself thoroughly to either policy. Much of the energy of his life is dissipated in a useless struggle between wishing to grow up and being unequal to the task.

The size of the modern family and the greater amount of leisure with its tendency to sharpen the sensibilities make fixation a much commoner family fault than it has been in the past. Even when parents have tended toward habits that logically lead toward fixation on the part of the child, this has been largely corrected by the fact that in the family have been several children. In a home where there are four or five children few parents have had any opportunity to indulge their dangerous inclination to the extent of seriously hurting a child. Even when they have concentrated their affection upon a particular child he has somewhat escaped the consequences of this from his constant association with his brothers and sisters, who have counteracted the influence of the parent.

The larger place that fixation now holds as a parenthood problem is perhaps not so much due to a change in the disposition of parents as to the greater opportunity provided by our small families, especially in cases where there is only one child, with a natural increase in the solicitousness of the parents. We have every reason to suppose that the family of the future will commonly be small; the risk of fixation is therefore a danger that the parent must be prepared to recognize and trained to avoid. The parent's emotions run so strongly with reference to this situation that it is not at all difficult for him to deceive himself and assume that he is permitting the child to escape from his clutches, while at the same time in actual practice he is doing everything possible to make the child a victim of his indulgent affection. The good parent must be ready to guide his child from the very first to the normal impulses that, arising in the child and pressing toward independence, bring about the development of a self-reliant, autonomous personality.

Fortunately for human happiness the child's attainment of full maturity is not necessarily at the expense of a break in the affection between parent and child. Certainly children need abundant fellowship with their parents, provided this be an interpretive and stimulating rather than a dominating association. The neglected child who is thrown almost wholly on his own resources, has no real comradeship with either father or mother, and is made an emotional orphan, even though he escapes all risk of fixation, suffers a deprivation which, whether it be a conscious loneliness or not, means that he has inadequate parental help in the formative years of childhood.

It is the child's right, because it is his need, to have from the parent a contact which is something more than simply physical proximity. He must have inspiration from the parent that he may have incentive to develop his resources, understanding that he may be given assistance in his inevitable struggles toward maturity; he most especially needs a personality toward whom his affection can flow. The crushing effect of the short-sighted, neurotic parent who cannot see his child grow up and develop self-support must not blind us to the equally obvious fact that no child goes safely through childhood unblighted by his experience if denied parental affection.

The home is a social institution which has developed to satisfy human need; if it is to function there must be affectionate association between the child and the parent, not only for the sake of the child, but also for the parents. They cannot have the full taste of human satisfactions without this interplay of affection. Just how large a place in the evolutionary process this parental love has had in developing the social qualities that we prize, it is not possible to know. The indispensable place of sympathy and other social qualities, in part at least, derivative from mother love show us that even from the point of view of racial perpetuation the experience of parental attachment has made an indispensable contribution. If Henry Drummond's theory of the ascent of man has exaggerated the place of mother-love in biological survival, the social significance of parental affection is not to be questioned. The temptations that it brings the parent toward over-indulgence give testimony to the depth of human satisfaction it provides.

Certain social qualities that are desperately needed in modern life are stimulated in parents by their association with children. Mistakes are always more easily seen than opportunities, and this accounts for the fact that our modern psychology is at present emphasizing the danger of parental fixation more than the need of the child's receiving wholesome comradeship. Serious pathological cases more commonly reveal the risk of parents doing too much than the opposite mistake of denying the child a reasonable amount of fellowship. The observer of the average family life of to-day in this country cannot, however, fail to notice that one of the great dangers is the preoccupation of parents who are content to let their children form all their significant contacts after the very early years of infancy with persons outside the home circle. There is nothing in recent psychology that encourages this sort of family neglect. On the other hand sociology is replete with illustrations of the bad social consequences that come to homes where the parents have made no investment of themselves in time and sympathy through fellowship with the growing boy or girl.

The Goals of Childhood.—A positive program of child-training will put stress upon the goals of childhood rather than upon hard and fast rules of procedure. One of the conditions of normal childhood is giving to the child at every stage of his growth the joy of life. A physically well, rightly treated, socially secure child is naturally happy. Adult memory so falsifies past experience as one looks backward to his earlier years that one is likely to forget how easy it is for childhood not always to be happy, indeed how inevitable certain experiences of tragic character are in every child's career. No parent has full control over such circumstances, but he must have the disposition, if he is to be efficient at all as a parent, to make the child love life. The tendency toward youthful, even childhood, suicide in our country should attract attention. The burden of life is felt by the more serious kind of adolescent. It is at this period that the child is most affected by the collisions that come between his own desires and the will of his parents and the other adults who try to control him. The physical changes going on in his body also influence his reactions to life. Passing through the storm and stress of these experiences of mind and body it is not strange that his philosophy at times takes on a tinge of melancholy.

A second goal, which has already been discussed, is that of inner self-control. To bring it about the adult must plan to retreat from the child's life from the very beginning, gradually leaving as the child matures and proves himself able to assume responsibility. Sometimes a child can be given considerable freedom with reference to certain activities, but must have less in regard to others, as, for example, he may be trusted to maintain good physical habits while requiring supervision concerning his recreation. Of course each child has to be treated by himself. The parent finds in actual experience that he cannot use the same policy for his different children.

Another important goal, which modern psychology is constantly emphasizing, is the need of the child's passing through his early years without accumulating any morbidity. There are three

15

dangers at this point that are common enough to demand attention. One is fear. Even those who consider fear a necessary part of childhood development agree that it can easily be made morbid, and that it has a baneful influence over the life of the individual who comes under its dominance. Parents surely should protect their children from fear as much as possible. Fear control is the most unwise method of disciplining the child.

Danger must be taught, and in these days of the automobile must be taught early. It should, however, be taught with calmness and as far as may be without exciting the emotional reactions that are the characteristics of true fear. Those who stress fear as a means of protecting the child from danger forget that by accident or even by the strange fascination that fear sometimes exercises the child may find himself in the place of danger. Then the strong emotion that has been created will act adversely in enough cases to make this a very foolish method of protecting the child even from danger. The paralyzing effect of severe fear may make it impossible for the child to escape from a menacing situation from which a child free from panic could easily flee.

Curiosity is another attitude of the child that can easily become morbid. Such a result is due to the parent's allowing the child's curiosity to be stimulated and at the same time blocked. The parent's attitude, particularly with reference to matters of sex, is often itself the stimulating influence that operates upon the child, while the parent's reticence is repressive and leads to a morbid curiosity which apparently in some cases continues into adult life and becomes a social menace. Undoubtedly there are forms of vice and criminal behavior that go down, as far as psychic cause is concerned, to early experiences of intense curiosity.

A more common form of morbid reaction in our day, due to the competitions and constant tendency in schools and homes to compare and standardize children, is an exaggerated sense of insufficiency which we call the inferiority complex. As opportunity becomes more widespread and the struggle for success and distinction unhampered by the acceptance of class restrictions, the risk of developing an inferiority complex, both for adult and child, becomes correspondingly greater. It appears that the childhood period is more likely to develop the inferiority complex, although, once made a part of the personality, adult experience furnishes innumerable ways by which it can be intensified and expressed.

The craving for power which is called by some psychiatrists the will-to-power is a characteristic human craving. Modern American life has tended to emphasize it by magnifying the competitive and acquisitive motives. The parent must not only guard himself against making appeals to the child that will encourage inferiority attitudes, as for instance, adversely criticizing one child constantly or praising one much more than another; the parent must also be quick to discover the coming of an inferiority reaction, from whatever source it originates, and, by providing the child with some opportunity for establishing self-confidence that will remove the stings of his real or fictitious failure, keep the inferiority complex from becoming chronic.

Modern psychology is also making clear the constant risk that the child, to protect himself from the unpleasantness of his real environment, may construct a world of daydreams which will enfeeble him in his actual responsibilities. The moral waste of personalities unable to face the actualities of life is a practically new discovery of our modern science. We now know what has been one of the most retarding of human weaknesses. We realize why so much apparently good enthusiasm has never proved of social service. Without forgetting the value of creative art or the therapeutic significance of the imagination it is necessary for the parent to teach the child to face actual facts squarely. If he is to meet his environment in this wholesome way, it must not be made too stern a reality for him to accept. In no place can the parent serve the child more wisely than by introducing the every-day world in such a fashion as to make it seem to the child both real and inviting.

If the harsh program of making the child push his way violently into an environment so distasteful as to sap him of his courage is forced upon him, the result is bound to be in many cases a looking to the world of fancy for relief. With the moving-picture opening an entrance for the child's fancy that captivates the most prosaic type it is not difficult for any child overwhelmed by the burdens of his environment to escape reality by developing the day-dreaming habit. The child needs to be thoroughly cognizant of the fact that the mischief comes when he imagines himself doing or being what he is unwilling to attempt to do or be. In other words, the moral risk is a substitution of fancy for real experience. By keeping this in mind the parent can easily distinguish the creative and recreational use of the imagination from its morbid expression.

Another goal that the parent is not free to forget if he is to bring his child to full maturity is the necessity of building up in the child confidence in moral principles rather than in rules of conduct that are purely traditional and are maintained by the dogmatic assertion of the parent. In a changing civilization such as ours moral progress demands a constant change of behavior; the principles of moral conduct afford a safe foundation, but in the midst of shifting standards it is easier for the parent merely to give the child a set of habits in conformity to the usual doings of his time and place. If he does nothing more, he leaves the child to the mercy of future disturbances when for the first time he comes in contact with different customs or moral circumstances that require something more than inflexible traditions. If the child is to go out from the home eventually able to adapt himself to the moral demands made of him in a future which the parent could only partially anticipate, at best, he must have the rock-bottom moral basis which comes from a sense of security that principles rather than rules or habits produce. Nowhere so much as in dealing with the moral problems of his maturing child must the parent realize that he lives in the present and that the child in his maturity is to live in the future.

CHAPTER XIV

SOCIAL PROBLEMS RELATED TO FAMILY LIFE

Poverty in Its Relation to Family Life.—Poverty makes impossible a satisfactory family life. It is true, as workers with the poor have so often testified, that we frequently find in families suffering from poverty intense sympathy and a sacrificial spirit. One who is familiar with families that have suffered economic disaster knows that a proportion of such homes express in their misfortune a magnificent courage and loyalty that intensify family spirit. Inwardly however, unless the family is able to crawl out of its predicament the dire effects of its low standards of living are shown in the life of the home.

Although it is clear that poverty blights family life, it is impossible to state accurately the extent to which poverty in the United States menaces good home life. This is not only because of the difficulty of getting reliable statistics concerning poverty in this country but also because of the task one encounters who attempts to define poverty in order to measure it. In the Chicago Standard Budget for Dependent Families appears a very careful and detailed statement of the minimum normal standard of living, which is defined as follows: " The minimum normal standard must furnish everything necessary for a manner of living that will make possible a high standard of physical, mental and normal health and efficiency for adults, the full physical and mental growth and development of children, and provision for their normal welfare."

No one at all familiar with our actual social conditions can doubt that we have a considerable number of families, both in cities and in the country, who because of inadequate income cannot maintain a normal standard of living. When a student of the family attempts to discover how large a proportion of our population is made up of such families, he has to be content with estimates that show considerable variation. For example, Parmelee judges that if we assume that all, or the majority, of the families of this country are supported by one male adult wage-earner, then at least one-half, and probably more than half, of the families in this country are in a state of poverty.[1] Robert Hunter in his book entitled "Poverty," published in 1904, stated that there were not less than four million of our population living in poverty and he regarded ten million as the more probable number. Professor Ely of the University of Wisconsin and others have estimated that about four per cent of our people are in poverty. Poverty in its family aspects cannot be satisfactorily treated on the basis of mere income. In the effort to discover whether an individual family has adequate financial resources, many factors have to be taken into account. Some of these are: the place where the family lives, whether in the city or a rural district and in what section of the country, the size of the family and the ages of the children, the family habits and particularly the housekeeping skill of the mother. It is also true that bad family life and poverty are so interlinked that it is difficult to find out which is cause and which is result. In many cases they are both products of other causes, such as feeblemindedness, disease, ignorance or psychopathic personality.

At no time in the past and in no other place in the world have the material standards of family life reached the high level that now exists in the United States. The general trend appears to be toward still higher standards. This is as it should be, for in a country as rich as ours in natural resources, enjoying the advantages of twentieth century science, an increasing rather than a decreasing poverty would represent a pathological condition in our national life. Nevertheless, in spite of our great wealth and the progress that is being made in its more equitable distribution we have an immense number of families that suffer from poverty. In whatever form the unsatisfactory home life of such families expresses itself, the essential problem remains economic, and therefore, an adequate income is a prerequisite of satisfactory family experience.

In helping the family that suffers from chronic poverty to get over its difficulties it is not enough to provide for the breadwinner earnings that are sufficient to support the family; it is also necessary that the income be spent wisely, for the margin of safety of

[1] "Poverty and Social Progress," p. 93.

a family is so slight that unwise expenditures force the home
ck into the poverty from which it is attempting to emerge. Fam-
y poverty, therefore, has both its economic and its social aspects.

Housing.—A house is not a home, but housing conditions
fundamentally influence home life. There are, as every social
worker knows, individuals who are equal to the seemingly impossible task of creating a fine type of home in spite of wretched
quarters, a social miracle too much to expect of many mothers and
fathers. Moreover, it is contrary to public policy to permit home-
loving people to struggle against such obstacles. The majority of
slum-dwellers show the bad effects of their miserable surroundings
more clearly in their home-life than in anything else. A suitable
dwelling-place is the first demand of those who would build up a
home. Good housing will not create a satisfactory home, but bad
housing entails conditions that make it easy for the home to fail
and difficult for it to succeed.

If one realizes the significance of bad housing conditions upon
the life of the home, travel in almost any section of our country
through cities, villages and even rural districts starts serious and
depressing thoughts as one looks out upon the dismal city tenement
with its narrow iron balcony filled with airing bedclothes or
crammed with small children, the dilapidated village dwelling
which is actually worse inside than its outside shell suggests, or
the unpainted rural shack, often as crowded and dirty and sometimes even as insanitary as the eighteenth century slums of London.

The housing problem may be considered as having two sides.
In its positive aspects it represents the attempt to provide decent
housing conditions for those who wish for themselves and their
children a proper home life; on the negative side the housing problem presents the task of finding means to prevent those who prefer
a low type of family life or who, left to themselves, could achieve
nothing better, from becoming a social menace. From whatever
angle one views it, housing becomes a community problem, not a
matter of mere individual taste as the complacent American is so
likely to regard it. The influence of its homes appears at once in the
social life of every community, and housing conditions have a
determining effect upon the home. It is as contrary to public policy

to tolerate the slums as it is to permit a carrier of disease infec
to deliver milk; the one attacks the home, the other, the body. ',
difference in public attitude is primarily due to the more wid
spread knowledge of the danger of the spread of disease, througi
the popularizing of the sciences of bacteriology and sanitation.

In the attack upon bad housing conditions in the United States,
especially in the cities, progress has been made. Our largest city,
New York, furnishes perhaps the best illustration. Attention
appears first to have been consciously directed to the housing
problem in New York City after the war of 1812 as a consequence
of an increase in immigration, and warning of the danger of disease from the Health Department. Several investigations were
made of housing conditions in the city and various efforts were put
forth to combat existing evils. After the Civil War when conditions
were getting worse a death rate of 35.32 in 1865 led to a careful
investigation by the Council of Hygiene and Public Health, a
citizens' association of New York, and the discovery of most appall-
ing conditions. This publicity brought about the establishment of
the present Department of Health in 1866, and the passage of the
first tenement-house law in the following year.[2]

If New York City because of its size and congestion has furnished the most spectacular problem, it has merely disclosed on a
larger scale bad housing conditions that have existed in all our
cities. The attack on housing evils has also been similar in our
various cities. We have had investigations by public officials and
private agencies, surveys, publicity, attempts to get improved legislation through state and city government against the opposition of
vested interests that feared a loss of profit as a consequence of
housing reform. For example, it still gives an unpleasant shock
to learn that the Trinity Church Corporation carried on in the
court until 1895 its opposition to the provisions of the New York
Tenement-house Act of 1887 requiring running water on each floor
of a tenement-house.

During the World War a new departure was made in the effort
for good housing. The concentration of workers in certain localities where manufacturing essential to the prosecution of the war

[2] Wood, E. E., "Housing and the Unskilled Wage-earner," pp. 35–37.

was carried on led to such a shortage of houses that government assistance became necessary. Appropriations were made as an emergency war measure and building programs on a large scale were put into execution at places where war-materials were being extensively manufactured. Although this policy of the government attracted national attention to the housing problem it did not have as beneficial effects as some prophesied. American public opinion is still largely indifferent to bad housing and in dealing with this particular evil our nation is backward in comparison with many of the countries of Europe.

In recent years, due to the increase in rents, the high cost of building, and the lessening of the construction of dwelling-houses, housing has become a matter of anxious concern not only to the poor but also to people of moderate means. It is the belief of many that the movement for better houses has actually slipped backward. The shortage of dwelling-places is felt most acutely in our cities; on the other hand in some of our villages where there have been industrial changes, as mills have curtailed production or moved away to more favorable localities, the quantity of houses that are for rent or for sale present the opposite type of problem.

Dr. Edith E. Wood, authority on American housing conditions, estimates that about one-third of the people of the United States are living in subnormal housing conditions and that about one-tenth are in circumstances that menace their health, morals and family life.[3]

One of the most serious results of our housing situation is the falling off in home ownership; this decrease has been going on since 1900. The conditions in our cities of 100,000 or more population have not been the same everywhere; some have had an increase, some a decrease in home ownership, but it is stated that in every one of these cities there has been a striking decrease in the number of persons owning their homes free from debt.[4] The trend is unfortunate, for home ownership encourages attitudes of social value. He who owns his house has an incentive to be interested in the community. Ownership also shows its influence in subtle ways in family life: the children are more apt to be

---

[3] *Ibid.*, p. 7.
[4] " Conference of Social Work," 1923, p. 345.

taught the value of property, neighborhood contacts are regarded more seriously, the home is more likely to reflect a sense of permanency and self-respect than when the family merely rents. A decrease in home ownership tends toward greater social restlessness and instability.

The housing problem is of concern to the family along other lines than those of health and comfort. The home that is forced to exist in bad quarters is undermined in every aspect of its life. The proper privacy is denied, family clashing is fostered, the right relationship between parents and children becomes more difficult, slovenly habits are stimulated, a sense of shame smothers family loyalty, and the ambitious come to feel that the home represents an obstacle to success. The young man and woman seek their pleasures as much as possible apart from the wretched home surroundings and at the first opportunity slip from the home to try to hide their family connections as something that brings them disgrace.

A student friend was recently given an interesting illustration of the young person's reaction to bad home conditions. Meeting at a church entertainment in a mill-town a rather attractive working girl, he asked permission to escort her to her home. She led him to the better residential section of the town and bade him goodnight at the gateway of a substantial middle-class home. Somehow he became suspicious that this was not the place where she really lived and he loitered near, soon to discover that she went only part way up the path, turned about and retraced her steps to the street and then hurried homeward. My friend followed, and when she reached her house fully understood why she had been unwilling to let him see where she lived. The house was one of those box-like two-family dwellings so frequently found in mill-towns, bare and uninviting on the outside, distinguishable from twenty others only by its individual number over the porch door.

Bad housing lifts the death rate, especially of children, provides breeding-places for disease, develops and attracts vice, establishes anti-social attitudes and, most serious of all, crushes the inner life of the family and makes the home an affliction difficult to endure.

Roomers.—A considerable part of the population of our American cities live a life practically destitute of family experience; they are renters of furnished rooms. When they are through with their day's work it may be said that they start homeward, but the statement is euphemistic for actually many of them seek their sleeping-place and change from their working-clothes to seek the recreation of the city streets. Their existence as roomers does not give them even a semblance of family life. Of all city-dwellers, they are the farthest removed from the atmosphere of a normal home, birds-of-passage in the highest degree free from social responsibility. The extreme mobility of the rooming population (for we are told that in a typical section the whole population is turned over every four months) provides little opportunity in the area where he has sleeping-quarters, for the roomer to break away from his social isolation; he lives an anonymous existence, often not having even a speaking acquaintance with those who seek shelter under the same roof, and feeling that nobody knows or cares what he does. Roomers come and go with such rapidity that they do not develop even what the sociologist would call " secondary contacts," but experience merely personal proximity.

An investigation of a rooming-house area on the lower North Side of Chicago was summarized in a most interesting report, replete with meaning for the student of the family, at the twentieth meeting of the American Sociological Society. In that section 20,007 people were living in various sorts of furnished rooms. Ninety blocks in the better rooming area were studied intensively by a house-to-house census. Seventy-one per cent. of all the houses in the district took roomers, and the renters of these rooms were fifty-two per cent. single men and ten per cent. single women; thirty-eight per cent. were couples, supposedly married, but actually sixty per cent. of these were maintaining a companionate merely upon mutual consent.[5]

The study of this Chicago district reveals the social strain and the moral risk of an existence so empty of permanent ties and home satisfactions. Even suicide, we are told, becomes a way of relief for some; others turn to daydreaming and fiction. This explains

---

[5] Zorbaugh, " The Dweller in Furnished Rooms, an Urban Type," *American Journal of Sociology*, July, 1926.

in part the large circulation of highly colored romantic magazines of the cheaper sort. Some roomers get rid of their loneliness by starting a companionship with a member of the opposite sex in the same predicament, an association which, however intimate it may become, is understood by both not to contemplate ending in matrimony. There are those, also, who find substitutes for their human craving for friendship in animal pets, most often canary birds, parrots, dogs and cats.

This problem brings out clearly the strength of the human impulses that make future parenthood attractive, and demonstrates the bad effect of denying or starving out the almost universal yearnings for contact with home life.

Illegitimacy.—Unmarried motherhood presents another problem that is of significance to the family. Illegitimacy represents an abortive type of family life which has all the misfortunes of a home without a father, and other handicaps in addition. The plight of a woman who brings a child into the world without the prospect of a home of her own for its protection is sad enough without the cruelties that society in the recent past has been wont to heap upon her and her offspring.

Our changing social policy regarding illegitimacy is evidence of an increasing sense of the meaning of motherhood as an achievement in our interpretation of human values. The present trend is away from the brutal treatment of the unmarried mother which used to be dealt out in blind confidence by those who supposed that their severity was the best means of protecting society from the birth of illegitimate children. Thanks to the new psychology, we now recognize that this old program of harshness was to many individuals a subtle source of pleasure. Fortunately, we are now moving not in the direction of a sentimental attitude with reference to the offender, but toward an understanding of her situation and an effort to help her return if possible to a normal status in society.

The new policy does not permit attempting to solve the problem by a forced marriage in the reckless manner of the past, when the guilty man was commanded to choose between jail and marriage, with the consequence that the family life begun so hopelessly all too often ended either in divorce or in desertion. The modern method of dealing with illegitimacy as a conduct-problem rather than an act betraying social viciousness is both more humane and successful, judged by its results, than was the vindictive policy which was so apt to chastise the woman while allowing the man to escape all punishment.

The effort to handle cases of unmarried motherhood as special and difficult problems of adjustment is the only proper scientific procedure and is socially just, since an analysis of the facts of illegitimacy, by revealing the situations that encourage unmarried motherhood, more often shows the woman to have been weak or exploited than a person of evil intent.

The tendency is at present, as recent legislation proves, to make the father of the illegitimate child more responsible. The tightening up of the law appears particularly in the effort to require the man to provide for the support of the child. The purpose of the non-support laws already passed and the still more stringent ones advocated is socially justified, but the complexities of the problem of illegitimacy, including the possibility of false accusation and the great difficulty in many cases of proving the paternity, make it evident that we must not expect legislation by itself to solve all the practical problems of illegitimacy.

It is easy to overestimate the change that has taken place with reference to illegitimacy. The majority of people still react to actual cases of illegitimacy in the cruel manner of the past, although usually the manner of their expression is somewhat milder. It is easy for the student of the problem in sympathy with the scientific attitude to overestimate the change of thought in regard to illegitimacy. It is not difficult to find isolated rural communities where there has been no departure at all from the spirit of vengeance that Hawthorne gives a Puritan setting in " The Scarlet Letter."

Illegitimacy is doubly related to a discussion of the social problems of the home. On the one side illegitimacy involves practical questions regarding the mother and child. Shall the mother keep her child? If not, shall the child be legally adopted? Can marriage be brought about between the mother and the child's father in such a way as to offer the hope of a satisfactory family life? If not, is the woman likely later to marry some other man, and, assuming this probability, what disposition had best be made of her child? Each case of illegitimacy presents these baffling questions that in one way or another have family aspects. Illegitimacy is also linked with family life by the fact that it is so often the result of a bad home. Sometimes the sex irregularity that finally ends in unmarried motherhood began in the home, with an older relative the person responsible. More frequently than one might suppose the woman's predicament has resulted from family negligence along lines of sex instruction. The poverty, incompatibilities, drab existence and vicious atmosphere found in the home often become influences in the early life of the girl that contribute largely to her later misfortune. Illegitimacy is one of the most bitter fruits of family failure.

Prostitution.—Prostitution is another social problem related to the family, concerning which progress is being made. Instead of being an ally of the monogamous family, as some have called it, prostitution always has been a menace to the home, and its evil effect upon family life appears in a multitude of ways. Wherever prostitution appears it becomes productive of influences that contaminate family life. Its clientele acquire sex habits that frequently spoil their marriage relations, and their attitude toward sex and their thinking about sex are discolored by their familiarity with the low standards and practices of the prostitute. The idealism that normally surrounds sex experience is torn away with the consequence that to the home is brought the coarseness and perhaps also the perverted cravings with reference to sex that reveal social deterioration. The man who patronizes any form of prostitution, whether he be single or married, loses little by little, if not at once, qualities of thought and feeling that are prerequisite to matrimonial happiness. Eliminating the venereal disease peril, prostitution undermines the home.

The venereal diseases are indissolubly connected with prostitution. Syphilis and gonorrhœa are the arch enemies of the home. In popular thought syphilis has been considered a just scourge for those who left the path of virtue; gonorrhœa was regarded lightly. Thanks to advances made in recent years in the sciences of bacteriology and medicine, we now at last know the seriousness of both diseases. Their attack upon human well-being is often insidious and long concealed. The tragedies they cause are inflicted on the innocent and the guilty alike. They are no more to be thought of as moral penalties than small-pox or typhoid. The diseases are transmitted by infection, and the chief carrier of them is the prostitute. Recent science has made no larger contribution to human welfare than has come from tracing causally the effects of syphilis and gonorrhœa on the body in their many ramifications.

Fortunately social progress has released multitudes of people, particularly in the United States, from the clutches of the social taboo that in the past suppressed all discussion of sex and venereal diseases, so that the new knowledge of medicine can be popularized. The modern campaign against veneral diseases is not limited merely to a revelation of their peril; progress has also been made in the prevention and cure of both syphilis and gonorrhœa. In this country the attack on the venereal danger has been concentrated in the Social Hygiene movement; it has stressed legislation, recreation and education. Prostitution, being the chief medium of venereal infection, has received no quarter.

Quite apart from any attempt to rid society of venereal disease, the effort to eliminate prostitution has been carried on with aggression. While social standards have been lifted to a higher level, public opinion is increasingly intolerant of the thought of prostitution. The new opportunities of women and their achievement of higher social status necessarily antagonize this evil. Progress already made in the elimination of houses of prostitution, as, for example, in the city of New York, would have seemed to many students of the problem fifty years ago impossible. This has come about primarily because of our clearer knowledge of the meaning of prostitution and an increasing public hostility to commercialized vice. Prostitution, whether looked upon from the point of view of its physical menace or its effect upon character, is plainly a menace to the home and its elimination is for the advantage of family life.

Intemperance.—Intemperance has long been recognized as one of the major problems that concern the family. Although there is no way by which the bad effects of alcoholic beverages upon family life can be measured, intemperance has unquestionably been one of the chief causes of home troubles. In the temperance reforms of the past there has doubtless been an exaggeration of the evils of intemperance because it was not so well understood as at present that it often results from bad social conditions rather than being a primary cause of the evils charged against it. However, even when its rôle is secondary, it contributes prolifically to our social evils, particularly to family misfortunes.

The arraignment of alcoholic beverages by modern science is increasingly severe. For instance, turn to Rosenau's " Preventive Medicine and Hygiene " and read the summary he gives of the attitude preventive medicine takes toward the problem of alcohol. Rosenau tells us that it is a habit-forming drug that lowers resistance to disease, shortens life, decreases efficiency, fosters poverty, stimulates crime, causes accidents, stirs up the passions, impels toward vice and provides favorable conditions for venereal infection; it also promotes economic waste and slows up social progress. Although part of its harmfulness comes from its local irritating action and its toxic results upon nerve-tissue, the worst thing about it is that, taken even in small amounts, it lessens the ability to think clearly, hampers will-power, and dissolves the inhibitions that protect self-restraint.[6] Such is the detailed indictment of alcohol as a drink, as drawn up by a specialist in preventive medicine, and this statement is in accord with the growing conviction of science, which, in spite of the widespread prejudice in favor of alcohol among those who have formed the habit of using it, is becoming increasingly intolerant of alcohol as a beverage. Each item in Rosenau's list of the bad effects of alcohol used as a beverage concerns the home. Every inch of progress made in the decrease of alcoholic drinks favors family life by relieving the home of a part of the load that for so long has pressed heavily upon it.

The headway that is undoubtedly being made against intemperance, which, as with all social progress, does not proceed without its occasional setbacks, is, like the attack on prostitution, a product of general social advance and a wider and better understanding of the significance of the evil. When an intelligent public opinion has been securely established that forbids alcohol to the surgeon, the sea captain, the locomotive engineer, the automobile driver, the pregnant woman and the conceiving father,

---

[6] *Op. cit.*, p. 493.

the question naturally arises: Must not modern civilization attempt, for its safety, to do away with the use of this drug as a beverage altogether? The seriousness of the problem of alcohol from the point of view of the family is a matter of common knowledge. Alcohol is rightly held responsible for at least part of our poverty, quarreling, vicious sex behavior, lack of employment, neglect of children, cruelties, venereal infection, physical breakdown, insanity and loss of affection. It contributes to divorce and desertion. In short, nothing is more ruinous in its effect upon the home than intemperance.

Recreation and the Home.—It is an optimistic fact that recreation has become a major social problem of immense interest to the home. This situation has come about from the rapid increase in leisure, and the subsequent demand for recreation. It has been the democratizing of leisure rather than its mere increase that has elevated the problem of recreation to the position it now holds in public attention. Leisure is no longer the prerogative of the wealthy; it has become the normal thing in all classes of American society, and discloses the great distance we have already traveled from the time when living conditions afforded too precarious an existence to give many people the luxury of leisure.

As leisure has increased and recreation has come to occupy a larger place in the daily life of most people, recreation has become commercialized. Whereas formerly, to a large extent, particularly in rural communities, those who enjoyed play and entertainment had the task of providing their own amusement, now recreation has become a business. This change automatically reduces the opportunity of the home to provide recreation for its members. The family at this point has suffered loss, for it no longer has the almost exclusive opportunity it once had to construct family sympathy by promoting among its members recreational experiences of various sorts. Mechanical invention has been enlisted by modern commerce to provide new and stimulating forms of recreation that are cheap enough to become for a multitude habitual forms of entertainment. The outstanding examples are of course the movies, the automobile and the radio.

Commercial and mechanical recreation have not only robbed the family of a part of its former function; they have also affected the

16

family life by their influence upon conduct. No form of public amusement has ever rivaled the moving pictures in the intensity and cumulative effect of its influence. The filmed play has now gone into every part of the world and pleases all classes and races; it has become the most nearly universal public entertainment. Its faults are notorious. Recently leaders in the moving-picture industry, recognizing that the prevailing standards endangered the popularity of the business in which they were engaged, voluntarily organized in an effort to lift the standards. Already various states have legislated in the effort to protect public morals from the menacing influence of demoralizing plays. In this crusade we see the influence of the home and the parent, and conversely we can now detect in the homes that are being established influences that emanate from the moving picture.

In like manner the automobile has in countless ways influenced family life; it also has become a cheap means of entertainment. Its effect upon the family life is both good and bad. It permits, for example, the entire family to have an outing together, while on the other hand its association with vice offers a new form of temptation, and it thus becomes instrumental in bringing about the saddest of family tragedies. The automobile is having a large influence in giving many people a desire for luxury beyond their means, and probably is the chief cause of the increase in mortgages on homes, which already has been noted in the discussion on housing. The automobile is also doing much to make the family members look outside the house for their recreation, and in this way has had no small part in bringing about the restricted function of the American family which seems characteristic of our time.

The radio is so new that it is not possible yet to detect its ultimate effect upon the home, but at present it has done not a little to draw the family back into the house and to offer a common form of recreation for all members of the household. Its happiest result so far has been protecting the family from isolation. In the contact with the outside world that it provides for people in the country, or for those who are confined to the house, it furnishes a unique service to the home.

The Problem of Health.—The modern health movement has contributed directly to the efficiency, happiness and stability of the family. To a large extent the task of dealing with disease has passed from the family as a unit to the community, and the trend in this direction still continues. This change of program was inevitable as science made increasingly clear the social aspects of both disease and health. The development of bacteriological knowledge has convinced people of the futility of asking the family to protect itself from diseases which are spread by social conditions beyond the control of the individual family.

The fundamental changes that have recently been made in medical and health service emphasize the social character of the effort to maintain health, and hospitals and clinics demonstrate the necessity of organized community coöperation in the treatment and cure of diseases. Chemical analysis, the taking of bacteriological cultures, the inspection of food, health examinations and public health education are some of the requirements in the conflict against disease that the private family cannot provide. These modern methods of increasing good health are made possible only by resources furnished by private organizations and by the community.

In present-day health activities we have an increasing emphasis upon prevention rather than cure. This program necessarily stresses community effort rather than the work of the individual family. Medical inspection of school children, school nurses, and in the more progressive communities clinics for school and preschool children, all bear witness to the greater attention given preventive health work on the part of our towns and cities. We have discovered that it is contrary to public policy to leave the health problems of the child entirely to the intelligence and resources of the individual home.

With the tendency to put more and more upon the community the responsibility for a good health program, medical practice has been moving away from the atmosphere of authority and mystery which the old-time practitioner maintained with his patients toward intelligent coöperation on the part of those needing medical assistance. This gradual change of policy in medicine requires more attention to education by the community, for patients who have no understanding of the general facts of health and disease cannot easily coöperate with their physicians. Although the family has a large responsibility, especially with reference to habit training, it cannot adequately accomplish health education without the assistance of schools and other organizations.

These recent trends of modern medical practice, coöperation, prevention, and education, do not destroy the interest of the family in the problem of health, but change the form of the family's concern. It is dangerous and criminal for the family to attempt to do what was once its function, but still the home must contribute its share in the development of a public opinion that demands adequate public education in the ways of health and that insists that the community in its dealings with the problem of disease keep in accord with the growing knowledge of science. Only a beginning has yet been made in our community health program because so many people are still traditional and individualistic in their health outlook.

Prophecy as to what can be accomplished when our communities are widely conscious of their power to control and eliminate disease appears in the Community Health Work of Framingham, Massachusetts.[7] The effect of this vigorous socialized campaign for public health in adding to the conditions that make for family happiness is revealed by such statistical facts as the 16 per cent decrease in the general death rate as compared with the pre-demonstration decade average, and the 50 per cent decrease in the infant mortality rate. The common backwardness in our community practices which leaves so much of the problem of health and disease to individual initiative and family resources is an intolerable condition, whose penalties appear in large measure in the home. Our future progress in socializing medicine, inevitable if the attack on disease is to continue, will prove of the greatest value to the family as an institution by protecting it from many of the misfortunes that in the past have resulted from diseases which we now know to be preventable if the community so wills.

Problems of Mental Hygiene.—The family has shared in the benefits of the modern movement in mental hygiene. This has come about not merely from the attack upon mental disease, but also through the better insight that has been gained into the mechanisms that control human behavior. Mental disease, like physical disease, adds greatly to the burdens of family life. Insanity,

[7] "Conference of Social Work," 1923, p. 40.

especially, has been in the past a family catastrophe, for not only has it produced every sort of family disaster, but also it has tagged the family with what has been interpreted as a disgrace.

Mental hygiene also serves the family by revealing the pernicious influences that come out of the wrong kind of home and spoil personality. As I have elsewhere stated, a large part of the momentum of science in its attack upon bad home life must be credited to mental hygiene. The part the home plays, even in the development of mental disease, is so large that mental hygiene of a certainty must concern itself with the home. The greatest benefit from mental hygiene thus far has been that it has popularized the idea that the conduct of man, like his body, is in the domain of natural law; and since this concept is fundamental in any effort to safeguard and improve family life, the contribution mental hygiene is making to the home is of inestimable value.

CHAPTER XV

CONSERVATION OF THE FAMILY

Conservation of the Family.—It is indeed true that the family has been too much taken for granted, but even though it has been relatively neglected, it has not been destitute of social support. Multitudes of educational and social agencies have contributed to the welfare of the home. Movements of various sorts have come into being in the effort to conserve the family. The results of these efforts, especially as expressed in legislation, have done much to promote the happiness and efficiency of the modern home. In a study of the social problems of the home the more important of these social influences furnished by organizations and measures that are attempting to assist the home require brief mention.

Legislation.—Although good homes cannot be created directly by legislative acts, laws seriously influence the home. Some of the recent changes in legislation affecting the family are of fundamental importance. They may be classified in three primary groups: laws concerning the status of women, laws for the protection of women and children, and laws regulating marriage, divorce and family behavior. In the first group we find in the United States a steady trend toward the social equality of women. Beginning in 1847, laws have been passed by the various states giving to married women their so-called " property rights "; these laws continued for the married woman the same control over her property which she had enjoyed before entering matrimony. In harmony with this legislation were laws which were designed to give to the mother rights over her own children. These acts were known as Equal Guardianship Laws, although as a matter of fact the mother was seldom given equal rights with the father. Enactments faltered, generally refusing to give the mother the same rights as the father, but the interpretation of these laws by the courts was usually even more backward. While the statutes fixing woman's legal status and defining her rights vary from state to state, the trend away from the brutalities of the English Common Law is unmistakable. This movement is of very great importance as it concerns the

246

family, since it must become increasingly true that the normal home in this country can have no secure foundation unless it is built upon an absolute equality before the law of husband and wife.

Child Labor Laws.—Laws regulating child labor have become a necessity in modern civilization. The child who in his early years enters regular industrial employment and thus loses the schooling and the more subtle development of normal childhood suffers a handicap that decreases his value when he arrives at citizenship to such an extent that the matter cannot safely be left to the ignorance, indifference or necessity of parents. The prevention of child labor, because of its social consequences, has now become a major obligation of the state. At an earlier time when our surplus of wealth was smaller the results of child labor were not so serious; but this fact offers no valid argument for the neglect of the child under the economic conditions now prevailing. It has been necessary thus far to depend upon state laws for the regulating of child labor. This has hampered the getting of desirable legislation since it has permitted backward states to gain an unfair advantage in industrial competition by the employment of children at a lower age than that allowed in the more progressive states.

According to the Census of 1920 there were 1,437,783 children from seven to thirteen years of age out of school and 2,221,364 between seven and fifteen not at school.[1] These children were for the most part child laborers. Child workers are found at present chiefly in the following industries: the cotton-mills of the South, canning, mining (especially in the anthracite coal-mines of Pennsylvania), glass-manufacturing, and perhaps in greatest numbers in the various types of farming and the raising of tobacco, fruits, berries, hops and sugar-beets.

The decision of the United States Supreme Court that Congress, through its power to regulate interstate and foreign commerce or to lay and collect taxes, does not have the right to prohibit child labor makes the federal government impotent in dealing with the problem of child labor until an amendment is added to the Constitution, specifically granting to Congress the authority to pass

---

[1] "Conference of Social Work," 1923, p. 414.

restrictive legislation. On account of the widespread hostility to the amendment prohibiting alcoholic beverages, it will be for some time to come difficult if not impossible to educate public opinion to an understanding and approval of a constitutional amendment, particularly with so many child-workers employed in industries that find such labor profitable.

Although child labor is frequently defended as a family necessity, the premature employment of the child is actually an attack upon the welfare of the home. It is not easy for the typical American to face this fact squarely, since the tradition of the pioneering period still lingers, and with it the idea that the boy-worker can if he will make a place for himself in society without the aid of school. Public opinion is so eager to take this attitude toward child labor that a few spectacular successes hide the tragedy of a multitude of handicapped persons, who, not only in their industrial career, but in every aspect of living show a stunting of personality that discloses how much they have missed by their lack of opportunity to be reasonably prepared for life.

The handicap of these individuals becomes in turn a burden to society itself. They become homemakers in due time, and the great majority of them exhibit in their family life the same limitations that shackled them in their employment. From this group in large proportion come those who in old age, in a period of industrial unemployment or when they suffer from illness or accident, have to come to the social relief societies for assistance. Exploited in the beginning of their life, they are denied the full heritage which belongs to them as potential citizens, and in the end they force society to pay in one way or another for their losses, and add to the burden that has to be carried by the more successful citizen.

While the individual family close to the bread-line may welcome the time when the older children can go to work, without any thought of the effect of sacrificing their opportunity for a minimum education, the predicament of poverty blinds the parent to the fact that the employment of children lowers the wage and shortens the working season of the unskilled adult laborer. In other words, such families as a class profit from an increase of the school age and the decrease of child labor. It is more fundamentally a family problem than one that concerns industry. Child labor is not a necessity in any form of industry, but the prolonging of childhood so that every normal individual can be given suitable education for a fair start in life is a basic requirement of homemaking.

Labor Legislation for Women.—The United States has been backward in the passage of legislation for the protection of the woman worker. In 1893 the first eight-hour law for women was passed by the state of Illinois as the result of the leadership of the trade unions and the settlements, especially Hull House. Two years later the Supreme Court of Illinois held that the law denied women the right guaranteed them by the Fourteenth Amendment, since as citizens they could not be deprived of the right to work more than eight hours. The effect of this decision was such that no legislation was attempted by any state until, in 1907, Oregon adopted a ten-hour law for women. This later was upheld by a decision of the United States Supreme Court. In 1917 the court also allowed the decision of the Oregon court in support of a minimum wage law to stand. In April, 1923, the Supreme Court declared the minimum wage law passed by Congress for the District of Columbia unconstitutional, and this decision dealt a severe blow to the effort to protect the wage-earning woman by legislation, since it reversed what had come to be accepted as an established constitutional principle.

Laws regulating the hours and conditions of women's work and establishing a minimum wage influence family life by preventing avaricious employers from exploiting the female worker, and by encouraging higher standards in the lines of work where women are employed. It must not be forgotten, also, that these laws directly influence some families since widows, deserted wives, and single women who are responsible for dependent relatives are the actual economic heads of households, and laws that protect them from excessive hours of labor or low wages contribute to the well-being of the families they represent.

Eugenic Marriage Laws.—A modern effort to conserve the family is expressed in legislation that requires of candidates for marriage a medical certificate stating that they are physically fit for wedlock. These laws, passed by several of the more progressive states, refer to venereal diseases and concern men. In 1925, Wisconsin, Alabama, Indiana, North Carolina, North Dakota, Oregon and Wyoming had such laws. The law of Wisconsin has received most attention. In many other states similar laws have been introduced into the legislature only to be defeated; for example, in 1923 in fourteen different states legislation of this sort failed of passage. In Europe also there has been considerable discussion concerning the advisability of passing laws requiring medical examination to detect the presence of venereal disease, but Norway and Turkey appear to be the only European countries that have passed certification laws.

On account of the controversy that has gathered about Wisconsin's law, it may well be given in detail as it stood in 1917, after having been twice amended:

1. All male persons making application for license to marry shall, at any time within fifteen days prior to such application, be examined as to the existence or non-existence in such person of any venereal disease, and it shall be unlawful for the county clerk of any county to issue a license to marry to any person who fails to present and file with such county clerk a certificate setting forth that such person is free from venereal diseases so nearly as can be determined by a thorough examination and by the application of the recognized clinical and laboratory tests of scientific search, when in the discretion of the examining physician such clinical and laboratory tests are necessary. When a microscopical examination for gonococci is required such examination shall upon the request of any physician in the State be made by the State laboratory of hygiene free of charge. The Wassermann test for syphilis when required shall upon application be made by the psychiatric institute at Mendota free of charge. Such certificate shall be made by a physician, licensed to practice in this State or in the State in which such male person resides, shall be filed with the application for license to marry, and shall read as follows, to wit:

I,...... (name of physician), being a physician, legally licensed to practice in the State of......, my credentials being filed in the office of ......, in the city of......, county of......, do certify that I have this ......day of......19.., made a thorough examination of...... (name of person), and believe him to be free from all venereal diseases.

.... (Signature of physician).

2. Such examiners shall be physicians duly licensed to practice in this State or in the State in which such male person resides. The fee for such examination, to be paid by the applicant for examination before the certificate shall be granted, shall not exceed two dollars. The county or asylum physician of any county, shall, upon request, make the necessary examination and issue such certificate, if the same can be properly issued, without charge to the applicant, if said applicant be indigent.

3. Any county clerk who shall unlawfully issue a license to marry to any person who fails to present and file the certificate provided by subsection I of this section, or any party or parties having knowledge of any matter relating or pertaining to the examination of any applicant for license to marry, who shall disclose the same or any portion thereof, except

as may be required by law, shall, upon proof thereof, be punished by a fine of not more than one hundred dollars or by imprisonment not more than six months.

4. Any physician who shall knowingly and wilfully make any false statement in the certificate provided for in subsection I of this section shall be punished by a fine of not more than one hundred dollars or by imprisonment not more than six months.[2]

Although Rosenau thinks it is improbable that we can prevent the marriage of many syphilitics by legislation,[3] a conclusion shared by many physicians, the Wisconsin law appears worth while if only as an educational influence. The following statements of Wisconsin physicians express a judicial appraisal of the effect of the Wisconsin legislation.

Dr. W. F. Lorenz writes:

The law does not operate as a strict preventive to the marriage of those suffering from an inactive form of syphilis, but I am firmly convinced that it has had a tremendous educational value.

The following is the opinion of Dr. George C. Ruhland, until recently the health officer of Milwaukee:

At the beginning I was opposed to the law as I did not think it would work, but I am now much in favor of it. It has educated the people of the State in this matter. In some cases where men would otherwise have married while they were infected, it has been a deterrent. I know of men who, as a result of the law, have postponed their marriage until they have been cured. Many men also, knowing they are diseased, do not try to get certificates. There is a general impression that some men have obtained certificates while diseased, but I know personally of no such cases.[4]

The law has helped a greater number of men to appreciate the risk of venereal infection. It has led many of those planning matrimony to make sure that they were legally fit to marry before applying for certification; and in some cases the law has operated to reveal, through examination, contagious conditions that have brought about the postponement of marriage. On the other hand, the law suffers from ambiguity and from the absence of any provision for state supervision. It seems also not to have won the coöperation of the medical profession in its practical administration, although a majority of the physicians in the state appear to be favorable to the idea of a medical certificate for marriage. In cases

[2] "Hall, F. S., "Medical Certification for Marriage," pp. 83–84.
[3] *Op. cit.*, p. 65.
[4] Hall, *op. cit.*, p. 40.

not a few the examination is merely perfunctory, for the physician has issued a certificate upon the declaration of the man that he is not suffering from any form of venereal disease.

The law is at least significant as a pioneering expression of a sentiment already strong among the educated classes and bound to spread, that no person harboring venereal disease in an infectious form should be permitted to marry. Any legislation that contributes to the educational campaign for the elimination of venereal disease is from a family viewpoint socially justified.

Eugenical Sterilization.—Many of those who have been impressed with the apparently hereditary foundation of certain types of social problems have advocated eugenical sterilization. Sterilization laws have been passed by many of the states of the Union. The first law of this type was passed in 1907 by the state of Indiana. This law was finally declared unconstitutional by the state Supreme Court in 1921, on the basis that it violates the Fourteenth Amendment to the Federal Constitution, in that it denies due process of law. The law of the state of California advising sterilization has led to the largest number of operations. Although this law provides for compulsory sterilization, those responsible for its administration have stopped to obtain the consent of the nearest relatives in cases where the operation has been performed. Usually it has not been found difficult to get this consent; often, indeed, the patients themselves have desired to be made sterile.

Sterilization as a punitive measure has been generally held unconstitutional, and at any rate is repugnant to present-day public opinion. Sterilization legislation is thus far advocated only from a eugenical motive and is considered by those who favor it an effective means of preventing the reproduction of the most degenerate and defective human family stocks. Since from such families come offspring incapable of meeting the responsibilities of modern living, the cutting off of these lowest human family strains becomes one of the obligations of the state in its effort to promote the general welfare.

Its advocates believe that eugenical diagnosis has arrived at such a point that its findings can be put into legislative form, so that by eugenical sterilization we can eliminate the worst strains of constitutionally inferior stocks. The difficulty of legally defining persons that are to be prevented from reproducing is easily recognized. Harry H. Laughlin, of the Eugenics Record Office, has defined the type to be sterilized as that potential parent " whose hereditary nature is such that the immediate offspring, or the descendant family stock of such person, would, because of inadequate or defective inheritance from such person, be represented, in abnormally great percentage, by individuals who, under the normal environment of the state, would fail to function as socially adequate persons."[5]

He defines the socially inadequate person as " one who by his or her own effort, regardless of etiology or prognosis, fails chronically, in comparison with normal persons, to maintain himself or herself as a useful member of the organized social life of the state; *provided* that the term *socially inadequate* shall not be applied to any person whose individual or social ineffectiveness is due to the normally expected exigencies of youth, old age, curable injuries, or temporary physical or mental illness, in case such ineffectiveness is adequately taken care of by the particular family in which it occurs."[6]

Sterilization as a compulsory program for the elimination of inferior stocks is at present far in advance of public opinion and assumes greater certainty than science yet has regarding the hereditary determination of social inadequacy. Sterilization is scientifically premature. The general opposition of the psychiatrists to compulsory sterilization has been well expressed by Dr. George K. Pratt of the National Committee of Mental Hygiene as follows:

One of the most outstanding objections to sterilization is founded on a conviction that sterilization is not the solution to the problem of the feeble-minded, and that it may even create other problems.

The advocates of sterilization put forward their claims chiefly on biologic and eugenic bases. If mentally defective persons—they say—are rendered surgically unfit for procreation, in a certain length of time there will be, obviously enough, no more mental defectives. This premise fulfills many requirements. It is seductive, it sounds plausible, it arouses hope in a sorely tried citizenry, and it ought to work. Its chief drawback consists in being founded on unproven (in some cases even discredited) theories and on unscientific reasoning.

---

[5] " Eugenical Sterilization," 1926, p. 74.
[6] *Ibid.*, p. 65.

Eugenical sterilization presupposes a proven and universally accepted law of heredity. As a matter of fact no such final law exists. Our theories about heredity are constantly changing. Once we thought tuberculosis was inherited. Now we know differently. Once we were positive that personalities and characters were familial hand-downs. For some time past we have been discovering that they are acquired instead. And so we feel it premature, at least, to base as monumental a policy as that of sterilization on a belief that because a thing ought to be true, it therefore must be true.[7]

TABLE XVI[8]

Statistical summary, by states, of operations for eugenical sterilization in the United States, to July 1, 1925.

State	Operations performed				Total
	Males		Females		
	Vasectomy	Castration	Salpingectomy	Ovario-tomy	
1. California......	2,624	1	1,936	75	4,636
2. Connecticut....	6	0	75	12	93
3. Delaware......	2	0	3	0	5
4. Idaho..........	0	0	0	1	1
5. Indiana.......	118	0	2	0	120
6. Iowa..........	41	0	15	0	56
7. Kansas........	148	58	104	25	335
8. Maine.........	0	0	0	0	0
9. Michigan......	7	0	39	2	48
10. Minnesota.....	0	0	0	0	0
11. Montana......	11	0	12	0	23
12. Nebraska......	141	0	115	6	262
13. Nevada.......	0	0	0	0	0
14. New Hampshire	4	0	37	0	41
15. New Jersey....	0	0	0	0	0
16. New York.....	1	0	36	5	42
17. North Dakota..	18	0	14	1	33
18. Oregon........	6	91	184	32	313
19. South Dakota..	0	0	0	0	0
20. Utah..........	0	0	0	0	0
21. Virginia.......	2	1	88	0	91
22. Washington....	1	0	0	0	1
23. Wisconsin......	26	0	118	0	144
Total.........	3,156	151	2,778	159	6,244

This table gives an interesting summary of the operation of sterilization laws up to the present time.

[7] *Journal of Social Hygiene*, May, 1925, p. 262.
[8] Laughlin, *op. cit.*, p. 60.

Compulsory sterilization as a means of eliminating the unfit must wait for increased knowledge regarding the conditions of heredity and a changed public opinion if it is to become an effective program; but voluntary sterilization is often highly desirable, especially when sought by the patients themselves. It is also the obligation of education to stress in every way possible the necessity of the individual's developing a deep sense of eugenical responsibility. Unfortunately there is not now any short cut to eugenical welfare. To a considerable extent modern philanthropy checks the more brutal processes of eugenical elimination characteristic of lower stages of culture. For family welfare it is imperative, therefore, that intelligent public opinion shall be developed that will make possible in many cases voluntary sterilization of individuals who in their opinion and that of their relatives, guided by the diagnosis of competent officials, should not have children.

Reform of Child-marriages.—In 1925 in fourteen of our states the minimum marriageable age of girls was only twelve years; in nine states it was fourteen years; in eight states it was fifteen years; in seventeen states it was sixteen years, and in one state, New Hampshire, it was eighteen. In the practical administration of the existing laws we find even greater diversity among the states. There is also laxity in many localities in the enforcing of laws relating to the marriageable age, and misstatements concerning their age are frequently made by one or both of the parties applying for a license to marry. When the consent of the parents or guardians is necessary because of the age of those seeking to enter matrimony, many parents show little insight or sense of responsibility respecting the child-marriage. The children in some cases forge the names of their parents to written statements of consent, and by means of this false document obtain their marriage license.

Richmond and Hall, after a careful study of the problem of married children, estimate that in this country there are at present 343,000 women and girls who began their married life as child-brides within the last thirty-six years.[9]

The marriage of the immature is hostile to the prevailing standards of modern culture. Many such marriages are of short duration, are contracted lightly, and reach their logical anti-

9 " Child Marriages," p. 57.

climax in the divorce court; others are ended by seeking an act of annulment from the court, based on the fact that one or both of the contracting parties were below age when the marriage was performed. When, as is often the case, the man is much older than the girl he marries, the home is bound to be one of masculine dominance, with the likelihood that the girl's personality will receive little chance for development. Although there is need of greater knowledge concerning the biological aspects of child-marriage, Carr-Saunders tells us that such evidence as we now have seems to show that when marriage is consummated at an early age there is a marked tendency for the premature death of the wife from tuberculosis or some other form of respiratory disease or some type of ovarian complication; he also tells us that in India, where the Hindoos practice child-marriage and Mohammedans do not, fertility is much higher among the latter than among the former.[10]

Efforts to lift the minimum marriage age are complicated by the attitude of the general public regarding illegitimacy. In the popular mind adequate solution of the pregnancy of a young girl is immediate marriage. In spite of this handicap of sentiment the trend toward the fixing of a minimum age for marriage is unmistakable. It is also true that progress is being made in the improvement of the administration of the laws we now have.

The friend of the family will seek to encourage the coming of the following reforms. In states where the minimum marriageable age is low, it needs to be advanced as rapidly as public opinion will permit until it corresponds with the age at which children are now permitted to leave school in the more progressive states. Eventually the intelligent leadership is bound to insist on eighteen years as a minimum age for the marriage of girls. There is need also of requiring reliable evidence of the age of the contracting parties and the only satisfactory method of bringing this about is by the presentation of the birth certificate when the marriage-license is issued. Since parents are not always to be trusted to exercise wisely their power of granting consent for the marriage of a child whose age is below that required by the law, it appears necessary to make some additional provision such as that of the New

[10] " Population Problems," p. 104.

Hampshire law, which insists upon the court's consent as well as that of the parents. To reduce the temptation of those in charge of the issuing of licenses, as much as possible, the fee system should be abolished and the authorities in charge of the licensing of marriages should be paid a salary. The requirement that both the parties contemplating marriage should appear for the license would also safeguard the home.

Although these reforms and others that are needed are likely to come about gradually, those who have the welfare of the family at heart must bear in mind that this is not a social problem that can be solved merely by legislation. Laws can be passed that will have an educational value, but they must not be far in advance of the prevailing public opinion of the states enacting them. Social strategy demands that the emphasis be primarily at present upon the necessity of educating public opinion. Progressive legislation regarding the marriageable age cannot go far unless there be a more intelligent and reasonable attitude toward child-pregnancy.

Family Allowances.—Well-established as the principle of a living-wage is in social thought, its interpretation has brought forth some fundamental problems. One of these is: How large a family should a worker be expected to support? The general answer to this question has been: A family of five, the husband, wife and three dependent children. Recent writers have challenged the idea that the living wage should be established on the basis of a typical family of five. In actual practice the payment of a wage sufficient to support a family of two adults and three children would yield an income in excess of the needs of from 70 to 80 per cent of American workers, while it would be inadequate for from 10 to 15 per cent.[11]

In the light of these facts some students of the family believe that the only just wage-system is one built on the actual, not the theoretical, size of the family. It is proposed that the minimum wage-scale vary with the actual needs of the worker who has the responsibility of maintaining a family. The single man does not need the same income as his fellow-worker who is the father of several children. It would, however, be futile to demand of

[11] Douglas, P. H., "Wages and the Family," p. 41.

17

employers that they pay more wages directly to married than to single men, for naturally if such an effort were made industrial concerns would give preference to single men and as a consequence the heads of families would be thrown out of employment and their second state would be worse than their first.

The program advocated by American proponents of family allowances is already operating in various parts of continental Europe and is rapidly winning adherents. The relative poverty of Europe as a result of the World War, the food-rationing experience of the people during the war period, and the insistent demand of the workers for a living wage explain the headway that the family allowance system is making in Europe. The European manufacturer cannot afford to pay a living wage that will support theoretical, non-existent dependents, but on the other hand it has not seemed wise to propose a scheme that would directly discriminate between single and married men or between married men with reference to the number of children they were supporting, so a minimum wage-scale sufficient to support single men has been adopted with the addition of allowances for wives, children and other dependents. This family allowance has been paid from a common fund assessed on each employer of a specialized group of industries in such a way as to make it of no advantage to the individual employer to seek single men rather than married. Thus the burden of family maintenance is distributed among the employers and the amount collected from each is entirely independent of the proportion of single and married men in that particular concern.

The plan of a family allowance system is supported not only as the most just wage scheme but as an effective means of preventing poverty and lessening the growing sense of sex competition between men and women workers, for there would be no discrimination between men and women in the operation of this type of minimum wage. The family allowance system is also a practical method of encouraging births among those who now find the coming of a child a serious attack upon the economic standards of the family. It would enable a multitude of parents to face life confidently without the fear that their children might suffer from inadequate support. It also would lessen the burden of the newly married and the youthful parent who often, under present circumstances, must because of his marriage or his parenthood sacrifice the standards of life to which he was accustomed during his single career. By thus lessening the strain of the earlier period of homemaking, this system would immensely conserve family life.

The proposal of a family allowance as an addition to a minimum wage calls attention to the necessity of industry as a whole recognizing its social responsibilities to the family. In the early period of modern industry the family was exploited; in more recent times family interests have been both ignored and neglected, but with the increasing consciousness that industry is essentially a social process, justified by its contributions to public welfare, the necessity of finding an effective way by which the income of the worker may be made somewhat proportionate to the individual's household responsibilities will become increasingly apparent. Students of the American family, therefore, will watch with intense interest the operation of the European experiments for providing one form or another of family allowance.

Pensions for Mothers.—Missouri in 1911 passed the first enactment in the United States providing for a regular allowance to be paid to mothers for the care of their own children. In spite of the doubt of many experienced social workers concerning the wisdom of such legislation, the idea of granting allowances to mothers caring for dependent children gained favor throughout the United States and by 1921 all the states of the Union save four had passed some form of a Mothers' Pension Law. The popularity of this legislation rests upon the general conviction that the home should, if possible, not be broken up. It is held better for the mother to be paid to take care of her children than to have them placed in an institution. The home environment gives the child a better chance for physical survival and offers opportunity for a normal moral development; it also seems just not to force the mother because of financial misfortune to separate from her child. Social experience has demonstrated the superiority of individual homes as compared with an institution as a proper place for the bringing up of children. Allowances that come to the family through mothers' pensions also escape the stigma connected with public relief or private charity.

The laws vary from state to state. For example, in some states either parent may be given an allowance, in other states, only mothers or only widows. Deserted wives, divorced wives, unmarried mothers, mothers whose husbands are prisoners, and mothers whose husbands are in state asylums for the insane or feebleminded are recipients as defined by the various statutes. The conditions under which the allowances are granted also show wide diversity. For instance, in some states aid must be necessary to save the child from neglect or to prevent the break-up of the home, while in others it must be required to prevent the child from becoming a public charge.

In most states the allowance is not granted unless the mother is deemed a fit person to bring up her child and the laws of some of the states do not permit her to work outside the home while she is receiving the allowance. The maximum age of the child whose mother may receive the pension runs from fourteen to eighteen years in the different states, while in two it is specified as the legal working age of the child. The amount of the allowance also differs from state to state. For example in Iowa it is two dollars a week per child, four states give ten dollars a month for one child and five dollars for each additional child; Colorado, Massachusetts and Nevada set no maximum but the amount must be sufficient to care properly for the child, but in Nevada this amount must not be more than it would cost to maintain and educate the child in a county or state home. In Oklahoma the amount given is equivalent to what would be the wages of the child if he were set to work.

There is no uniformity in the method of administration of mothers' pensions. Many states have the law administered by the Juvenile Court or some other county court with similar functions. In New Hampshire the county commissioners, upon the advice of the school-board, make the grant. In Massachusetts the allowance is given by the city or town overseers of the poor; in this state, however, supervisory powers are given to the state board of charities. In Pennsylvania the power is located in an unpaid county board of five to seven women, appointed by the governor.

Federal Aid for the Protection of Maternity and Infancy.— Congress in 1912 created the Children's Bureau and authorized it to investigate many subjects connected with child welfare, the foremost place being given to infant mortality. The first studies undertaken by the bureau had to do with this subject. In addition to its valuable investigations, which were published in the form of bulletins, the department also issued instructions to mothers regarding the proper care of children, stressing for example the value of breast-feeding and the importance of having a child who showed symptoms of disease immediately examined by a physician.

Since the studies of the department showed that little progress was being made in decreasing the mortality rate of infants, attention was necessarily directed to the question of helping mothers receive good treatment before, during and after childbirth.

In 1917, in making her annual report for the bureau, Miss Julia Lathrop directed attention to the coöperation between national and local governments in Great Britain in the carrying on of maternity and infant welfare work and suggested that this country should adopt a legislative program by means of which the federal government and the various states could conduct coöperative work for the purpose of reducing the high death rate of mothers and babies in the United States.

In 1921 the Shepard-Towner Act, for the promotion of the welfare and the hygiene of maternity and infancy, became a law. By this bill, an initial sum of $5,000 was given to each state and an additional grant on condition that the state appropriated a similar amount, the money to be expended according to a program originating in the state, but receiving the approval of a federal board. In 1926 there were only five states that had not accepted the terms of the act.[12] Of these states, Connecticut, Massachusetts and Maine, although not accepting federal assistance, appropriated money for the promotion of the hygiene of maternity. The conditions differ widely in the various states and the programs inaugurated are necessarily adapted to local situations. This public health work for mothers, like the other activities of the Children's Bureau, is of inestimable value in conserving home life.

---

[12] *Children's Bureau Pub. No. 156*, p. 1.

The Family Court.—To Illinois belongs the credit for having inaugurated the first Juvenile Court, an event of great significance in the modernizing of the treatment of the juvenile offender. Public spirited women of Chicago, thoroughly convinced that the conventional treatment of delinquent children by the methods then in vogue were both a miscarriage of justice and a social wrong, agitated for the creation of a separate court, exclusively for the child offender, and their efforts were rewarded in 1900 by the establishment of the first juvenile court in the world. The Juvenile Court movement owes much to two outstanding persons, Judge Ben B. Lindsey of the Denver Court, who popularized the movement and protected it in his native city from the assaults of regressive forces, and Dr. William Healy of the Judge Baker Foundation of Boston, who by his work in developing the psychopathic institute made available a scientific technic for dealing with problems of juvenile delinquency.

Since the problems of delinquent children usually arise in the home life of the families involved, there has developed in recent years a family court, or the Court of Domestic Relations, which has jurisdiction over all matters concerning the home. The establishment of the family court as central tribunal does not mean that all the cases regarding family problems are heard in the same court or by the same judge. Specialization is permitted, but the disposition of the case is not decided by the technical breach of law involved, but by what seems to be the underlying problem.

By the concentration of all types of family cases under one jurisdiction it becomes possible, for the advantage of all concerned, through the centralized filing of records to treat any member of a family in the light of the knowledge that has been gathered concerning the family as a whole through the different cases that from time to time have come before the various divisions of the court. Thus the family court, when rightly organized and authorized by law, is enabled to consider the family as a unit and to deal with problems of conduct so that the legal disposition conserves the family relationships.

The family court also makes possible the assembling of social data of the greatest value in dealing with family matters. This important aspect of its work is well demonstrated by the records kept by the Court of Domestic Relations of the city of Cincinnati, which is presided over by Judge Charles Hoffman. The family court truly stresses preventive work since its function necessarily turns away from traditional legal procedure towards a more human and scientific attitude in dealing with the problems that come before it. The family court provides not only the best method of legally disposing of divorce cases; it offers also a promising method of conciliating family-members who are at odds and bringing about the adjustment prerequisite to the establishment of family unity.

The Humanizing of Industry.—Although American Industry has paid little attention to the family in any direct way, the greater emphasis in recent years on the human factor in industry has proven a decided advantage to the home. The changed attitude toward the length of the working day, attempts to eliminate unnecessary fatigue, the provision of rest periods, devices resulting from the growth of the accident-prevention movement, the campaign against industrial health hazards, the introduction of periodic physical examinations, the establishment of a medical staff and clinics, attention to a mid-day lunch and noon-hour activities, utilization of recreational and educational interests, and perhaps most of all the effort to reduce the turnover by shifting the employee from a position in which he cannot do satisfactory work to some other job which he can do well: all these factors have lifted the standard of the worker and contributed to his efficiency as the head of the household. Since much of this is still pioneering and experimental, it is not too much to look forward to a time when industrial policy will be keenly conscious of its home responsibilities.

Newspapers and Magazines and the Conservation of the Home.—The newspaper is alive to the general interest in home welfare. Both in its news and editorial sections it constantly brings to the attention of the public matters that are related to the welfare of the home; but, as every newspaper-reader knows, it is not consistently on the side of the family in its news items for it prints a quantity of news, such as sensational reports of contested divorce cases among the wealthy and prominent, that tends to lower matrimonial standards and debase home life. Its excuse is, of course, the general interest in such matters, the same sort of morbid curiosity that expresses itself in the small community in village gossip.

Editors of newspapers realize more than most people the fundamental changes that are taking place in the modern family and it would be unfair to them to complain that they merely reflect in their newspaper policy public opinion, since they are as individuals often particularly friendly to the family and, in so far as their commercial responsibilities permit, contribute constructively to the establishment of modern, efficient family life.

Current magazines also are giving increasing attention to family matters. Their articles have put undue emphasis upon the problem of divorce but we are now beginning to have a new type of treatment, more concerned with the positive aspects of family problems, and especially the relationship of parents to children. Along with these serious and helpful articles in the better type of magazines, there have come into being periodicals that deliberately exploit sex interest; these circulate largely among the young and are written in a way to stimulate sex interest and at the same time keep within the law; they are a direct attack upon youthful morale and their influence upon the high school student who reads them is most certainly pernicious. Being naturally profitable, they are difficult to legislate out of existence, but they make no appeal to the boy or girl whose home atmosphere has developed proper standards.

Religion and Family Conservation.—The churches have long been interested in the problem of divorce, but they are now beginning to have a broader and more constructive attitude toward family problems. The subject of the family is becoming a topic of discussion in the religious periodicals and conventions and in ministerial meetings. There is a growing disposition to study the family rather than to be content with emotional outbursts against divorces or the moral problems of the youth. The Y. M. C. A. and the Y. W. C. A. are attempting to minister to the family, but both of them are hampered by the traditional idea of sex segregation. The Y. M. C. A. of Philadelphia, by emphasizing the policy of ministration to the family as a whole, points toward the greatest usefulness of these organizations. Their highest service cannot be rendered by one being a club of boys and young men and the other for young women. The Y. W. C. A. must face the problem of the family with the same seriousness that it has tackled other social problems of contemporary life; its Commission on the Family in the Life of To-day has already made valuable investigations of the attitude of young women with reference to marriage and family life. The organization has also conducted study clubs that are a distinct contribution to family welfare.

Educational Conservation of the Family.—There is at present a most promising interest in the family among educators and social workers. Civic organizations, women's clubs, colleges, normal schools, and educational societies are giving a liberal place to the family in their discussions and conferences. Of all the activities that endeavor to conserve family life, this educational movement is by far the most important; it is naturally leading toward training for marriage and for parenthood. This idea of preparation for the obligations of the home is so significant that it is treated by itself in the following chapter.

Matrimonial Counsel and the Conservation of the Family.—With the growth of a practical psychology and sociology capable of dealing with actual problems of conduct, the question naturally arises: Why should not science contribute more directly and helpfully to the problems of marriage and parenthood? Since June, 1922, in Vienna, Austria, there has been a matrimonial advice bureau which has especially stressed the physical problems of marriage, including health examinations and also for the syphilitic an adjustment of sex difficulties. There is even greater need of the establishment in this country of bureaus that can give to those seeking it advice with reference to the social problems that arise in home life. Such counsel has always been sought, particularly from doctors and ministers.

The work that has already been done in dealing with the delinquent child by such men as Dr. William Healy and Dr. Herman

Adler raises the question: Why cannot similar scientific service be provided for the family as a whole in a way that will make it possible to prevent the growth of adjustment problems that bring about serious divisions within the family? In a limited way the author of this book has been advising friends and students with reference to problems of marriage and parenthood for some years. Similar work has been done by others. The time is near at hand when bureaus for family counsel will be organized to make available scientific knowledge which is as valuable in dealing with family matters as it has proven itself with regard to other aspects of human life. It is the most intelligent people that seek the help of scientific counsel when they face the practical problems of the home. This is fortunate, for it will save the bureau of matrimonial counsel from coming into existence to deal primarily with the pathological problems of the family. We need matrimonial counsel not so much to prevent divorces as to make possible happier and safer homes.

CHAPTER XVI

EDUCATION AND THE FAMILY

Public Education and the Family.—It is, of course, impossible to estimate the influence of public education upon the family. Modern life is too complex to permit us to trace with clearness the effect of school training upon the home. There can be no doubt that the contribution of public education is largely indirect. Even the most severe critic of the school would admit that public education is in great measure responsible for our present social culture. The home is, as we have found, sensitive to current social conditions. Indirectly, therefore, our schools must act as a primary factor in making modern home life what it is. The demand for higher standards of life, as expressed in more comforts, greater leisure, and the craving for luxuries, is a product, to a considerable degree, of the ever increasing educational opportunities. The extension of popular education is in turn an evidence of our easier circumstances of life, the gift of machine production. Our appropriation of public funds for school purposes reveals the strength of home impulses, for it was the parent's desire to give to his child an adequate preparation for life, superior if possible to what he himself had had, that produced in America our democratic school system.

The results of our present school program are registered in the lives of the children. Thus the products of our education, both those that help and those that hinder normal development, become a fundamental constituent of the personality and show themselves in marriage and in parenthood as elsewhere. Although neither the school nor the home has a monopoly of the forces that form character in children, the opportunity of each is so great that they are held to be chiefly responsible for such personality defects as appear in adult behavior. Indeed, as one would expect, the school and the home show a disposition to blame each other for the failures that appear in the process of child-training. No institution that assumes a large social function can, in our time, hope to escape well-deserved criticism. Its failures are too obvious and naturally they attract more attention than its successes, which are taken as a matter of course. Both the home and the school are guilty of the attempt to hide their mistakes in the handling of children by each attacking the other institution for its own shortcomings.

So far as there is actual competition between the home and the school for the control of the child-training process, it is the school that is gaining power, the home that is losing. More and more the school is taking over responsibilities that once belonged to the parent. It is encouraged to do this by the fact that many parents are only too glad to hand over to the school duties that appear either irksome or difficult. The trend toward urban life increases the demand for a larger school program, since parents in the cities, however good their intentions, find that they cannot furnish children with the resources necessary for their proper development. The practices of the city schools are in turn imitated by the more progressive school organizations of the smaller communities, for in education as elsewhere city standards have prestige and spread outward until the most isolated rural school is somewhat influenced by the urban school program.

It would be better for the child if the school and the home were in closer contact, and each had a more sympathetic understanding of the task of the other. Those connected with the school organization are too prone to look with suspicion on any effort parents make to influence school practices. If schools are to continue to increase their dominance over the child by lengthening the period when he is at school and multiplying their resources for character-making, the family must more effectively present its point of view to those who administer our schools or the child will surely suffer loss.

If the home has a tendency to make too much of the individual child, the school is certainly amiss in making too little. The school emphasizes the group. It is still largely impersonal and formal and too greatly interested in the learning of facts and in objective and measurable accomplishments to be safely trusted with the predominant influence in the making of personality. The gulf that many a child feels between his home and his school leads in these days to a type of social discord that hurts any child who experiences it.

The functions of the school and the home are too different for the one ever to become a substitute for the other, but there now is grave need of a more sympathetic understanding, and it is the school that will suffer unless it learns to appreciate the other's social service. The Parent-Teacher Association has been a valuable help in bringing teachers and parents into greater accord, but it has accomplished far more in reconciling the home to the work of the school than in creating in the school administration any sincere desire to incorporate within itself home qualities. Thus far the school has been much more impressed by the efficiency of modern business organizations than by the more human activities of wholesome home life.

Before the school can successfully abstract from the home its human values and make them a part of the child's educational environment, more effort must be made to give teachers a larger quantity of normal home life. A considerable proportion of women teachers would in any case be deprived of an opportunity to share a family life of their own, but at present this situation is generally regarded as a thing to be expected, even desired. As a consequence we have too many women teachers whose outlook upon life and reactions to its occurrences are less normal than wholesome instruction requires. The teacher who has no family experience, no realization of a child's behavior in the home circle, develops as by instinct too great stress on discipline, too much confidence in technic, and a dangerous loyalty to routine.

Even though the school may be exceedingly interesting to the child, it is devoid of the atmosphere of personal relationship which in the past has done so much, through home training, to socialize personality. In the decoration of its buildings and in its architecture the school has evidenced its appreciation of the value of atmosphere as a molding influence in the life of the growing child. It now needs to recognize the same fact regarding the personality of the teacher. This means, if it is faced with sincerity, that marriage and family life for women teachers should be regarded, as in other occupations, as purely the business of the individual

teacher. The fact that school authorities have so widely banned the
marriage of their women instructors discloses how far the school
has wandered away from a normal life-attitude and how much has
been sacrificed in its social function by giving too great heed to
ease of administration and institutional efficiency.

It is not surprising that a school system which refuses to
permit the women members of its staff to marry and which so
seldom engages one who has been a mother should do little directly
to relate the school to family life by preparing youth for home
responsibilities. It is, of course, a question which only experience
can answer, how far the school can go in getting young people
ready for an association that lies in the future, but it can at least
use its opportunity to impress young men and women with the
advantage of later getting specific instruction that will help them
when they actually face home and parenthood responsibilities.

If public school instruction can function efficaciously for good
citizenship in anticipation of the time when individuals will arrive
at a voting age, there is no reason why similar teaching regarding
the problems of marriage and of the home cannot be made educa-
tionally successful. The development of our public school system
appears to have sapped the vitality of many homes, so that they
are incapable of giving their children instruction that will prepare the next generation for better home life. It follows that if
the schools are to give preparation for life they must not omit
specific instruction regarding the experiences that belong to a
sphere of activity which has so much to do with human happiness
and social prosperity as the home.

Private Schools and the Family.—Our private schools are
often more in harmony with family life than those that are public.
The private school provides opportunity for educational experiment
to an extent that is difficult in standardized public education. The
students in the private schools are also largely selected in such a
way as to give the school a less serious task in its efforts to socialize.
The private school maintains a more home-like atmosphere; it is
more interested in home problems and keeps closer contact with
parents. It necessarily has to regard the home, since from the
home comes directly its financial support. The result is that the

private school leads in its attention to home atmosphere and in the serious endeavor to have its teaching function in later home life.

The Nursery School.—In the whole range of education there is at present nothing more significant or characteristic of our time than the growth of the nursery school idea. Although not entirely new, since it is the direct descendant of the Infant School of Robert Owen and others of his time, it is so closely related to recent developments of science that it deserves to be treated as an innovation. It originated in the need of studying and caring for the young child. The realization on the part of the more thoughtful educators and parents of the social importance of the findings of psychological science in the last twenty years, which have demonstrated the overwhelming importance of the early years of childhood, led to the establishment of an organization for the guidance of the young child, which is neither nursery nor school, but a place where children can get an early start in their development amid such conditions as science teaches us that the child requires for wholesome growth.

Since the city child was so clearly deprived of the resources necessary for his proper development, the nursery school came first in the city and is still largely confined to our cities. The parents who have been willing to coöperate in this new educational activity have also been chiefly in the professional and intellectual class. Because of this some nursery schools have made special effort to enrol children from poorer and less fortunate homes.

The analysis of adult character defects has made it apparent that one of the troublesome social products of modern life is an unreasonable degree of fixation of the child on its mother, or less commonly on its father. The larger family of the past without doubt guarded children from this dwarfing experience. The nursery school provides the means by which the child in the small family of today can be given this protection so early that there are less likely to be mischievous results from too close contact between the child and his parent. The child also finds companionship that is more beneficial for him than that in the large family where there were so likely to be older children who over-stimulated or nagged and took advantage of their younger brothers and sisters.

The nursery school child is introduced to a society made up of other children of his own age. He learns to play with them and becomes accustomed to a reasonable program of rest and recreation, is guided in the early formation of habits, and has a happy opportunity to begin the exploration of life.

The nursery school is costly; its success depends upon an environment of abundant resources for its purposes and a skilled staff of superior personal qualities. The expensiveness of the nursery school is likely to restrict it at least for the present. This is fortunate. Already we find determined effort to incorporate the nursery school in our public school system. There are certainly a considerable number of parents who would welcome such an annex to our traditional educational equipment merely because it would relieve them of the irksome task of having charge of their young child during a large part of the day. It would without question be disastrous at present to develop nursery schools rapidly and place them widely throughout the land as the starting-place for our orthodox public school education. At once would appear grave risk of institutionalizing the whole effort and making it only an earlier beginning of formal instruction. Teachers thoroughly committed to present educational procedure would of necessity become instructors in the new type of school. The nursery school would soon largely lose the human qualities that have made possible its success.

The nursery school stands between the school and the home and becomes their mediator. It has no ambition to replace the mother, but coöperates with the home, encouraging the mother to see it in operation, and naturally its invitation is generally accepted. It stimulates the study club for mothers that takes up problems of motherhood with seriousness. Conferences are held with the mothers, who are given every opportunity to get an unbiased but sympathetic interpretation of their child's problems and needs. The nursery school is just now the one point at which education and the home come in close contact, the only place where instruction is sensitive to the values and needs of the home.

Home Economics.—Next to the nursery school the student of family interests finds in our home economics courses the greatest connection between instruction and the home. In its origin this type of teaching was a definite attempt to prepare young girls for the duties of the home. Actually the instruction had to do mostly with household activities; in content it embraced teaching concerning food, textiles, child care and home decoration. The present trend is to recognize the larger problems of human relationships; without neglecting chemistry and economics, home economics courses are beginning to do greater justice to the social elements of the home problems. If these courses are to contribute their proper values to educational preparation for life, they must be radically adjusted to the changing circumstances of home-making.

The social trend is unmistakably towards taking out of the house activities that can be commercialized and carried on more efficiently on a large scale. Canning, for example, is a pursuit that can never again have the significance for the housekeeper that it has had in the past. The home economics program has suffered in its adaptability to present needs from a reluctance on the part of its administrators to recognize the currents of change in the modern home and to keep clearly in mind that such courses, so far as they belong in our secondary education, must be adjusted to the home rather than to the laboratory.

Useful as home economics courses have certainly been, they are falling behind their promise to the extent that they forget that home-making is more largely a problem of relationships than of occupation. It is in the light of this fact that a solution may be had to the old-time topic for discussion, whether courses in home economics should be required of all high school girls. We may not be justified in teaching all girls to cook or to sew by forcing upon them a required high school course, but we are justified in insisting that instruction regarding the home as a human institution deserves a place in the required program not only of all high school girls, but equally and for the self-same reason, of all high school boys. Embedded in such a program are the three elements that are contained in a thoroughgoing discussion of the subject: Marriage, home responsibilities, and parenthood.

Our courses in home economics have suffered loss in their relationship with the home from the fact that their teachers have so often themselves been strangers to normal home experiences because they, like other teachers, have remained unmarried and have grown away from home habits. Familiarity with home economics

18

courses also convinces the impartial observer that such work in many schools is hampered by the unadapted teaching of instructors who have become specialists or at least have acquired the habits of specialists while at college. Certainly the instruction of our high school departments of home economics has made only a slight contribution to the progress of the modern family.

Co-education and Family Welfare.—Discussion regarding the advantages and disadvantages of teaching boys and girls together continues, but fortunately for the welfare of the family the trend is constantly toward co-education. Co-education, particularly as it concerns the adolescent girl, presents a problem but much of the criticism of co-education, so far as it has to do with the adolescent girl, is essentially an attack on the harmful influences that find favorable opportunity in a difficult age-period rather than on co-education. Some who object to co-education are really complaining of human nature itself, not of the association of boys and girls. For example, sex attraction is a perfectly normal element of the adolescent period. Co-education does not produce it: segregation cannot prevent it. It comes because it is due in the development of the young person. Society knows no more effective way of dealing with it than to provide everyday contacts for boys and girls in the wholesome associations of school activities. Co-education furnishes a very important means of giving boys and girls the contact that helps give a basis for later normal family life.

Perhaps if it were in our power, on account of changes in our social life due to modern ways of living we might hold back sex attraction until a somewhat later period. Whether that would work out better for society than nature's present method could be demonstrated only by actual trial, but it is clear that any attempt to retard normal development along this line, so far as the individual is concerned, is likely to be as hazardous a proceeding as any other attempt at social or mental retardation. The morbid risks of segregation of the sexes have been too frequently demonstrated to give any ground for supposing that sex attraction can be more satisfactorily met by separating boys and girls during the adolescent period than by letting them associate as they do in the co-educational high school.

Adolescence is not a sharply defined period; it comes gradually and fades away little by little. Every argument that justifies co-education in the high schools equally stresses its advantages in most institutions of higher learning. The atmosphere of the co-educational college is far more normal and educational than can ever be developed in any college exclusively for men or for women. Sex itself does not have the prominence, where constant association between men and women at college is possible, that it gets as a consequence of separation. The difficulties of teaching mixed classes are fictitious, the product of theory and self-consciousness. There are of course individuals in co-educational colleges who are led from their work by the attraction they feel for members of the opposite sex, but this is not less likely to happen in the segregated colleges, even when frequent association is impossible.

Co-education well expresses the family impulse, for it provides in the developing period, when they are acquiring an education, opportunity for boys and girls and men and women to know each other under circumstances that make understanding of one another the natural consequence of contact. The segregated college remains with us as a product, so far as the man's college is concerned, of the time when as a result of man's dominance higher education belonged exclusively to him; and so far as the woman's college is concerned it remains to remind us that when women first rose from their subserviency and sought opportunity to develop their own capacities as did men, they were forced to form colleges of their own where they in turn imitated male exclusiveness. It is the co-educational college that is in harmony with the present social status of men and women and it is therefore the institution that is best qualified to train most young men and women in the way that adapts them not only to the modern family but also to the conditions of modern life itself.

Origin of Idea of Parenthood Training.—Nothing is more characteristic of our time than the idea of training parents. It is evidence not only of our supreme confidence in the value of education, but also of our realization that the home is in trouble and needs help.

We cannot assume, however, that parenthood training is a

modern discovery. Even among savages there has been some understanding of the social advantage of giving candidates for parenthood
instruction that was expected to prepare them for their obligations.
Our discussion is the result of a breaking down of the methods of
instruction that prevailed in the past and even more of a better
knowledge of the good that can come from teaching parents how
to deal wisely with their children. The home once gave instruction
for marriage and parenthood which was reasonably successful in
those days when parenthood was much less difficult than it is
to-day. Now we find the home, if it attempts to meet its responsibilities, unfitted to succeed unless parents are themselves given
specific, scientific instruction.

The necessity of a new type of instruction for parents is a
modern discovery, and is still the conviction of a few, but among
thoughtful and experienced social workers it is spreading with
great rapidity. Soon all our leadership will accept it as a social
axiom. It is born of a better understanding of the problems of
human happiness and of the processes by which human nature is
made from its raw material into an adult personality.

Science, once it cast aside its philosophic fetters and took in
hand seriously the study of people and their ways of living, brought
into clear light facts that are certain to lead to the training of
parents as a social necessity.

It has been hard for man to think of himself as a product of
causes. The idea was resented, as now it is by many, because it
carried with it social consequences that destroyed the comfortable
assumptions we love to make as a protection against social
responsibilities.

The idea that the adult is made, not by his adult choices or
his inheritance, but by early influences that fashioned him when
he was sensitive and easily formed, is a fact which is bound in the
end to dominate all our thinking in regard to character making.
We hide from ourselves the revolutionary character of modern
social and psychological science when we consider that our idea
of childhood determination is merely a clearer appreciation of what
our ethical teachers have always thought.

The definite knowledge we now have of the process by which

children are developed into persons of fixed character, our insight into the impossibility of greatly modifying the personality, once it is set, our sense of the social importance of the home as the place of the first and therefore the greatest influences will soon alter every conception we have had of good preparation for life. Social science began with this recent discovery. Since in modern life changes come with surprising quickness, every aspect of man's life will be reconstructed in harmony with the new fact in human relationships. The home is one of the first institutions to feel the impending change since it is so obviously required to adjust itself to the new truth. Religion, industry, public school education and every other major social interest must, however, follow the home and prove its social efficiency by constructing its activities upon the fact that the determination that rules human life is not sin or instincts or knowledge, but the formative happenings of childhood.

We owe a great deal to mental hygiene for pioneering in the field of childhood determination. It was forced either to stress childhood experiences or turn aside from the clear pathway of social causation. Mental hygiene tried at first to reconstruct warped and spoiled personalities with confidence in its technic and its understanding of human needs. It quickly realized that both its failures and its successes harked back to childhood conditions, the strength of such factors, and the ability of the specialists to isolate and reform them. The early confidence of mental hygiene in its power to reëducate gave way, with an increase of knowledge, to the realization that the economical and efficient way of obtaining better mental health was a wiser use of childhood. Since the child is the partaker rather than the maker of childhood, the next logical step was an effort to bring science into the home. This in essence meant parenthood training. Science had the means of such training. It knew the need. It tried to popularize its findings and as a result parenthood training became at once the object of those who believed that the home could be made to contribute its maximum of wholesome social influences to the developing life of the child.

Development of Content.—It was natural that stress upon the responsibility of the parent for the physical welfare of the child should have come first. It was the physician who led the way to the conservation of child life. Medical science was more advanced than either psychology or sociology and far better prepared to emphasize the influence of early childhood as a preparation for good health in the adult. Not until another generation reaches middle life shall we begin to gather the first fruits of the remarkable progress made in safeguarding the physical side of childhood.

The physician skilled in literary expression undertook the task of producing books that could be widely circulated, easily understood and followed by conscientious mothers. Some of these books were read by more than a million mothers. Magazines read by women took up the discussion of the physical health of children. The consequence was a new technic in the handling of babies, widely practiced in spite of the protest of grandmothers, and decidedly for the advantage of the infants.

Next, attention was given to the psychic side of the child's early life, for it became apparent that his physical welfare was tied up with his mental development. Psychological science, about this time, shook itself free from abstractions and began to collect a vast amount of experimental knowledge of value to parents. It was not, however, until the mental hygiene movement got under way that the serious import of the mental life of young children was revealed.

As soon as attention was turned to the mental life of children it grew clear that this side of childhood could not be handled except from the social viewpoint. It was not mind as an isolated experience, but the mental life of contact that science had to interpret. Both psychology and sociology were involved. The child, to be understood, had to be thought of as a functioning personality whose impulses were expressed in the everyday life of association with parents and playmates. The analysis of character led straight back to childhood where it was discovered that difficulties originated, not because of defective impulses, but on account of the way the impulsive life was badly developed as a consequence of the unfortunate influences that played upon the mind of the child in his early years.

It is this social aspect of childhood that we have in mind when we advocate the training of parents. We realize to-day that the home failure is not so much along mental and physical as along social lines. Parents treat the physical needs of the child with far greater understanding than his social interests, born of his contacts. It is, therefore, at this point that science must help parents if it is to do anything of practical value in training for parenthood. The social needs of the child are not so easily handled as his physical needs because, though rules can often be made to apply very well in dealing with his physique, they can not give satisfactory guidance for parents in dealing with social conditions. A balanced diet can be formulated with considerable exactness, but the social side of childhood cannot be treated in so mechanical a way. If parents are to meet their social responsibilities in handling their children, they must be educated rather than trained. The task includes more than devolved upon the doctor when he undertook to help mothers give their children better physical care.

Science now is better prepared to assist parents than was true when the movement for physical conservation first started. Science is better acquainted with the kind of problem it assumes when it attempts popular instruction. Parents, also, are willing to accept help, in part because of their desperate plight, but largely because they have already learned the value of scientific assistance.

The Present Situation.—An analysis of the present status of parenthood education reveals the growing interest in the subject. Evidence of this comes from many quarters and is unmistakable. Although at present parenthood education is being discussed mostly by social workers and students of the home, consideration of the subject is by no means confined to the social specialist. The idea that parents need special preparation for their life task appears in magazine articles, and occasionally even in the more popular newspaper. Courses for parents are already being offered by universities and various types of social organizations. Although this instruction is clearly experimental in character, its appearance is proof of a concern with parenthood training which seems to be developing rapidly.

It is possible to exaggerate this interest. It is a happy fact that so many people are at least talking about the need of training parents, but we can easily over-value the significance of this discussion. The great majority of those, even, who are committed to the idea of training parents have vague notions as to what such instruction really involves. To a large extent the discussion means no more than that people are beginning to realize that parents are not satisfactorily meeting their responsibilities and that they need help if they are to be more efficient. In other words, the attention given to parenthood training is to a great extent merely another illustration of the American habit of turning to education whenever a social perplexity arises, but without any clear conception as to how education can make its necessary contribution.

A multitude of parents, in spite of the fact that many of them are having difficulties with their children, are either indifferent or hostile to the idea of special instruction for parenthood. The reasons for their attitude are many. A few at least deserve attention, they are so commonly found. Some parents are indifferent because they see no need of parents receiving other instruction than that which comes, in their opinion, from the very fact of parenthood; they have confidence in some mystic resource which is supposedly given to the parents when the child comes, and qualifies them to handle the child wisely. Such persons explain the manifest failures of home life by the evil ways of the child; they see no need of training the parent, since they feel that he is endowed with the needed insight; to them the one question is, "Are the children obedient?" They have no recognition of the fact that obedient children are as likely as others, if they have not been given understanding parents, to have difficulties of social adjustment.

There is also another group of parents who resent as criticism of themselves any suggestion that parents should be given special education. Here we find ourselves dealing with a form of inferiority reaction. These parents do not have genuine confidence in their ability to handle their home problems, but they are unwilling because of self-pride to look squarely at the facts and admit their need of assistance. Moreover, some of them are antagonistic since they realize that science is bound to get a foothold in family life if the idea of parenthood education prevails, and they are hostile to science because all their life they have been trying to protect themselves from the personal adjustments they would have to make in their thinking and acting if they were to listen without prejudice to the teachings of science. To them education is safe so long as it keeps away from life, but it becomes treacherous the moment it is applied to any social situation; they want to keep it out of the home because they fear its social implications. These parents are perfectly willing that the young mother should be taught to cook or to care for the child's physical needs, but to use science in the construction of the human character of the little child is to them a treasonable idea at variance with all their life philosophy.

There is enough indifference and hostility to make any program of parenthood training more difficult to popularize than the enthusiast, who sees only the keen interest of a minority of parents, is likely to suppose.

Inspection of the present status of parenthood education uncovers another fact which is most encouraging. Those who seriously advocate education for parenthood with an understanding of what they wish to accomplish have an idea of the relation of cause and effect in home life. This is a forward step that has decided significance. It is always hard to bring any part of social experience under the concept of cause and effect; this is due in part to the difficulty of establishing such relationships and even more to the reluctance of human nature to deal with its own situations with the impersonal open-mindedness that is always necessary when one attempts to trace the workings of cause. Naturally we would expect the home to be the last place to accept the idea that its relationships are conditioned by the same law of causation that science has demonstrated in the other territories it has investigated. It is because we are already beginning to see how home conditions operate as causes in the life of the developing child that we are anxious to train parents. In so far as such education is carried out with success it will build up in the thought of parents the conception of causation in the character-making of the child. This, of course, does not mean that the parent has an exclusive control of factors that affect the child, or even that the home is the only source of determining influences in his social life, but rather that the parent has the most substantial grasp of opportunity and must therefore be the best prepared to deal with the child with the knowledge that what is done will surely have a large part in shaping his career.

The development of education for parents will do much more than enable parents to deal adequately with their children; it will further extend the idea of social causation which is fundamental to all our progress; it will lead the home to turn to science with the same eagerness to know the facts of social contact that the housekeeper has so long shown in dealing with the problems of the kitchen.

To bring to parents even a faint realization that the behavior of the child is due to influences that have operated upon him, and that such influences are in large measure under the control of the parent, is a social victory of large importance; but it must be confessed that we do not have exact knowledge as to how such causes operate, to the extent we might wish. Science in this field is young. It has worked against serious obstacles. As a consequence, we have neither the knowledge nor the standards with respect to the home that we need to get the best results from parenthood education. We find wide differences of opinion regarding certain aspects of family life. It is not strange that there should be such lack of agreement among students; indeed it is remarkable that the differences are not more numerous and held with greater tenacity. Experimentation is practically impossible. Observation is particularly difficult; every character study involves the untangling of a multitude of social influences, only a portion of which can be rightly charged to the home life. It is easy to exaggerate the seriousness of the differences of opinion that we now find among child specialists. There is certainly abundant material about which general agreement exists, and which seems to be substantiated by actual experience, that is available for the instruction of parents.

It is clear, however, that parenthood instruction requires a constantly developing body of scientific material which will show us more plainly and in greater detail just how the happenings of early childhood construct the personality that possesses the adult. Part of the material we now have has come to us from experiences that we usually catalogue as abnormal. Attention has been turned to badly adjusted personalities because these have required assistance, and they could not be helped without first being understood. Out of these investigations has come a large part of our ideas concerning good and bad parenthood. But we must, if our instruction of parents is to be reliable, pay much more attention to those homes that have been considered successful, where parents seem to have led their children into wholesome development.

It will some day appear strange that institutions of higher learning have made so little effort to investigate normal social relationships and have been so slow in developing courses of instruction in regard to marriage, parenthood, and home life. Education, with a strange perversity, started with the remote interests and has moved reluctantly toward those things that make up the core of our living and concern us most. The Institute of Euthenics at Vassar College discloses the growing sense of responsibility on the part of the colleges for parental education.

A study of the present status of parenthood education discloses another thing which its advocates need to realize. As interest in the problems of the home and the child is stimulated, opening will be made which the social promoter will be eager to enter as an easy way to distinction or big profits. We all know how the widespread interest in psychology was exploited; as mental hygiene attempted to distribute the findings of the psychiatrist and the psychologist, it soon found itself confronted with the exploiter. A considerable portion of the public who most needed the help of science were easily victimized by the fakir who mixed truth and falsehood in such a fashion that his teachings were generally more mischievous than helpful.

Once parents realize how desperately they need help and how much help can be given them, a still greater opportunity than was offered by the mental hygiene movement is likely to be snatched up by the pseudo-scientist who may be clever in presentation but utterly unreliable. Not only will the interests of parents be betrayed and science perverted into sentiment, but immediately scientists in the other fields, whose coöperation we who advocate parenthood instruction need, will become disgusted and eventually hostile to the movement. Any attempt to popularize science invites the promoter who learns a smattering of the new facts and then goes out to gather a harvest of dollars or applause, according to whether he enters the field for money or mere distinction.

The only thing that will secure the movement and save it from the risk of being exploited will be constant stress upon science. We must keep before the mind of the parents whom we attempt to teach the fact that we are getting our material from science, that it is a product of scientific investigation, and that although it seems simple, any one who is unscientific in temperament and training is as unfitted to teach it as the layman would be in expounding medical knowledge.

An analysis of our present status in parenthood education shows also that parents are for the most part demanding recipes rather than insight. They want formulas and expect from the teacher the definite statement, " Do this; don't do that," without qualification and without due regard for the concrete situation.   Even among those who are asking for instruction, where naturally we expect to find a high level of intelligence, we discover that not a few parents are interested in taking courses or hearing lectures or reading books in the same spirit that the illiterate person runs to the drug store, asking for something good to take for a self-diagnosed ailment.

Parenthood instruction can never successfully become the imparting of rules. Parents require understanding, not a statement that will permit them to deal with the child in the same manner that they follow directions in making a cake. Much of the craving parents express for concrete assistance is really a demand for rules that they can automatically follow. It is true that the instruction of parents will issue in a new technic, but it cannot become a procedure blind to circumstances or applied without discrimination and insight. Parenthood instruction must aim at better parents. The movement will accomplish nothing if it degenerates into an easy way by which the mother can learn how best to punish Johnny and keep Sarah from the movies.

It is interesting to note how frequently in our discussion of parenthood instruction we say *mother* and how seldom, *father*. It is to be expected, of course, that the mother should be more sensitive to the necessity of adequate preparation for parenthood; but the movement from the first must insist that it is training parents, not mothers. A large part of the problem in our homes at present is the little actual influence fathers contribute. If parenthood instruction confines itself entirely to the interests and problems of mothers, it will accomplish good but not so much good as we have a right to expect. Heroic effort must be made to prevent the parenthood instruction crusade from becoming a woman's club enterprise. One of the practical ways of stressing the education of fathers is to encourage education for marriage. Men appear nearly as anxious to have this instruction as women. Their interest provides a good basis for the building up of an interest that will carry over from the idea of preparation for marriage to that of training for parenthood, when at a later time a child appears. Indeed, instruction for marriage and for parenthood are inseparable, but at present public attention is primarily centered on the second. Eventually it will be seen that to train parents adequately we must also train youth for marriage.

APPENDIX

BIBLIOGRAPHIES

The student of social problems of the family will find the following bibliographies of assistance in original research:

Burgess, E. W., *American Journal of Sociology*, July, 1926.
Calhoun, A. W., " Social History of the American Family," pp. 332–358.
Groves, E. R., " Social Problems and Education," pp. 431–438.
Howard, G. E., " A History of Matrimonial Institutions," vol. 3, pp. 263–402.
Popenoe, P., " Conservation of the Family," pp. 255–258.
Robertson, A. I., " Guide to Literature of Home and Family Life."

CHAPTER I

SOCIAL SIGNIFICANCE OF THE FAMILY

References

Goodsell, W., " A History of the Family as a Social and Educational Institution", ch. 1.
(Especially Recommended)

Bosanquet, H., " The Family," Introduction.
Cutler, J. E., Durable Monogamous Wedlock, *American Journal of Sociology*, vol. xxii, No. 2.
Dealey, J. Q., " The Family in its Sociological Aspects," ch. 1.
Flügel, J. C., " The Psycho-analytic Study of the Family," ch. 12.
Groves, E. R., " The Drifting Home," chs. 1, 2, 3.
Lee, P. R., Changes in Social Thought and Standards which affect the Family, " National Conference of Social Work," 1923, pp. 286–294.
Levitt, A., Love and the Law, *Journal of Social Hygiene*, vol. xi, No. 8.
Ogburn, W. F., Factors Affecting the Marital Condition of the Population, " Pub. Am. Sociological Society," vol. xviii, pp. 47–59.
Parsons, E. C., " The Family," ch. 1.
Robertson, A. I., " Guide to Literature of Home and Family Life."
Williams, J. M., " The Expansion of Rural Life," ch. 22.

Topics for Discussion

1. Why are the first years of childhood so important?
2. What illustrations can you give of injury to children in their early years because of bad home life?
3. Why is the home so commonly interpreted as free from change?
4. What changes do you detect in the home life of your community?
5. Will the five-day working week proposed by the American Federation of Labor prove an advantage to the home?
6. Is the best test of a person based on his home-conduct?
7. Will the functions of the family continue to decrease?

Subject for Reports

1. The home and the conditioned reflex.
2. The home and the emotional life of children.
3. The political significance of the home.
4. The danger of family privacy.
5. Sectional variations in American family life.
6. The influence of traditions upon family life.
7. The Family Section of the American Sociological Society.

CHAPTER II
THE PRIMITIVE FAMILY
References

Westermarck, E., "The History of Human Marriage."
(Especially recommended)

Bosanquet, H., "The Family," ch. 2.
Dealey, J. Q., "The Family in its Sociological Aspects," chs. 2, 3.
Dow, G. S., "Society and its Problems," ch. 10.
Ellwood, C. A., "Sociology and Modern Social Problems," chs. 5, 6.
Freud, S., "Totem and Taboo."
Goldenweisser, A. A., "Early Civilization," chs. 3, 12.
Goodsell, W., "A History of the Family as a Social and Educational
    Institution," chs. 2–6.
Hobhouse, L. T., Wheeler, G. C. and Ginsberg, M., "The Material Culture
    and Social Institutions of the Simpler Peoples," ch. 3.
Hooker, E. H., "The Laws of Sex," ch. 2.
Howard, G. E., "A History of Matrimonial Institutions," pt. 1.
Knight, M., Peters, I., and Blanchard, P., "Taboo and Genetics," pt. 2.
Lowie, R. H., "Primitive Society," chs. 2, 3, 4, and 8.
Malinowski, B., Prenuptial Intercourse Between the Sexes in the Trobriand
    Islands, *Psychoanalytic Review*, vol. xiv, No. 1.
Mason, O. T., "Woman's Share in Primitive Culture."
Spencer, A. G., "Woman's Share in Social Culture," ch. 1.
Spencer, B., and Gillen, F. J., "The Native Tribes of Central Australia,"
    chs. 2, and 3.
Thomas, W. I., "Sex and Society," pp. 55–223.
Todd, A. J., "The Primitive Family as an Educational Agency."
Tozzer, A. M., "Social Origins and Social Continuities," ch. 4.
Tucker, E. F. G., and Gilbert, L. H., Primitive Promiscuity and Group
    Marriage, *Sociological Review*, vol. xviii, No. 4.
Wallis, W. D., "An Introduction to Anthropology," chs. 28–30.

Topics for Discussion

1. How do you explain the high standards of child discipline among
    savages?
2. Is modern woman happier than was the savage woman?
3. What should be the missionary's attitude toward savage family customs?
4. Does the urban or the rural environment offer at present the more
    favorable environment for modern family life?

5. Is it wise for individuals who have shared from childhood the same social environment to marry?

6. Do you believe there could be changes in social conditions that would lead to a revival of polygyny or polyandry?

Subjects for Reports

1. The study of the family life of an American Indian tribe.
2. The Iroquois matriarchate.
3. The Australian savage's marriage system.
4. Freud's theory of the mother-in-law taboo.
5. Social causes of infanticide among savages.
6. The power of old men in Australian savage society.
7. The marriage of cousins.

CHAPTER III

HISTORY OF THE AMERICAN FAMILY

References

Calhoun, A. W., "Social History of the American Family." (Especially recommended)

Dealey, J. Q., "The Family in its Sociological Aspects," ch. 8.
George, W. L., "The Story of Woman."
Goodsell, W., "A History of the Family as a Social and Educational Institution."
Harper, I. H., "Life and Work of Susan B. Anthony," 3 vols.
Hecker, E., "A Short History of Women's Rights."
Howard, G. E., "A History of Matrimonial Institutions," chs. 12–16.
Kempf, E. J., Charles Darwin, The Affective Sources of his Inspiration and Anxiety Neurosis, *The Psychoanalytic Review*, vol. v, No. 2; also "Psychopathology," pp. 208–251.
Kenton, E., The Ladies' Next Step, *Harpers Monthly*, February, 1926.
Keyserling, H., "The Book of Marriage," pp. 216–243.
Macy, J., Equality of Woman with Man: A Myth, *Harpers Monthly*, November, 1926.
Mill, J. S., "Subjection of Women."
Nearing, S., "Woman and Social Progress."
Phillips, R. L., The Real Rights of Women, *Harpers Monthly*, October, 1926.
Rich, A. M., The League of Women Voters and Family Social Work, *The Family*, vol. vii, No. 4.
Schiermacker, K., "The Modern Woman's Rights Movement," pp. 2–42.
Spencer, A. G., "The Family and its Members," ch. 15.
Stanton, E. C., Anthony, Gage, and Harper, "History of Woman Suffrage," 4 vols.
Taylor, C. C., "Rural Sociology," ch. 9.
Visher, S. S., "Who's Who" Among American Women, *The Scientific Monthly*, vol. xv, No. 5.
Williams, J. M., "Our Rural Heritage," chs. 6, 9.
Wollstonecraft, M., "Vindication of the Rights of Women."

Topics for Discussion

1. How do you explain the harsh treatment of children in the early theology of New England?
2. What was the origin of the New England conscience?
3. Do hard economic circumstances weaken or strengthen family affection?
4. What did Abraham Lincoln owe to his frontier childhood?
5. Was polygyny an advantage in the early period of the Mormon settlement in Utah?
6. Would woman suffrage have come without agitation?
7. Has woman suffrage failed?
8. What influences has the World War had on American family life?

Subjects for Reports

1. Woman's status in English common law.
2. Home life in the Puritan colony.
3. Home life in colonial Virginia.
4. Home life in Dutch New York.
5. Influence of negro slavery upon southern family life.
6. A critical study of *Vindication of the Rights of Women*.
7. The early history of the American woman suffrage movement.
8. Mormon family life under polygyny.
9. The National Women's Party and its program.

CHAPTER IV

HUMAN NEED OF THE FAMILY

References

Groves, E. R., " The Drifting Home."
(Especially recommended)

Bosanquet, H., " The Family," ch. 10.
Colcord, J. C., The Fabric of Family Life, *The Family*, vol. v, No. 7.
Groves, E. R., " Rural Mind and Social Welfare," pp. 86–97.
Huxley, J., " Essays of a Biologist," ch. 4.
Kelly, F. F., The Future of the Family, *Century Magazine*, vol. cxii, No. 5.
Keyserling, H., " The Book of Marriage," pp. 263–270.
Mayo, E., Should Marriage be Monotonous? *Journal of Social Hygiene*, vol. xi, No. 9.
Morse, L. B., Cultural Contributions of the Home to Child Life, *Progressive Education*, vol. iii, No. 4.
Parsons, A. B., " Woman's Dilemma," pp. 180–188.
Popenoe, P., " Conservation of the Family," Part IV.
——"Modern Marriage," ch. 1.
de Schweinitz, C., Social Work as it Contributes to the Strengthening of Family Life, *Journal of Social Hygiene*, vol. ix, No. 8.
—— The Cultivation of Family Life, *The Family*, vol. v, No. 8.
Spencer, A. G., " The Family and its Members," ch. 1.

Todd, A. J., The Family as a Factor in Social Evolution, "Nat'l Conf. of Social Work," vol. xxii, pp. 13–21.

Woodhouse, C. G., The New Profession of Homemaking, *Survey*, vol. 57, No. 5.

Topics for Discussion

1. Why is it an advantage to the doctor to marry?
2. Why is the unmarried minister so apt to be socially popular?
3. Do you believe that most married couples are frank with one another?
4. How far is the desire of women for children a result of social suggestion?
5. How does parenthood socialize?
6. Is Platonic friendship between men and women possible? If possible, is it desirable?
7. Should unmarried women of culture who do not expect to marry be encouraged to adopt children?
8. Which is apt to be the more hazardous, a first or a second marriage?
9. What are the norms of family life?

Subjects for Reports

1. Motives that impel people to marry.
2. Social conditions that antagonize marriage.
3. Advantages of marriage for the business man.
4. The family life of the Brownings and its influence upon their poetry.
5. The political significance of the family life of Abraham Lincoln.
6. The domestic failures of Percy Shelley.
7. Kempf's interpretation of family influence upon the life and work of Charles Darwin.

CHAPTER V

ECONOMIC CONDITIONS AFFECTING FAMILY LIFE

References

Pruette, L., " Women and Leisure."
(Especially recommended)

Abel, " Successful Family Life on a Moderate Income."
Abbott, E., " Women in Industry."
Andrews, B. R., " Economics of the Household; Its Administration and Finance."
Baber, R. E., and Ross, E. A., " Changes in the Size of American Families in One Generation," ch. 5.
Bosanquet, H., " The Family," ch. 9.
Bulletins of Women's Bureau: Women in Four Selected Cities, No. 41; Women in Ohio Industries, No. 44; The New Position of Women in American Industry, No. 12; Women in New Jersey Industries, No. 37.
Collier, V. M., " Marriage and Careers."
Dow, G. S., " Society and its Problems," pp. 232–245.
Dublin, L. I., Home Makers and Careers, *Atlantic Monthly*, September, 1926.

Gilman, C. P., "Women and Economics."

Gordon, M. J., State Laws Affecting Working Women, "Bulletin of Women's Bureau, No. 40."

Groves, E. R., "Social Problems and Education," ch. 5.

———"The Drifting Home," ch. 5.

Hammond, J. L., and B., "The Town Labourer," ch. 2.

Hansl, E. v B., What About the Children? *Harpers*, Jan., 1927.

Hinkle, B. M., Changing Marriage, A By-Product of Industrialism, *Survey*, vol. 57, No. 5.

Hughes, G. S., "Mothers in Industry."

Kingsbury, S. M., The Relation of Women to Industry, "Pub. American Sociological Society," vol. xv, pp. 141-158.

LaFollette, S., "Concerning Women."

Mavity, N. B., The Wife, the Home and the Job, *Harpers Monthly*, July, 1926.

Parsons, A. B., "Woman's Dilemma."

Parsons, E. C., "The Family," ch. 10.

Ross, M., Shall We Join the Gentlemen? *Survey*, vol. 57, No. 5.

Schreiner, O., "Woman and Labor."

Snedden, D., Probable Economic Future of Women, *American Journal of Sociology*, vol. xxiv, No. 5.

Spencer, A. G., "Woman's Share in Social Culture," chs. 8, 11.

Stone, G., "A History of Labour," ch. 9.

Winslow, M. N., Married Women in Industry, *Journal of Social Hygiene*, vol. ix, No. 7.

Wolfson, T., "The Woman Worker and the Trade Unions."

Woods, R. A., and Kennedy, A. J., "Young Working Girls," chs. 2-4.

Topics for Discussion

1. Could the Industrial Revolution have been so directed as to prevent the economic suffering and family demoralization of the English working classes?
2. Has woman attained economic independence?
3. What are at present the educational handicaps of women?
4. How are modern American wives made parasitic?
5. Must women in the earning of a living sacrifice preparation for home making?
6. Are women as gregarious as men?
7. Do the experiences of the wage-earning woman alienate her from marriage and the home?

Subjects for Reports

1. Woman's contributions to primitive industry.
2. Family life of the English working classes during the Industrial Revolution.
3. The early history of secondary education for girls in the United States.
4. The development of higher education for women in the United States.
5. The influence of the automobile upon American home life.
6. The family budget.
7. The social significance of matrimonial competition among women.

CHAPTER VI

THE ARRESTED FAMILY

References

East, E. M., " Mankind at the Crossroads."
(Especially recommended)

Carr-Saunders, A. M., "The Population Problem," pp. 314–321.
Fishbein, M., Birth Control: An Unsolved Problem, *The American Mercury*, vol. iii, No. 10.
Groves, E. R., " The Drifting Home," ch. 7.
Hibbs, H. H., Infant Mortality and the Size of the Family, *Quar. Pub. Am'n Statistical Ass'n.*, vol. xiv, pp. 629–641.
Hollingworth, L. S., Social Devices for Impelling Women to Bear and Rear Children, *American Journal of Sociology*, vol. xxii, pp. 19–29.
Inge, W. R., " Outspoken Essays," ch. 3.
Malthus, R., " Essay on Population " (2d edition or later).
Meyers, A. W., Neo-Malthusianism, *Journal of Social Hygiene*, vol. ix, No. 9.
Newcomer, M., and Gibson, E. S., Vital Statistics from Vassar College, *American Journal of Sociology*, vol. xxix, No. 4.
Newsholme, A., " The Elements of Vital Statistics," ch. 9.
Popenoe, P., " Conservation of the Family," Part II, chs. 7, 9–11.
———— Family or Companionate, *Journal of Social Hygiene*, vol. xi, No. 3.
Reuter, E. B., " Population Problems," ch. 11.
Swinburne, J., " Population and Social Problems," ch. 22.
Thomson, W. S., " Size of Families from which College Students Come."
————" Population: A Study in Malthusianism."
Worthington, G. E., Statutory Restrictions on Birth Control, *Journal of Social Hygiene*, vol. ix, No. 8.
Wright, H., " Population," ch. 6.

Topics for Discussion

1. Among your acquaintances is the companionate increasing?
2. What seem to you the chief causes of the companionate as you find it among people you know?
3. Do you detect greater or less happiness among your friends who have children than among those maintaining companionates?
4. Do you believe women have an instinctive desire to have children? Do men?
5. Is the having of children a public duty or a matter merely of private concern?
6. Do you expect the popularity of the companionate to increase or decrease? Why?
7. Would you advise a young man just entering a profession to delay marriage or to establish a companionate?

Subjects for Reports

1. Venereal disease and sterility.
2. The problem of abortion in the United States.

3. Marriage and family statistics of graduates of Vassar College.
4. Taxation and the companionate.
5. The influence of education upon the size of families.
6. Malthus' Theory of Population and the companionate.
7. The birth-rate trend among native Americans.

CHAPTER VII

COURTSHIP

References

Popenoe, P., " Modern Marriage," chs. 3, 4.
(Especially recommended)

Allen, G., " Falling in Love and Other Essays."
Blanchard, P., " The Adolescent Girl," ch. 6.
Booth-Clibborn, C., " Love and Courtship."
Edson, N. W., " Choosing a Home Partner."
———— Love in the Making, *Journal of Social Hygiene*, vol. xi, No. 5.
Exner, M. J., " The Question of Petting."
Gans, B. S., ed., " Concerning Parents," pp. 137–159.
Groves, E. R., " Personality and Social Adjustment," chs. 13–14.
Hart, H., The Eugenist on Early Marriage, *Journal of Social Hygiene*, vol. xiii, No. 1.
Key, E., " Love and Marriage," ch. 4.
Keyserling, H., " The Book of Marriage," pp. 273–305.
Popenoe, P., Early Marriages and Happiness, *Journal of Social Hygiene*, vol. xii, No. 9.
Pruette, L., What's Happening in the Daydreams of the Adolescent Girl, *Journal of Social Hygiene*, vol. x, No. 7.
————" Women and Leisure," ch. 8.
Thomas, W. I., " Sex and Society," pp. 223–247.
Westermarck, E., " The History of Human Marriage," vol. 1, ch. 13.

Topics for Discussion

1. What is the purpose of animal courtship?
2. How do adolescent girls win the attention of boys?
3. Has there been in recent years a decrease of the male's desire to lead in courtship?
4. Is deception a necessary element in courtship?
5. How far does age influence the character of courtship?
6. Are men right in complaining of the high costs of modern courtship?
7. How long ought courtship to last?
8. What are the causes of petting?
9. Do you favor an elaborate or simple wedding? Why?
10. What kind of honeymoon is the best preparation for happy family life?

Subjects for Reports

1. Darwin's description of animal courtship.
2. Courtship among savages.
3. Fashion as a function of courtship.

4. The psychology of courtship.
5. Changes in American wedding ceremonies.
6. The history of the honeymoon.
7. Day-dreams of adolescent girls.
8. Day-dreams of adolescent boys.
9. The history of courtship in America.

CHAPTER VIII

FAMILY INCOMPATIBILITIES

References

Flügel, J. C., " The Psycho-Analytic Study of the Family."
(Especially recommended)

A Modern Ruth, Meditations of a Daughter-in-Law, *The Atlantic Monthly*,
   January, 1925.
Burgess, E. W., The Romantic Impulse and Family Disorganization, *Survey*,
   vol. 57, No. 5.
Davis, K. B., A Study of the Sex Life of the Normal Married Woman,
   Journal of Social Hygiene, vol. viii, pp. 173–189; vol. ix, pp. 126–146.
Gans, B. S., " Concerning Parents," pp. 5–23.
Groves, E. R., " The Drifting Home," ch. 7.
———" Personality and Social Adjustment," ch. 12.
Flinn, H., and Jacoby, A. L., One Hundred Domestic Relations Problems,
   Mental Hygiene, vol. x, No. 4.
Kempf, E. J., " Psychopathology," ch. 2.
Keyserling, H., " The Book of Marriage," pp. 348–363.
Knight, M. M., Peters, I. L., and Blanchard, P., " Taboo and Genetics,"
   Part III.
Myerson, A., " The Nervous Housewife."
Mowrer, E., " Family Disorganization."
——— City Life and Domestic Discord, *Survey*, vol. 57, No. 5.
Tannenbaum, S. A., Jealousy and its Treatment with Reports of Cases,
   Journal of Sexology and Psychanalysis, vol. 1, Nos. 2, 3.
Warner, F. L., Love's Minor Frictions, *Atlantic Monthly*, December,
   1920, pp. 746–751.
Weininger, O., " Sex and Character," ch. 9.

Topics for Discussion

1. Why do women more often than men desire an elaborate wedding?
2. Why are newly married women often excessively ambitious and super-sensitive in regard to their housekeeping?
3. Should a newly married couple entertain relations and friends the first year of their housekeeping?
4. Do you believe that young women are less prepared for housekeeping now than were their mothers?
5. What preparation for marriage should boys receive?
6. Is marriage disillusionment normal and necessary?
7. Why do many married persons deteriorate soon after marrying?

Subjects for Reports

1. A high school program for girls in preparation for marriage.
2. A college course for men in preparation for home responsibilities.
3. Analysis of cases of matrimonial jealousy.
4. Personality defects as a cause of marriage incompatibilities.
5. Home influences as causes of chronic day-dreaming.
6. Excessive novel reading as an escape from marriage dissatisfaction.

CHAPTER IX

DIVORCE AND DESERTION

References

Lichtenberger, J. P., " Divorce."
(Especially recommended)

Breckinridge, S. P., Family and the Law, " Nat'l Conf. Social Work," 1925.
Bromley, D. D., The Ethics of Alimony, *Harpers*, Feb., 1927.
Catholic Encyclopædia, vol. v, pp. 54–69. ix, pp. 691–707.
Colcord, J. C., " Broken Homes."
Dealey, J. Q., " The Family in its Sociological Aspects," ch. 9.
Devine, E. T., " The Principles of Relief," ch. 11.
Dow, G. S., " Society and its Problems," pp. 217–232.
Encyclopædia Britannica, 11th ed., Article on Divorce (by Willcox, F.)
Fiske, C., Marriage, Temporary or Permanent, *Atlantic Monthly*, September, 1926.
Ellwood, C. A., " Sociology and Modern Social Problems," ch. 8.
Eubank, E. E., " A Study of Family Desertion."
Groves, E. R., " Social Problems and Education," ch. 6.
Howard, G. E., " A History of Matrimonial Institutions, chs. 17–18.
Key, E., " Love and Marriage," ch. 8.
Norcross, F. H., " Christianity and Divorce."
Patterson, S. H., Family Desertion and Non-Support, *Journal of Delinquency*, vol. vii, Nos. 5, 6.
Richmond, M. E., and Hall, F. S., " Child Marriages."
———" Marriage Laws."
Sorokin, P., Influence of the World War upon Divorces, *Journal of Applied Sociology*, vol. x, No. 2.
Spencer, A. G., " The Family and its Members," ch. 12.
Stevens, D., vs. Hale, R., Freedom in Divorce, *Forum*, vol. 76, No. 3.

Topics for Discussion

1. Do children tend to prevent the desire for divorce or merely to make it difficult to carry out the desire?
2. Do you believe in a national divorce law?
3. Do you believe in divorce? On what grounds?
4. When do you think alimony should be granted divorced wives?
5. Why were there so many divorces among war-brides?
6. What is the minimum marriage age in your state? What ought it to be?

7. What is the law of your state regarding common-law marriage? What is the attitude of your community?
8. What is the law of your state regarding family desertion?

Subjects for Reports

1. Early divorce legislation and practices in New England.
2. The teaching of the Roman Catholic Church regarding divorce.
3. Recent changes regarding divorce in England.
4. Trial divorce.
5. Legislative program advocated as a means of decreasing divorces.
6. Influence of the World War upon divorce.
7. An analysis of cases of family desertion.
8. Treatment of the family deserter.

CHAPTER X

THE BROKEN FAMILY AND ITS SOCIAL RESULTS

References

Colcord, J. C., " Broken Homes."
(Especially recommended)

Ansted, H. B., The Auto-Camp Community, *Journal of Applied Sociology*, vol. ix, No. 2.
Buffington, A. A., Automobile Migrants, *The Family*, vol. vi, No. 5.
—— Automobile Migrants, " Nat'l Conf. Social Work," pp. 258–264.
Eubank, E. E., " A Study of Family Desertion," ch. 4.
Karpf, M. J., The Demoralized Family, *Journal of Social Forces*, vol. 1, No. 4.
Shideler, Family Disintegration and the Delinquent Boy in the United States, *Journal of Criminal Law*, vol. viii, No. 5.
Slawson, J., Marital Relations of Parents and Juvenile Delinquency, *Journal of Delinquency*, vol. viii, Nos. 5, 6.
Stream Pictures from Family Records: A Broken Home, *The Family*, vol. iv, No. 8.
Sutherland, E. H., " Criminology," pp. 134–148.
Woodbury, R. M., Maternal Mortality, " Children's Bureau, No. 158."

Topics for Discussion

1. Do you believe in restricting the publicity of divorce trials?
2. What bad effects on character have you known to result from divorce?
3. Should a mother wait, on account of her children, thirty years for a divorce from an unhappy marriage?
4. Can anything be done to help families suffering from religious discord?
5. Should a child's treatment be influenced by the bad reputation of the home from which he comes?
6. What motives in your experience have led people to Wanderlust?
7. What was the effect of the World War upon the American children of that period?
8. Do you believe in requiring all men who marry to take out life insurance?

Subjects for Reports

1. Needed reforms in divorce trials.
2. The influence of the divorce lawyer upon family discord.
3. Life insurance as a family protection.
4. Child-placing societies as substitutes for the asylum—their policy and success.
5. Problems of the immigrant home.
6. The passing of the frontier and automobile migrants.
7. War and desertion.

CHAPTER II

MODERN CRITICISMS OF THE FAMILY

References

Kirchwey, F., " Our Changing Morality."
(Especially recommended)
Breuer, E., Feminism's Awkward Age, *Harpers Monthly*, April, 1925.
Carpenter, E., " Love's Coming of Age."
Ellis, H., " Little Essays of Love and Virtue," chs. 5, 7.
Ellis, Mrs. H., " Life of James Hinton."
George, W. L., Feminist Intentions, *Atlantic Monthly*, vol. 112, pp. 721–732.
Goodsell, W., " A History of the Family as a Social and Educational Institution," ch. 14.
Johnson, G. G., Feminism and the Economic Independence of Women, *Journal of Social Forces*, vol. iii, No. 4.
Key, E., " Love and Marriage," ch. 9.
Leuba, J. H., The Weaker Sex, *Atlantic Monthly*, April, 1926.
Margold, C. W., " Sex Freedom and Social Control."
Newkirk, F., The Case Against Marriage, *Journal of Sexology and Psychanalysis*, vol. i, No. 4.
Phillips, R., The Worthless Woman Triumphs, *American Mercury*, January, 1925.
Swinburne, J., " Population and Social Problems," ch. 17.
Russell, D., " Hypatia."
Symposium, The Mind of Youth, *The World Tomorrow*, vol. xv, No. 1.
Værting, M., and M., (tr. Paul, E., and C.,) " The Dominant Sex."
Wells, H. G., " Socialism and the Family."

Topics for Discussion

1. Is skepticism concerning the family growing?
2. Is modern literature just to the family?
3. What influences of the home are hampering social progress?
4. What faults of the home do you regard most harmful to children?
5. What influence does the emotional newspaper have on home life?
6. How do parents alienate youth from the home?
7. What makes such attacks on American family life as Lewis' Main Street popular?

Subjects for Reports

1. Plato's attitude toward the family.
2. Study of a newspaper with reference to its material of concern to the family.
3. A critical study of Herrick's "The Healer."
4. Mental Hygiene as a critic of the home.
5. A comparison of the faults of rural with those of urban family life.
6. Art and family happiness.

CHAPTER XII

FAMILY ADJUSTMENT

References

Groves, E. R., "Personality and Social Adjustment."
(Especially recommended)

Aikman, D., Amazons of Freedom, *Harpers Monthly*, June, 1926.
Angell, K. S., Home and Office, *Survey*, vol. 57, No. 5.
Bosanquet, H., "The Family," chs. 11, 12.
Burgess, E. W., The Family as a Unity of Interacting Personalities, *The Family*, vol. vii, No. 1.
Duflot, J. L., The Study of Critical Situations in the Organized Family, *Journal of Applied Sociology*, vol. x, No. 2.
Dutcher, E., Principles Underlying Modern Case Work with Relations, *The Family*, vol. v, No. 5.
Flügel, J. C., "The Psycho-Analytic Study of the Family," chs. 10, 14–18.
Freud, S., "A General Introduction to Psychoanalysis."
Gans, B. S., ed., "Concerning Parents," pp. 24–43.
Gregg, Mrs. A. J., What Women Are Thinking; The Y.W.C.A. Talks it Over, *Survey*, vol. 57, No. 5.
Groves, E. R., "The Drifting Home," ch. 8.
High, S., "Revolt of Youth."
Kempf, E. J., "Psychopathology," ch. 2.
Peters, I. L., Repressions and Problems of the Family, *Journal of Applied Sociology*, vol. viii, No. 6.
Raymond, S., Individualization of the Parent, "Nat'l Conf. Social Work," vol. xxii. pp. 257–261.
Richards, E. L., Practical Aspects of Parental Love, *Mental Hygiene*, vol. x, No. 2.
Sayles, M. B., "The Problem Child in School," ch. 1.
Spencer, A. G., "The Family and its Members," ch. 4.
Taft, J., The Effect of an Unsatisfactory Mother-Daughter Relationship upon the Development of a Personality, *The Family*, vol. vii, No. 1.
Van Waters, M., "Youth in Conflict," ch. 2.
Weininger, O., "Sex and Character."
White, W. A., "Mechanisms of Character Formation," ch. 7.
———"The Mental Hygiene of Childhood," chs. 5, 9.
Williams, J. M., "Our Rural Heritage," ch. 10.
Woods, R. A., and Kennedy, A. J., "Young Working Girls," ch. 6.

Topics for Discussion

1. What family influences can you detect in your adult friends?
2. Is it necessary for youth to experience a conflict between family teaching and the conditions he finds outside the home?
3. Is the present trend toward greater self-expression for children in their school training adding difficulties to family association?
4. What marriage problems are due to childhood experience?
5. Do you believe that parenthood training is practicable?
6. Can you give illustrations of the love-and-hate attitude of children?

Subjects for Reports

1. The psychology of homesickness.
2. The grandparent in the modern home.
3. An analysis of cases of child jealousy.
4. The rôle of the girl who is the oldest child in a large family.
5. Problem children in school, who show effects of family repression.
6. Failures to marry due to family suggestions.
7. Freud's interpretation of the risks of parents.

CHAPTER XIII

PARENT AND CHILD

References

Van Waters, M., "Youth in Conflict."
(Especially recommended)

Bigelow, M. A., Unchanging Youth, *Child Study*, vol. iii, No. 3.
Bosanquet, H., "The Family," ch. 13.
Burnham, W. H., "The Normal Mind."
Cheley, F. H., "The Job of Being a Dad."
Cleveland, E., "Training the Toddler."
Edson, N. W., The Youth of Today, *Journal of Social Hygiene*, vol xii, No. 4.
Ellis, H., "Little Essays of Love and Virtue," ch. 1.
Fisher, D. C., "Mothers and Children."
Flügel, J. C., "The Psycho-analytic Study of the Family," chs. 6, 7.
Groves, E. R., "The Drifting Home," ch. 6.
———"Personality and Social Adjustment," chs, 13, 14.
——— and G. H., "Wholesome Childhood."
Gruenberg, B. C., "Guidance in Childhood and Youth."
———The Adolescent in Modern Society, *Child Study*, vol. iii, No. 3.
———"Outlines of Child Study."
Gruenberg, S. M., "Sons and Daughters."
———"Your Child Today and Tomorrow."
Kenworthy, M. E., Some Emotional Problems Seen in the Superior Child, *American Journal of Psychiatry*, vol. iv, No. 3.
Kirkpatrick, W. H., New Methods of Discipline, *Children*, vol. i, No. 2.
Mateer, F., "The Unstable Child."

Miller, H. C., " The New Psychology and the Parent."

Mudgett, M. D., The Development of Greater Sympathy and Understanding between Parents and Children, "Nat'l Conf. Social Work," 1924, pp. 280–284.

Richardson, F. H., " Parenthood and the Newer Psychology."

———Is Your Child Jealous? *Children*, vol. i, No. 3.

Seham, M., and G., " The Tired Child."

Stearns, A. E., " The Challenge of Youth."

Van Waters, M., Nineteen Ways of Being a Bad Parent, *Survey Graphic*, Jan., 1927.

Walsh, J. J., and Foote, J. A., " Safeguarding Children's Nerves."

Wile, I. S., " Good " Education and " Bad " Children, *Mental Hygiene*, vol. ix, No. 1.

Williams, F. E., What Are Parents For? *Survey*, vol. 57, No. 5.

Wise, S. S., " Child Versus Parent."

Topics for Discussion

1. Do you believe the present-day child is happier as a result of the greater complexity of life?
2. Which do you think coöperate more with the home—public or private schools?
3. What important contributions have been made in the last decade by scientific child study?
4. Do you believe in protecting the child from temptations outside the home?
5. Is childhood best regarded as a period for the happiness of the child or for his preparation for adult life?
6. Why do adults exaggerate the happiness and the suffering of childhood?
7. Can a child develop without having experiences of fear?
8. Can a child be trained to accept a changing, progressive morality? If so, how?

Subjects for Reports

1. Recent changes in public education that concern the home.
2. Progressive movements in education that promise to aid family life.
3. Recent progress in the science of heredity of importance to the home.
4. The impulsive life of children.
5. The causes, results and treatment of child fixation.
6. Dangers of the one-child family.
7. Adler's doctrine of the inferiority complex.

CHAPTER XIV

SOCIAL PROBLEMS RELATED TO FAMILY LIFE

References

Addison, C., " The Betrayal of the Slums."

Aronovici, C., " Housing and the Housing Problem."

Baber, R. E., and Ross, E. A., " Changes in the Size of American Families in One Generation," chs. 8, 10, 12.

Breckinridge, S. P., and Abbott, E., " The Delinquent Child and the Home."

Chicago Council of Social Agencies, " The Chicago Standard Budget for Dependent Families."

Devine, E. T., " The Principles of Relief," ch. 5.

Dugdale, R. L., " The Jukes."

Estabrook, A. H., " The Jukes in 1915."

Groves, E. R., " Social Problems and Education," ch. 7.

Heagerty, J. J., Education in Relation to Prostitution, *Journal of Social Hygiene*, vol. x, No. 3.

Hooker, E. H., " Laws of Sex," chs. 2, 8–12.

Johnson, F. E., The Moral Hazards of Child Labor, *Journal of Social Hygiene*, vol. x, No. 6.

Kammerer, P. G., " The Unmarried Mother."

Kleinschmidt, H. E., Milestones of Progress in the Control of Syphilis, *Journal of Social Hygiene*, vol. ix, No. 7.

Lenroot, K. F., The Delinquent Girl and the Unmarried Mother, *Journal of Social Hygiene*, vol. x, No. 2.

Lies, E. T., Juvenile Delinquency and Recreation, " Proceedings Nat'l Probation Ass'n," 1924.

Lonza, A. J., Venereal Diseases and the Family, *Journal of Social Hygiene*, vol. xi, No. 7.

Lovejoy, O. R., and Gonzala, W. E., The Twentieth Amendment—A Deba⁺e, *The Forum*, vol. lxxiii, No. 1.

Parmelee, M., " Poverty and Social Progress," ch. 8.

Patten, S., " The New Basis of Civilization," ch. 3.

Popenoe, P., " Conservation of the Family," Part II, chs. 5, 6, 8.

Publications of Children's Bureau: " Child Labor in North Dakota," No. 129; " Child Labor in Representative Tobacco Growing Areas," No. 155; " Child Labor In Fruit and Hop Growing Districts of the Northern Pacific Coast," No. 151; " The Welfare of Children in Cotton Growing Areas of Texas," No. 154.

Marquette, B., Are We Losing the Battle for Better Homes? " Nat'l Conf. Social Work," 1923, pp. 344–349.

Menken, A. D., A Social Aspect of the Unmarried Mother, *Journal of Delinquency*, vol. vii, No. 2.

Reed, R., " Negro Illegitimacy in New York City."

————Illegitimacy Among Negroes, *Journal of Social Hygiene*, vol. xi, No. 2.

Wood, E. E., Must Working People Live in Frayed-Out Houses? " Nat'l Conf. Social Work," 1923, pp. 349–352.

————" Housing Progress in Western Europe."

————" The Housing of the Unskilled Worker."

Woods, R. A., and Kennedy, A. J., " Young Working Girls," chs, 8–11.

Woodbury, R. M., The Need of Improved Child Welfare Statistics, " Publications American Sociological Society," vol. xix, pp. 109–122.

Worthington, G. E., Law for Children Born out of Wedlock, *Journal of Social Hygiene*, vol. x, No. 3.

Zorbaugh, H. W., The Dweller in Furnished Rooms, " Publications American Sociological Society," vol. xx, pp. 83–89.

Topics for Discussion

1. Does poverty cause bad home life or does bad home life cause poverty?
2. What are the building laws in your community?
3. Is home-ownership increasing or decreasing in your community?
4. Will a humane treatment of the unmarried mother tend to increase illegitimacy?
5. What are the causes of the passing of prostitution?
6. Is prohibition an advantage to the home?
7. Are the movies of your community helping or hurting the home?
8. What is the influence of the radio on the home?

Subjects for Reports

1. The history of the Jukes family.
2. The housing reforms of Octavia Hill.
3. Bad housing in the rural community.
4. The housing problem of New York City.
5. The influence of the automobile on home-ownership.
6. The settlement's program for roomers.
7. The work of the American Social Hygiene Association.
8. The Mental Hygiene movement.
9. Recent advances in preventive medicine.

CHAPTER XV

CONSERVATION OF THE FAMILY

References

Bowers, P. E., The Necessity for Sterilization, *Journal of Delinquency*, vol. vi, No. 5.
Colcord, J. C., The Matrimonial Advice Bureau, *The Family*, vol. v, No. 3.
———The Family Wage, *Survey*, vol. 57, No. 5.
Douglas, P. H., "Wages and the Family."
Hall, F. S., Marriage Legislation in 1925, *The Family*, vol. vi, No. 9.
———"Medical Certification for Marriage."
Kelley, F., Progress of Labor Legislation for Women, "National Conference Social Work," 1923, pp. 112–116.
Laughlin, H. H., "Eugenical Sterilization," 1926.
Parsons, A. B., The Parent's Wages, *Survey*, vol. 57, No. 5.
Parsons, E. C., "The Family," ch. 15.
Petersen, A. L., Mothers' Pensions, *Survey*, vol. 57, No. 5.
Popenoe, P., and Johnson, R. H., "Applied Eugenics," ch. 10.
Popenoe, P., "Conservation of the Family."
Rathbone, E. F., "The Disinherited Family."
———Wages According to Family Needs, *Hibbert Journal*, vol. xix, pp. 712–723.
Richmond, M. E., and Hall, F. S., "Child Marriages."
Ryan, J. A., Our Self-Amending Constitution, *The Survey*, Aug. 1, 1923.
Seager, H. R., The Minimum Wage—What Next? *The Survey*, May 15, 1923.
Villard, O. G., Sex, Art, Truth and the Magazines, *Atlantic Monthly*, March, 1926.
Waite, E. F., "Child Marriages."

Topics for Discussion

1. What are the child labor laws of your state? What changes should be made?
2. Do women workers need special protection by legislation?
3. Do you believe in compulsory examination of men who desire to marry?
4. Is eugenical regulation of human offspring practicable?
5. Do you believe in forcing marriage when possible in cases of pregnancy?
6. What is the law in your state regarding mothers' pensions? Is it working well?
7. Do you favor Federal aid for maternity education?

Subjects for Reports

1. The present condition of child labor in the United States.
2. The Supreme Court's decisions concerning Federal child labor laws.
3. The history of American labor legislation for women.
4. A critical study of the Wisconsin law requiring a medical certificate for marriage.
5. European experiments in wages for families.
6. The evolution of the Family Court.
7. The work of Judge Charles Hoffman of Cincinnati.
8. The Sheppard-Towner act.
9. The Children's Bureau.

CHAPTER XVI

EDUCATION AND THE FAMILY

References

Gans, B. S., ed., "Concerning Parents."
(Especially recommended)

Baber, R. E., and Ross, E. A., "Changes in the Size of American Families in One Generation," ch. 4.
Dealey, J. Q., "The Family in Its Sociological Aspects," ch. 11.
Dummer, E. S., Changing Ideals of Parenthood, *Progressive Education*, vol. iii, No. 2.
Goodsell, W., "The Education of Women," ch. 6.
Hooker, E. H., "Laws of Sex," ch. 13.
de Lima, A., "Our Enemy the Child."
Parsons, A. B., "Woman's Dilemma," ch. 9.
Popenoe, P., "Conservation of the Family," Part III, ch. 1.
Reeve, M. W., Educating for Parenthood, *Journal of Social Hygiene*, vol. x, No. 8.
Richards, F. H., Training for Parenthood, *Journal of Social Hygiene*, vol. xii, No. 3.
Spencer, A. G., "The Family and Its Members," ch. 14.
———The Social Education of Women, *Publications American Sociological Society*, vol. xiii, pp. 11–28.
———"Woman's Share in Social Culture," ch. 7.

Van Waters, M., and Others, Why Do Parents Need Special Training?
"Child Study," vol. ii, No. 7.
Watson, A. E., and F. D., Opportunities for Parental Education, *Progressive Education*, vol. iii, No. 2.
Woods, R. A., and Kennedy, A. J., "Young Working Girls," ch. 13.

Topics for Discussion

1. Do Americans have too much confidence in public school education?
2. Would the individual treatment of public school children prove too expensive?
3. Should married women be permitted to teach?
4. Do you favor a compulsory public nursery school?
5. Is co-education desirable in high school? In college?
6. Why is co-education in college generally favored in the West and not in the East?
7. Is science prepared to help solve the social problems of the family?
8. Can preparation for parenthood be taught in high school? If so, how?
9. Is home-life getting better or worse?

Subjects for Reports

1. The work of the Parent-Teacher Association.
2. Robert Owen and the origin of the nursery school.
3. The nursery school in England.
4. The nursery school movement in the United States.
5. Recent changes in home economics in the high school.
6. The history of college co-education in the United States.
7. The history of the baby hygiene movement in the United States.
8. A college program for parenthood instruction.
9. The Vassar College Institute of Euthenics.

FICTION

In literature we find material of great value in studying the social problems of the family. When such material is used for class reports the student must take care not to lose in the telling of the story the meaning of the author's treatment of the family problem. The following novels and plays have been chosen as representative of the modern writers' discussion of various phases of family relationships:

Novels

Anderson, S., "Tar, a Midwest Childhood."
——"Dark Laughter."
Baldwin, F., "Three Women."
Ballamann, H., "Petenera's Daughter."
Banning, M., "The Women of the Family."
Bennett, A., "These Twins."
Benson, B. F., "Mezzanine."
Beresford, J. D., "An Imperfect Mother."
Bodenheim, M., "Ninth Avenue."
Booth, E. C., "The Tree of the Garden."

20

Canfield, D., "The Brimming Cup."
———"The Home Maker."
———"Her Son's Wife."
———"The Squirrel's Cage."
Cather, W. S., "The Professor's House."
———"My Antonia."
Crompton, R., "Dread Dwelling."
Deeping, W., "Sorrell and Son."
Deutsch, B., "A Brittle Heaven."
Ferber, E., "So Big."
———"Girls."
George, W. L., "The Second Blooming."
———"Gifts of Sheba."
Gibbs, H., "Soundings."
Gibbs, J. P., "Portia Marries."
Glasgow, E., "Virginia."
———"Life and Gabriella."
Hamilton, M. A., "Slings and Arrows."
Hamsun, K., "Growth of the Soil."
Héman, L., "Maria Chapdelaine."
Herrick, R., "The Healer."
———"Chimes."
Hutchinson, A. S. M., "If Winter Comes."
———"This Freedom."
Jerome, J., "Passing of the Third Floor Back."
Lawrence, D. H., "Kangaroo."
———"Sons and Lovers."
Leech, M., "Tin Wedding."
Lewis, S., "Babbitt."
———"Main Street."
Marshall, A., "The Allbrights."
Morley, C., "Thunder on the Left."
Norris, K., "Mother."
———"Sisters."
Onions, O., "The Spite of Heaven."
Poole, E., "His Second Wife."
———"His Family."
———"With Eastern Eyes."
Sinclair, M., "The Helpmate."
Stern, G. B., "The Matriarch."
Tarkington, B., "The Turmoil."
Van Doren, D., "Strangers."
Wassermann, J., "Wedlock."
Wasson, M., "The Big House."
Wells, H. G., "The Wife of Sir Isaac Harman."
Wharton, E., "Sanctuary."
Wilson, M., "The Able McLaughlins."
———"The Painted Room."
Wolf, R., "Springboard."
Young, E., "Custody Children."

Plays

Andreyers, L., " He Who Gets Slapped."
Beach, L., "Ann Vroome."
———" The Goose Hangs High."
Cotton, J. and Randolph, C., " Rain."
Davis, O., " Icebound."
Ervine, St. John, " John Ferguson."
Fisher, D., " Lavender Ladies."
Galsworthy, J., " Old English."
———" A Family Man."
Hughes, H., " Hell-Bent fer Heaven."
Ibsen, "A Pillar of Society."
———" A Doll's House."
———" Ghosts."
Kaufman, G. S., and Connelly, M. C., " To the Ladies."
Maeterlinck, M., " Monna Vanno."
Maugham, S., " The Circle."
O'Neill, E. G., " Desire under the Elms."
———" Beyond the Horizon."
Robinson, L., " The Whiteheaded Boy."
Williams, J. L., " Why Marry ? "
———" Why Not ? "

To the Instructor

SOCIAL PROBLEMS OF THE FAMILY has been planned for use as a text in a one-semester course three hours a week. Its purpose is to open up the problems of the modern family and to stimulate the student's thinking for himself. The text attempts to avoid giving the student any sense of finality in its interpretation of the social problems of the present-day American family.

In the author's experience students can best be encouraged to contribute serious thought in discussion by the instructor's giving in advance to individual students the responsibility of planning a class program for the first two days of each week. The other students are expected to coöperate by undertaking the assignments given them by the individual who has the week's program in charge. On the third day the instructor takes up in an informal manner problems that have arisen during the first two sessions or matters that should be brought to the attention of the class. The topics for discussion and subjects for reports are presented as suggestive in helping students plan the programs week by week. Whatever the method adopted by the instructor it is hoped that the topics, subjects and references will prove of assistance to the student.

Every effort should be made to make the course practical in its appeal to the student by emphasis upon his need of interpreting the social problems of the families he has known through personal experience. The more the student senses the fact that his goal is not to know about family-life, but to know family-life, the greater will be the profit of his study.

The following minimum reference library is suggested for those giving the course for the first time:

Books

Calhoun, A. C., "A Social History of the American Family."
Children's Bureau Bulletins.
Colcord, J. C., " Broken Homes."
Flügel, J. C., " The Psycho-Analytic Study of the Family."
Goodsell, W., " The Family as a Social and Educational Institution."
Groves, E. R., " Personality and Social Adjustment."
Hughes, G. S., " Mothers in Industry."
Popenoe, P., " Conservation of the Family."
Pruette, L., " Women of Leisure."
Spencer, A. G., " The Family and Its Members."
——"Woman's Share in Social Culture."

Magazines

Children, The Magazine for Parents.
The Family.
Social Hygiene.
Mental Hygiene.
Journal of Social Forces.
American Journal of Sociology.
The Survey.

Additional Books

It will prove an advantage to add books from this list:
Gans, B. S., ed., " Concerning Parents."
Groves, E. R. and G. H., " Wholesome Childhood."
Groves, E. R., " The Drifting Home."
Howard, G. E., " A History of Matrimonial Institutions."
                    (Invaluable but out of print)
" Intelligent Parenthood," Proceedings of the Mid-West Conference on
    Parent-Education, 1926.
Kirchwey, Freda, " Our Changing Morality."
Myerson, A., " The Nervous Housewife."
Richardson, F. H., " Parenthood and the Newer Psychology."
Richman, M. E. and Hall, F. S., " Child Marriages."
Westermarck, E., " The History of Human Marriage."
Wood, E., " The Housing of the Unskilled Wage Earner."

INDEX

DATE DUE

OCT 22	MAY 14	NOV 19	
OCT 29	DEC 1	APR 9	
DEC 1	MAY 16	MAY 19	
JAN 4	OCT 15	DEC 14	
FEB 1	DEC 2	MAY 15	
MAR 14	APR 30	DEC 19 '85	
MAR 30	APR 24	DEC 19 '85	
APR 27	APR 26	NOV 21 '86	
MAY 5	APR 29		
MAY 22	MAR 4		
DEC 15	MAY 1	DEC 2 1988	
JAN 29		NOV 28 1994	
MAR 22	NOV 3	APR 13 1996	
APR 29	DEC 6		
MAY 13	MAR 27		
DEC 9	APR 7		
DEC 20	APR 28		
APR 9	NOV 22		
	MAY 7		